The Bush Doctrine and the War on Terrorism

This new volume gives a balanced critical analysis of the Bush Doctrine and its profound effect on global politics and international security.

The Bush Doctrine and the War on Terrorism is a collection of 15 analyses of the global consequences of, and responses to, US foreign policy under George W. Bush. Offering competing interpretations of the origins and effects of Bush's policies, this book provides a detailed examination of the post-September 11 world and America's contested role and influence therein. Examining the key features of the Bush Doctrine, American primacy, preventive war, the war on terrorism, the promotion of democracy and their practical application in Afghanistan, Iraq and the broader Middle East, the chapters provide a comprehensive and timely assessment of Bush's proclaimed commitment to 'end tyranny' worldwide. Eight chapters written by regional specialists consider the particular factors driving divergent responses to Bush's leadership, and a further five chapters analyse the consequences of the Bush Doctrine for global security, the global economy, the UN, international law and multilateralism.

Providing a balanced and dispassionate assessment of continuity and change in American foreign policy, national/regional responses to it and the impact of US foreign policy on a set of 'big picture' discrete issues, this book will be essential reading for scholars and researchers of international relations, politics, contemporary history and area studies.

Mary Buckley is Visiting Fellow at Hughes Hall, Cambridge. She has written on Soviet ideology, gender, state and society under Gorbachev, Stalinism, Russian domestic and foreign policy, terrorism and human trafficking.

Robert Singh is Professor of Politics and Head of the School of Politics and Sociology at Birkbeck College, University of London. His research interests are in the field of domestic US politics and the politics of US foreign policy.

The Bush Doctrine and the War on Terrorism

Global responses, global consequences

Edited by Mary Buckley and Robert Singh

LONDON AND NEW YORK

First published 2006
by Routledge
2 Park Square, Milton Park, Abingdon, Oxon OX14 4RN

Simultaneously published in the USA and Canada by Routledge
29 West 35th Street, New York, NY 10001

Routledge is an imprint of the Taylor & Francis Group

Typeset in Baskerville by Prepress Projects Ltd, Perth
Printed and bound in Great Britain by Antony Rowe

British Library Cataloguing in Publication Data
A catalogue record for this book is available from the British Library

Library of Congress Cataloging in Publication Data
The Bush doctrine and the War on Terrorism : global responses, global
    consequences / edited by Mary Buckley and Robert Singh.
    p. cm.
    Includes bibliographical references.
    1. War on Terrorism, 2001– . 2. United States – Foreign relations
    – 21st century. 3. World politics – 21st century. 4. Bush, George W.
    (George Walker), 1946– . I. Buckley, Mary (Mary E. A.) II. Singh,
    Robert.
    HV6432.B875 2006
    327.73′09′0511–dc22
    2005014982

ISBN10: 0-415-36831-6 (hbk)
ISBN10: 0-415-36997-5 (pbk)

ISBN13: 9-78-0-415-36831-5 (hbk)
ISBN13: 9-78-0-415-36997-8 (pbk)

Contents

Tables

Contributors

George Blazyca (1952–2005) was Professor of European Studies at Paisley University. His main research interests focused on social and economic affairs in Poland since the early 1970s. He wrote for a wide number of publications contributing to both books and journals as well as writing articles for the *Guardian*, the *Herald* and the *Scotsman*. His most recent publications include Blazyca (ed.), *Restructuring Regional and Local Economies: Towards a Comparative Study in Scotland and Upper Silesia* (Ashgate, 2003) and 'EU Accession: The Polish Case', Chapter 10, in Hilary Ingham and Mike Ingham (eds), *EU Expansion to the East: Prospects and Problems* (Edward Elgar, 2002). His last article was 'A note from the Victoria Infirmary', *Scottish Left Review*, 26 January/February 2005, pp. 20–1.

Mary Buckley is Visiting Fellow at Hughes Hall, Cambridge. She is author or editor of ten books and over 40 articles in journals or anthologies. She has written on Soviet ideology, gender, state and society under Gorbachev, Stalinism, Russian domestic and foreign policy, terrorism and human trafficking. Her most recent books are *Mobilizing Soviet Peasants: Heroines and Heroes of Stalin's Fields* (Rowman and Littlefield, 2006) and *Global Responses to Terrorism*, co-edited with Rick Fawn (Routledge, 2003).

Anoushiravan Ehteshami is Professor of International Relations and Head of the School of Government and International Affairs at the University of Durham. He was also Vice-President of the British Society for Middle Eastern Studies (BRISMES) 2000–2003. His most recent publications include *The Middle East's Relations with Asia and Russia* (co-ed.) (Routledge Curzon, 2004), *The Foreign Policies of Middle East States* (co-ed.) (Lynne Rienner, 2002) and *Iran's Security Policy in the Post-Revolutionary Era* (co-author) (RAND, 2001).

Malcolm Evans OBE is Professor of Public International Law and Dean of the Faculty of Social Sciences and Law at Bristol University. His areas of interest include the international protection of religious liberty and issues concerning torture and torture prevention. His principal publications include *Religious Liberty and International Law in Europe* (Cambridge University Press, 1997), *Preventing Torture* (Oxford Universiry Press, 1998) and *Combating Torture in Europe* (Council of Europe, 2001). He is a member of the OSCE Advisory Council on the Freedom of Religion and Belief.

Alastair Finlan is a Lecturer in Strategic Studies at Aberystwyth, The University of Wales. He has written on military culture, special forces, the war on terror and the US counterinsurgency campaign in Iraq. His most recent major monograph is *The Royal Navy in the Falklands Conflict and the Gulf War: Culture and Strategy* (Frank Cass, 2004).

Robert Grey is a Professor of Political Science at Grinnell College, Iowa. He has written about both African politics and Russian politics. He edited *Democratic Theory and Post-Communist Change* (Prentice-Hall, 1997). He is now working on *The Russian People and the Fate of Democracy* as well as *Learning from the Post-Communist and African Experiences: Revisions in Democratization Theory*.

M. Donald Hancock is Professor of Political Science at Vanderbilt University. He is the author or senior editor and co-author of nine books on European politics. His most recent publications include *Politics in Europe* (Congressional Quarterly Press, 2003) and *Transitions to Capitalism and Democracy in Russia and Central Europe* (Praeger, 2000).

Daphne Josselin is Lecturer in International Political Economy at the London School of Economics. She is the author of *Money Politics in the New Europe* (Macmillan, 1997) and co-editor (with Professor William Wallace) of *Non-State Actors in World Politics* (Palgrave, 2001). Her current research interests include the political economy of international monetary integration and debt relief initiatives, with recent articles in *West European Politics* and *French Politics, Culture and Society*.

Rex Li is Senior Lecturer in International Relations at Liverpool John Moores University. He lectures regularly at the Joint Services Command and Staff College, UK Defence Academy. A specialist in Asia-Pacific security and defence issues, he has served as an Associate Editor of *Security Dialogue* and spoken at various track-two security conferences. His recent works have appeared in *Journal of Strategic Studies*, *The World Today*, *World Defence Systems* and a number of edited books.

Brendon O'Connor is a Senior Lecturer in the Department of Politics and Public Policy at Griffith University, Australia. He is the author of *A Political History of the American Welfare System* (Rowman & Littlefield, 2004) and the co-editor with Martin Griffiths of *The Rise of Anti-Americanism* (Routledge, 2005).

Phoebe N. Okowa is Senior Lecturer in Law at Queen Mary College, University of London. Her teaching and research interests are primarily in the field of public international law. She is the co-editor (with Malcolm Evans) of the series *Foundations of Public International Law* (Oxford University

Press) and the author of *State Responsibility for Transboundary Air Pollution in International Law* (Oxford University Press, 2000).

Stephen Ryan is a Senior Lecturer in the School of History and International Affairs at the University of Ulster. He has published articles and chapters on UN involvement in ethnic conflicts and on UN peace-keeping. His most recent book was *The United Nations and International Politics* (Palgrave, 2000).

Robert Singh is Professor of Politics and Head of the School of Politics and Sociology at Birkbeck College, University of London. He is the author and editor of six books on US politics, most recently *Governing America* (Oxford University Press, 2003) and *Contemporary American Politics and Society* (Sage, 2003). He is currently working on a monograph on Anti-Americanisms.

Brandon Valeriano is Assistant Professor in Political Science at the University of Illinois at Chicago. He completed his PhD at Vanderbilt University in 2003 and taught there full time in 2003–4. His main research interests are the causes of war and peace. His dissertation explores the onset of interstate rivalries from 1816 to 1992, and his research interests include the role of theory and empirical observations in explaining international conflict.

Samina Yasmeen is a Senior Lecturer in International Politics in the Department of Political Science and International Relations at the University of Western Australia (UWA), Perth. Dr Yasmeen is a specialist in political and strategic developments in South Asia and the role of Islam in world politics. She has written a number of articles on Indo-Pakistan relations, political changes in Pakistan and the Kashmir issue, and is a regular commentator on developments in South Asia and the Middle East on national radio, TV and in the print media.

Acknowledgements

We should like to record our warm thanks to Heidi Bagtazo, Craig Fowlie and Harriet Brinton, our editors at Routledge, for showing enthusiasm for this project. We should also thank our copy-editor, Heather Hynd, and indexer, Jim Henderson, for all their hard work. In addition, we are indebted to Wendy Blazyca for so kindly and willingly liaising with us after George's sad and premature death in 2005. His professionalism, smile and positive outlook will be much missed by his colleagues and friends alike.

MB

RS

1 Introduction

Mary Buckley and Robert Singh

When huge world 'events' take place, scholars subsequently reflect upon their meaning for global politics, their comparative historical importance and the extent to which the world has significantly changed, remains the same, is somehow 'qualified' or 'altered' in the short, medium or long term or confronts greater threats of instability than before. Themes of rupture, revolution, reform, continuity, stability, threat, balance of power, alliances and types of polarity are revisited in the light of what has just occurred. Existing approaches to international relations such as liberalism, realism, neo-realism, rationalism, constructivism, Marxism and post-modernism also come under the critical spotlight for re-evaluation. Examples of such key international events since 1940 include the Japanese bombing of Pearl Harbor in 1941, the exploding of atomic and then hydrogen bombs by the US and Soviet Union, the Cuban missile crisis in 1962, Soviet intervention in Hungary in 1956 and Czechoslovakia in 1968, the fall of the Berlin Wall in 1989, the Gulf War of 1991, NATO intervention in Kosovo in 1999 and the terrorist attacks on the World Trade Center and Pentagon by al-Qaeda on 11 September 2001, and a string of subsequent ones in Madrid, London and Bali, with more feared.

That leaders formally adopt sets of principles or 'doctrines' to make explicit how they wish to deal with issues of state security and responsibility after such events is neither new nor surprising. In setting out the principles that underpin a state's international relations, the public declaration by political leaders of a doctrine serves a dual purpose. On the one hand, it reflects and reinforces the values, beliefs and preferences of a particular domestic audience, setting out the goals, ends and means by which a state seeks to chart its course in the world. On the other, it speaks to an international audience of allies, adversaries and neutrals, making clear what the state's leadership wishes to achieve, how it seeks to do this and what, in turn, other states should expect from its behaviour. Doctrines therefore represent more than mere political rhetoric or symbolic statements of passing academic interest and marginal practical consequence. Such statements of grand strategy represent promissory notes and warnings alike, elevated far above the day-to-day interactions of foreign relations or the opaque communications of diplomats.

To issue a doctrine, then, places a powerful burden on the proponent. Not only may the doctrine's content prove controversial or misguided, but its intent may be misunderstood at home and abroad. Moreover, setting out a doctrine is not synonymous with implementing it, and its practical application may be deeply problematic. In setting out one's principles at face value, the danger arises of appearing two-faced if the principles outlined in such a statement are breached, dishonoured or applied in a selective, partial or biased fashion. It is hardly surprising, then, that neither scholars of international relations and foreign policy analysis nor practitioners agree on the utility of such grand declarations of statecraft. For some, foreign policy is a highly fluid, unpredictable and events-driven enterprise, one that demands pragmatism rather than inflexible adherence to doctrinal principles. The ship of state is rarely able to sail smoothly without being buffeted by unexpected forces that require adaptation and revision of its charted course. Setting out an unwavering route in advance therefore appears at best misguided, at worst utterly self-defeating. For others, however, making explicit the central compass by which the state will proceed is a surer way of advancing. In the case of a particularly – even uniquely – influential nation-state, especially, the expectations that its leaders can set for others can induce a greater sense of stability, predictability and clarity in interstate relations. To fail to announce a doctrine would be to leave the international arena dangerously unclouded by principle and precedent.

In the American case, the public declaration of doctrines long predated the republic's 'rise to globalism' in the post-1945 era. As early as 1823, the Monroe Doctrine warned European powers not to meddle in the continental sphere of the Americas, the province of the US alone. In the years following World War II, few presidents resisted the temptation to issue clear messages to ally and adversary alike as to what they could expect from the US. On 12 March 1947, President Harry S. Truman proclaimed that 'it must be the policy of the United States to support free peoples who are resisting attempted subjugation by armed minorities or outside pressures'. Although aimed rhetorically against totalitarian regimes, the Truman Doctrine generalized America's particular commitments to Greece and Turkey to a global promise to resist Soviet expansionism wherever it appeared, thereby setting out the principles of containment that would guide US policy for the next 44 years. The Eisenhower Doctrine of 1957 pledged the US to defend the Middle East against 'overt armed aggression from any nation controlled by International Communism', while the Nixon Doctrine sought to bolster influential regional powers in order to advance containment and maintain international order by proxy. The Reagan Doctrine reaffirmed the American commitment not simply to contain but to roll back communism around the globe through assisting guerrilla groups, the president stating in January 1985 that the US would defend 'freedom and democracy [on] every continent from Afghanistan to

Nicaragua'. Even Jimmy Carter and Bill Clinton proclaimed doctrines that bore their names. That the president occupies a unique position in having the legitimacy to speak both to and for the American nation adds particular force to the issuing of such sweeping public declarations.

Nor is the phenomenon of issuing doctrines distinctively or uniquely American. What was known in the West as the Brezhnev Doctrine of 1968 made clear that the Soviet state had the responsibility to ensure that no communist party lapsed into a 'one-sidedness' that damaged socialism in their own country or another. An article in *Pravda* on 'Sovereignty and the International Obligations of Socialist Countries' made clear that leaderships who valued autonomy and independence reneged on international obligations.[1] Alexander Dubcek's 'Prague Spring' was unacceptable to Brezhnev's views on bloc solidarity and communist monopoly power. Brezhnev perceived developments in Czechoslovakia as threatening to the norms and values of the Soviet state and to the Warsaw Pact. From the Politburo's perspective, action was necessary and tanks were sent in to overthrow Dubcek and to reinstate 'normalcy' Soviet-style. Leaders elsewhere reacted with varying degrees of condemnation, criticism, passive acceptance and support.

Doctrines – no more than specific foreign policies – are therefore rarely complete ruptures with, or comprehensive rejections of, the past. Nor need they arise fully formed or be proclaimed with pristine clarity at the outset of a new political leadership. Although the Truman Doctrine is conventionally regarded as the fundamental point of departure for the Cold War, for instance, it can be better seen as the ultimate expression of the strategy of the 'patience and firmness' that had been initiated several months previously. The Eisenhower Doctrine was not proclaimed until the first year of Ike's second term in office. The Reagan Doctrine, similarly, although effectively operative from 1981, was not articulated as such in public until 1985. In the Carter and Clinton cases, the declaration of a doctrine did not occur until their penultimate year in office. As such, the identification of a grand strategy and its relationship to a doctrine can sometimes muddy rather than clear the analytical waters. Similarly, the Brezhnev leadership's formal declaration of the international obligations of socialist states came four years after Brezhnev became General Secretary of the CPSU, but made explicit what had long been the Soviet intention regarding its fraternal allies.

The Bush Doctrine thus takes its place in an extended family of grand statements of global purpose. Although neither President George W. Bush nor the leading figures in his administration have publicly referred to it as such, it was unsurprising in the aftermath of 9/11 that a new foreign policy doctrine should be formulated. Bush immediately and viscerally understood the events of 9/11 as unacceptable and vile, necessitating a clear declaration to both the American people and the world as to how best to respond to the perpetrators of such a heinous attack and how, thereby, to make the US secure for the future. Following a series of landmark speeches that crystallized and advanced the re-evaluation of US policies, the National Security Strategy

(NSS) of September 2002 was the result. Therein, the four pillars of the Bush Doctrine were set out: the maintenance of American military primacy; the embrace of preventive war as a supplement to traditional deterrence; the war on terrorism; and democratization. More than any prior declaration by an American administration, however, the enunciation of this doctrine generated intense and widespread international controversy. The varied responses to the Bush Doctrine in distinct regions of the world, and the profound consequences of the doctrine for key features of the international system, form the central focus for this book.

That political leaders across the globe reacted in different and complex ways to the NSS of September 2002 and to the subsequent US-led war in Iraq in 2003 was predictable. Multifactoral explanations best account for why leaders behave the way that they do at a given point in time. Necessary variables include the political preferences of the particular government, historical and/or prevailing elite and mass attitudes towards the US, membership or aspiring membership of regional organizations, geo-politics, the structure of the world system, economic interests, views of the role of the United Nations (UN) and domestic political pressures. The chapters that follow analyse the ways in which leaders across regions and public opinion across states reacted to developments from 2002 to early 2005. Most illustrate how the interests of the state, as defined by its leaders, were in the forefront of decision-making. While approaches across these contributions are not uniform, included here to prompt debate, realist and neorealist perspectives nonetheless predominate in the chapters on specific regions. These are written mainly by area specialists steeped in the histories, politics, societies and languages of the systems they study. It is notable that the responses to the Bush Doctrine around the world, while mostly negative, did exhibit significant differences and were more complex than popular commentaries often suggested. It is perhaps appropriate, therefore, that the contributions in this volume are themselves reflective of distinct interpretations of the merits and flaws in the US approach to the world under Bush.

Before examining international reactions to the Bush Doctrine, Robert Singh in Chapter 2 outlines the Doctrine's origins and its relationship to 9/11, the defining event of the first decade of the twenty-first century. He argues that the Doctrine represents an intellectually coherent and distinctive marriage of Wilsonian idealist ends and muscular realist means. Its implementation, however, remains at best partial. Although the war in Iraq in 2003 demonstrated once again the supreme military capabilities of the US, the subsequent failures of the occupation graphically and gravely damaged American standing in the world. While the fundamental principles of the Bush Doctrine remain firmly in place as the lodestar of US foreign policy for Bush's second term, a combination of domestic and international factors powerfully constrain the likelihood of its practical implementation and, in particular, the prospect of a second preventive war by the US.

Bush's first-term policies placed strain on the transatlantic alliance that, if not without precedent, threatened a major rupture of lasting consequence. In Chapter 3, Donald Hancock and Brandon Valeriano contend that governance by centre–right coalitions in Western Europe was the 'decisive variable' behind support for the Bush Doctrine in the cases of Spain, Italy, Denmark, Norway, Portugal and the Netherlands. Ideology, however, was not a sufficient predictor, most notably in the contrasting cases of France under President Jacques Chirac – strongly opposing US action in Iraq – and the UK under Tony Blair. In the authors' view, Britain's 'special relationship' with the US accounted for 'New Labour' Prime Minister Tony Blair's unswerving backing. It is worth noting, however, that unease in the Labour Party ran high, with former Foreign Secretary and then Leader of the House of Commons, Robin Cook, resigning over the war and Development Secretary Clare Short eventually speaking out critically against war, along with the Liberal Democrats and the Scottish Nationalist Party. There was a view that it was only the government's misinterpretation of intelligence reports, taken earlier on trust by politicians across the spectrum, that gave Blair the decisive vote in the Commons that he needed. Certainly, debate among grass roots members was lively and acrimonious, and opposition to Iraq was a key reason behind Labour's loss of seats in the general election of 5 May 2005. Nuances specific to each state and European sensibilities fashioned responses. But, in affirming the existence of a 'post-modern' Europe, Hancock and Valeriano echo Robert Kagan's view of a Venusian continent sharply differentiated from a Martian America (Kagan 2003).

That notion, however, can be contested not only in terms of the divisions both across and within West European states but also in relation to Eastern Europe. The recent history of the collapse of the Soviet empire in Eastern Europe and the looking Westwards of states from Poland to Ukraine was an important factor in shaping the nature of support for Bush in Central and Eastern Europe. George Blazyca discusses in Chapter 4 how the historic fear of Russia underpinned governmental loyalty to the US, especially in Poland and the Baltic states of Lithuania, Latvia and Estonia. Polish President Aleksandr Kwaśniewski was also prompted to act, committing 2,400 troops to Iraq by the end of 2003, out of an interest in acquiring international prestige and contracts for post-war reconstruction. Blazyca discusses the relevance of the EU accession to decisions made in this region and observes the lack of public debate in the Polish press about the wisdom of war and troop commitments.

Much of the pro-US stance of East European governments can be explained by the legacy of the Cold War. Ironically, however, American relations with Russia were arguably improved by the Bush Doctrine's war on terrorism. In Chapter 5, Mary Buckley analyses the impact of terrorism inside Russia on support from President Putin for the war on terror, alongside the government's concern about what in the Bush Doctrine constituted 'good offence'. Putin and his ministers supported weapons inspectors in Iraq but not war, as did public opinion. Citizens, however, felt more positive about the USA in general than about the occupation of Iraq. Historic friendships with Iraq and Iran also affected reactions in Moscow, as did self-interest for oil contracts – the latter clouded by alleged corruption. It was Kazakhstan, not Russia, that sent troops from the region. Buckley also explores Russian security interests in Central Asia and the relevance to the region of Russia's partial displacement, the extent of military coordination, weak state capacity, terrorism in Uzbekistan and recent upheavals in Kyrgyzstan.

The other great power that demonstrated a marked ambivalence towards the Bush Doctrine was China. In Chapter 6, Rex Li examines alarm among Chinese leaders at what they perceived as an 'arbitrary expansion' of the USA's war on terror and a belligerent American unilateralism intent upon re-shaping the world. The Bush Doctrine was interpreted in Beijing as a shift in strategy that ran counter to international law and the UN Charter, although Chinese leaders did criticize terrorism. Concerns run both ways. Li discusses how the Bush administration is worried about the nuclear capabilities of an ascendant China and sees it as a strategic rival, unlike Japan. North Korea's withdrawal from the Non-Proliferation Treaty also antagonized Washington, a matter of immediate concern to the US, South Korea, China, Japan and Russia. Li explores the complexities of North-East Asian security, including the issue of Taiwan. He argues that the case of Japanese support was starkly one of maintaining the Japan–US strategic relationship, which was further strengthened after Cold War loyalties by documents signed in 1996 and 1997. Although Article 9 of its Constitution prevents Japan from taking part in military operations, Prime Minister Junichiro Koizumi was keen to despatch non-combat troops, despite criticisms from 54 per cent of Japanese citizens.

As with China, Japan and the other states and regions considered in this volume, national self-interest predominates in reactions in India and Pakistan – but with different outcomes due to both history and geo-politics. In Chapter 7, Samina Yasmeen charts how similar mixed responses in India and Pakistan suited the similar goals of both parties. Elites in both states wanted to see improvements in their national relations with the US. Yet they hesitated to make strong commitments to the Iraq war because of criticisms of unilateralism and support for multiculturalism. Yasmeen traces idealist and realist strands in Indian responses to the Bush Doctrine, strongly shaped by its adversarial relationship with Pakistan, and goes on to explore criticisms in Pakistan at a time when foreign policy had undergone a major shift to support the US war on terrorism. Here, the strongest criticism of the Bush Doctrine was that it was that it was part of a strategy to neutralize 'strong' Muslim states, thus with profound and potentially destabilizing implications for Pakistan itself.

The area most immediately affected by the application of the Bush Doctrine to Iraq was the Middle East, which was far more unsettled by the Iraqi invasion than the prior US intervention in Afghanistan. In Chapter 8, Anoushiravan Ehteshami assesses the complexities of the region and analyses various distinct responses. He argues that, whereas Bush's drive for democratization was generally criticized as neo-imperialism, the US war on terror also provided an opportunity for leaders to curry favour with Bush in order to obtain US backing for defeating Islamic-inspired violence at home. This pattern developed in Algeria, Egypt, Jordan, Morocco, Saudi Arabia, Tunisia and Yemen, alongside a defensiveness about the war on terror. Ehteshami traces the fear of preventive strikes against Iraq and how leaders in Jordan, the Arab League and even those unfriendly to Iraq – namely Syria, Saudi Arabia and Egypt – issued warnings of disastrous consequences to Bush. He goes on to examine different emphases in the responses across the region. Ehteshami stresses, however, how the notion of 'Islamic terrorism' was condemned outright with no-one linking it to Islam.

In stark contrast to Eastern and Western Europe, and shared with India, Pakistan and the Middle East, much of the continent of Africa is wracked by acute problems of poverty, AIDS and questions of basic survival. For most African leaders and citizens, the Iraq war was not their most pressing concern, although many nonetheless publicly condemned terrorism. Critics of war viewed economic development and an end to poverty as a surer way of preventing terrorism. In Chapter 9, Robert D. Grey addresses some of the complexities of US relations with African states and observes how, while Ethiopia and Eritrea joined the 'coalition of the willing', Libya and Sudan were perceived in Washington as supporters of international terrorism and, in Africa, it was thus feared that they were possible targets for the US in its war on terror. Whereas Europeans lacked any fear that states in their region might become US targets, with al-Qaeda as the most likely attacker, as the bombing of Madrid in March 2004 tragically illustrated, in Africa both the US and al-Qaeda were political actors of concern. Kenya and Tanzania had suffered terrorist attacks in 1998 and Kenya again in 2002.

Like the British under Blair, the Australian government offered what Brendon O'Connor in Chapter 10 sees as 'unreserved support' for the Bush Doctrine and preventive strikes. Dubbed by his critics as 'an American proxy' who has turned away from Asia, Prime Minister John Howard pursued highly pro-US policies and was keen to strengthen the US–Australia alliance. He sent troops to Afghanistan and Iraq and declared that Australia would use pre-emptive force in its own region against terrorism if necessary. O'Connor argues that the variable of political party alone, however, carries insufficient explanatory weight as the Australian Labour governments had been pro-US as well as Howard's Liberal Party/National Party coalition. In contrast, on a different foreign policy trajectory since 1984, the New Zealand government offered considerably cooler support to Washington.

If the responses to the Bush Doctrine differed significantly according to the complexions of distinct governments and their competing perceptions of national interests, the consequences of the Bush foreign policy were similarly varied and complex. Alastair Finlan's analysis of the security environment in Chapter 11 argues forcefully that the Bush Doctrine has caused more problems than it has resolved and, far from improving the security of the US and the world, has endangered it. The embrace of preventive war, unilateralism and militarism has caused untold damage to the traditional fabric of international relations while failing to address the most potent sources of threats to global peace.

In Chapter 12, Daphne Josselin examines an aspect of the Bush Doctrine of major consequence, the global economy. She notes that the 'consequences of Bush's spendthrift policies for the world economy have so far been largely beneficial, making the US the "engine" of world growth in a context of persisting economic sluggishness in Europe and Japan'. But Josselin highlights the important connection between the startling budget and trade deficits of the US under Bush and the problems these pose for an American imperium. Moreover, she argues that one of the key second-term challenges facing the administration is to reconcile the 'profound contradictions in the Bush Doctrine as it pertains to global economic trends: between short-term achievements and long-term prospects, and between claimed objectives and actual policies'.

Much of the international controversy over American policies was refracted through the prism of the US's relationship with the UN. As Stephen Ryan concedes in Chapter 13, the relationship was fraught and a major source of the illegitimacy that elites and publics attached to the US war in Iraq. But, as Ryan argues, the relationship was more complex than the Iraq imbroglio alone suggested and, when placed in historical context, 'apocalyptic visions were exaggerated'. Whereas the Bush Doctrine, along with other aspects of the foreign policy of the administration, represented a threat to certain basic UN principles such as non-aggression and respect for sovereignty, the actual record of the relationship was more complex than it appeared at first glance. The US under Bush maintained a close working relationship with the UN in many activities, even rejoining UNESCO after leaving the organization in 1984. Moreover, as Ryan notes, one consequence of the Iraq war was to cause the administration partially to reconsider the value of the UN and multilateralism.

The relationship of power and law is a central concern of the final two chapters of the book, As Malcolm Evans notes in Chapter 14, the implications of the Doctrine for international law were great. Although capable of being projected as a strategy to safeguard human rights around the world, the Bush Doctrine has instead been premised on the more cautious and introspective grounds of national security as a means to justify 'taking out the threat' rather than as a means of encouraging the export of standards of governance. A potentially transformational moment for shared views of the international order and the direction of international law was thereby lost. Moreover, with the symbolic image of the Iraq war less that of the fall of Saddam's statue and more the graphic photos of torture at Abu Ghraib, the US's moral standing was severely compromised. Phoebe Okowa reinforces Evans's deep concerns in the final chapter of the book, arguing that the multilateral legal order so painstakingly constructed over decades now confronts a potent challenge in the hegemonic position of the US and the Bush administration's clear – although not unprecedented – tilt towards unilateral action in the international arena. Although the US invasion of Iraq has caused potentially 'untold damage to the vitality of the norms constraining use of force as a set of neutral rules that applies to all equally', Okowa nonetheless offers reasons why multilateralism may yet revive. The very difficulties encountered by Washington in the Iraq occupation and the continued vitality of multilateralism in other fields – not least the coming into being of the International Criminal Court – point to an international order potentially less fractious than Bush's first term suggested.

Conclusion

By the end of the first year of Bush's second term as president, the Doctrine that bore his name had yielded a highly mixed set of results on the global stage. The heat that accompanied discussion of the Doctrine also remained intense, often to the detriment of the light of dispassionate analysis. Both proponents and critics of Bush's foreign policies could cite ample evidence to vindicate their respective positions.

Supporters of Bush argued that the president's boldness and unwavering support for the four pillars of the Doctrine had already produced remarkable and welcome changes. The two wars fought in Bush's first term had resulted in the overthrow of two of the world's most authoritarian, repressive and despicable regimes. The peoples of Afghanistan and Iraq, offered the opportunity to participate in self-government, seized it with relish. The supreme military might of the US, and the willingness to use such power to 'shock and awe', had been demonstrated clearly to those – especially in the Middle East – who had previously seen the US of the 1990s as a paper tiger. The US had extended its bases around the world to previously unimaginable nations such that America, uniquely, could project power around the entire globe. American relations with Russia and China had improved markedly while the support accorded Washington by the 'new Europe' proved how distant the EU remained from challenging, much less surpassing, American primacy. In the Middle East, Syria withdrew its troops from Lebanon in May 2005, and even hardened anti-American politicians reluctantly conceded that the ultimate cause of the 'Arab Spring' was the US invasion of Iraq. The emphasis accorded democratization, the determination to confront rogue states even by means of preventive and essentially unilateral war and the dogged pursuit of al-Qaeda by all means necessary together proved European cynics wrong (once again). Derision of the 'toxic Texan' blinded critics to the reality that a shrewd, fearless and carefully calculated strategy to reshape the world in freedom's favour was achieving remarkable results.

But, for many, more profound obstacles and disastrous outcomes obscured the nascent signs of progress. By the beginning of 2005, tens of thousands of Iraqis had been killed since the US invaded in March 2003, in comparison with some 1,700 Americans. Al-Qaeda had been denied its host state but, in disseminating more widely, the terrorist cells became ever more elusive. The Iraq war not only distracted the US from securing Afghanistan and tracking al-Qaeda in Pakistan but also resulted in a new and expanded cohort of *jihadists*, trained and tested in battle and ever more committed to the anti-western cause. The US military was, moreover, significantly overstretched at a time when serious threats outside the Middle Eastern theatre remained, and military morale was in serious decline. In addition, the Israel–Palestine conflict – for all the declarations of a 'roadmap' and US support for the establishment of a Palestinian state by 2005 – remained far from a clear, consensual and lasting resolution.

If the failure to defeat its enemies was not sufficient condemnation, America's breach with its allies was an equally disturbing development. Although the relationship between Washington and its European allies had been troubled throughout the Cold War era, and incipient signs of antipathy were clearly visible during the Clinton years, never had the transatlantic relationship been so acrimonious as during Bush's first term. Expression of anti-American sentiment became widespread, while America's standing plummeted to levels rarely seen before on the continent. At the same time, the priority accorded the war on terrorism helped Putin to step up his policy of 'securitization', interpreted by many as a halt to democratic reform, even its rollback. Arguably, however, some of the instabilities of the Yeltsin years – particularly in Moscow's varied relations with the regions and its discrete political deals – needed firm correction. Most non-Americans, and many millions of Americans (but, significantly, not Putin), had hoped for a John Kerry victory in the 2004 presidential election. Both were denied.

How much importance the president attached to international opinion after his first term was at best unclear. Bush's second term began with a ringing endorsement of his determination to spread democracy, safeguard American security and work tirelessly to – ultimately – 'end tyranny' in the world. Not since John F. Kennedy's address in 1961 had a presidential inaugural sketched such breathtakingly ambitious goals and expressed such an emphasis on the potency of American idealism and values. At the same time, in rewarding those who had demonstrated greatest fidelity to the Doctrine, Bush's appointments signalled his continued determination to control his administration in a way few predecessors had managed. Bush extended his policy reach by placing Condoleezza Rice as his Secretary of State, Alberto Gonzalez as his Attorney General and nominating Paul Wolfowitz to head the World Bank and John Bolton to be US Ambassador to the UN. Dick Cheney and Donald Rumsfeld remained as Vice-President and Defense Secretary respectively. Whatever emollient changes of tone with the rest of the world were initially flagged in 2005 – a 'dialogue' rather than a monologue, in Rice's words at her Senate confirmation hearing – there appeared to be limited reason to discern substantive alterations in US policy for the second term. The Bush Doctrine remained firmly in place in principle – whether it would also be so in practice remained to be seen.

In that respect, George W. Bush's place in the history books – a preoccupation of every second-term American president – hinges heavily on the success or failure of the Bush Doctrine. In particular, it rests centrally on the state of the Middle East by the time the president finally departs Washington in January 2009. Far more significantly, the fate of millions of people around the world rests directly on the outcomes of his administration's policies, at home and abroad. Rarely has an American president – and a foreign policy strategy – generated such worldwide attention, intense scrutiny and deeply divided opinions. Rarely, therefore, is dispassionate, serious and balanced critical analysis of the president and his policies more necessary and timely.

Note

1 Nogee and Donaldson (1985: 240); *Pravda*, 26 September 1968.

2 The Bush Doctrine

Robert Singh

This chapter examines the origins, content and contested meanings of the 'Bush Doctrine'. Although the Doctrine has never been formally articulated as such by President George W. Bush or his foreign policy principals, its four key elements – preventive war, confronting the nexus of weapons of mass destruction (WMD) and catastrophic terrorism, 'regime change' for 'rogue states' and democracy promotion – have become familiar themes in Bush's public rhetoric. These themes were outlined at length in the landmark speeches and publications of his first term in office (most notably, the State of the Union addresses of 2002 and 2003, the West Point address of June 2002 and the National Security Strategy (NSS) document published in September 2002). The NSS arguably represents as succinct and clear a statement of the Doctrine in its multifaceted dimensions as any US government publication that has sought to codify a broad foreign policy approach in a single document. After securing re-election in November 2004, the key themes of the Doctrine were also strongly reaffirmed in Bush's second inaugural address and State of the Union speech in 2005.

The analysis that follows locates the Doctrine's origins in a combination of structural and contingent factors: the dissensus among American elites over America's post-Cold War global role; the ascendancy within the Republican Party of a particular constellation of 'American nationalists' and 'neo-conservatives'/'democratic imperialists' to key positions within the foreign policy ranks of the executive branch; and the combination of threats and opportunities represented by the terrorist attacks of 11 September 2001. Contrary to many accounts of the Bush administration's response to 9/11, Bush both reversed some of his prior approaches to international affairs and maintained – even accelerated in more aggressive fashion – others. In particular, the tilt towards unilateral action and strengthening American primacy were features that 9/11 compounded rather than initiated. In engaging in an open and unapologetic embrace of American supremacy, however, Bush generated an unprecedented level of controversy over US foreign policy both at home and outside the US.

The central arguments advanced herein are threefold. First, the Bush

Doctrine represents an intellectually coherent amalgam of traditional 're-alist' approaches to international relations and an expansively muscular Wilsonianism. Second, as with the foreign policy of nation-states in general, and the US since 1945 in particular, the major problem with the doctrine lies less in its theoretical coherence than in certain inherent and abiding practical tensions that limit the degree to which the doctrine can be implemented – most notably the tension between its transformational objectives and the employment of appropriate means to realize them has yet to be reconciled by its proponents. Third, and despite this, while the Doctrine has generated widespread and intense opposition outside – and, to a lesser but significant degree – within the US, the scope of its departure from previous US policies and its relevance to the post-9/11 international system remains strongly contested. While some critics have alternately celebrated and censured the Doctrine as a 'revolution' in American foreign policy, others discern substantial elements of continuity with prior – and, in all likelihood, successor – administrations' approaches to international affairs and the imperative of American global primacy.[1] Like the Truman Doctrine previously, substantial elements of the Bush Doctrine seem likely to feature in US foreign policy not only during Bush's second term as president but also after Bush departs the White House in January 2009. Indeed, the domestic and international factors that underpin this continuity would probably have seen a John Kerry first term that departed less from Bush's foreign policies than either Kerry's supporters hoped or his opponents feared. Whether the key features of the Doctrine can realize both their proximate and longer term objectives, however, is considerably less certain.

This chapter proceeds first by examining the origins and content of the Bush Doctrine, arguing that its controversial international reception stemmed from its explicit embrace of a strategy premised unapologetically on an offensive strategy of preserving and strengthening America's global military supremacy. It then assesses the main criticisms of the Doctrine in the aftermath of the 2003 Iraq invasion, its principal practical expression. Despite the flawed planning and deeply negative features of the Iraqi occupation, the argument is advanced that the essential features of the Doctrine will probably remain in place as lodestars of American policy. However, a combination of political, diplomatic and logistical factors powerfully limits the prospect of a repetition of the central focus of international criticism – preventive and unilateral war – by the Bush administration in its second term. The rhetorical, stylistic and pacific changes that a second-term Bush administration makes should nonetheless not obscure the fundamental continuity in foreign policy principles that underpin Bush's approach.

The origins and content of the Bush Doctrine

Although widespread hostility to American foreign policies outside the US has been a staple feature of much of the republic's history, few – if any – presidents have excited the breadth, persistence and intensity of negative reactions that have accompanied George W. Bush's tenure in the White House. American presidents from Harry S. Truman and Lyndon Johnson to Richard Nixon and Ronald Reagan roused profound international ire on occasion, particularly in relation to their deployments of American military power. But, in his seemingly insouciant yet unwavering ability to symbolize all that many non-Americans most loathe about the US, Bush occupies a class entirely of his own. Moreover, while many of the objections to his administration rely on the most misleading and crudest stereotyping of both Bush personally and his administration's domestic and foreign policies, overwhelmingly it has been his (mis)conduct of foreign policy since 9/11 that has provoked the type of withering elite criticisms and mass disaffection towards America rarely witnessed previously. Whatever their many sources, few commentators dispute that the global anti-Americanism that has increased in breadth and depth since 2001 is firmly connected to Bush's leadership of America in the international arena and its declining standing therein.[2]

One of the many ironies that surround the Bush Doctrine, however, is that, in 2000, relatively few Americans or non-Americans had envisaged Bush presiding over such a provocative, muscular and pro-active phase in American foreign relations – including Bush himself. Although the Bush/Cheney campaign made references to rebuilding America's military and the need for a national missile defence system during the presidential campaign, the 2000 election was dominated – like those of 1992 and 1996 previously – by domestic issues. To the limited extent that they referred to foreign policy, both the formal and the informal signals from key Bush operatives suggested that the aspirant commander-in-chief would represent a return to his father's style of hard-nosed *realpolitik*. In his public comments during the campaign, Bush expressly rejected Clintonian humanitarian interventions, peace-keeping missions and 'nation-building' efforts abroad, favouring instead a coolly calculated appraisal of America's vital national interests. Neither terrorism (of global or localized reach) nor the proliferation of WMD figured highly in the Bush global agenda. Relations with the key 'great powers', most notably Russia and China, occupied the central focus of Bush's approach, while Iraq represented the main item of concern in relation to the Middle East. Most significantly, Bush argued that the way to earn international respect was for the US to display 'humility' in its foreign relations.

The attacks of 9/11 transformed Bush's approach. While academics disagree over the extent to which pre- and post-9/11 American foreign policy exhibited change over continuity, it is clear that the attacks were the catalyst for developments that otherwise would probably not have occurred at all or would have developed in far more piecemeal and fitful fashion. It is, for example, impossible to imagine a US military intervention in Afghanistan, US bases in several Central Asian states and the removal of US forces from Saudi Arabia, and difficult to conceive a US invasion and occupation of Iraq, without the intervention of the attacks. Similarly, the re-emergence of national security as a priority issue concern for all Americans, the signal priority accorded counter-terrorism, the centrality of the Middle East as the focus of US foreign policy for the first time in its history and the establishment of the Department of Homeland Security are merely some of the critical developments that owe their origin to 9/11. If, as Inderjeet Parmar (2005) rightly argues, 'the new more aggressive foreign policy pursued by the Bush administration [was] merely made more acceptable by 9/11, not made by 9/11 itself', it nonetheless remains the case that the tragic events of that day not only facilitated but forced a re-evaluation of America's world role as a 'reluctant sheriff'. Whether the Bush Doctrine represented a genuine consensus among the administration for a new approach or merely a rationalization for existing preferences, the Doctrine's provenance relied heavily on 9/11.

If the transformation of the Bush prioritization of, and key agenda items within, foreign policy owed the clearest and most direct debt to 9/11, however, notable fragments of the post-9/11 Bush approach were clearly identifiable long before the attacks. Most clearly, with the important but partial exception of Secretary of State Colin Powell, the administration's key decision-makers evinced an overwhelming commitment to promoting America's vital interests and a basic lack of faith in – to their critics, a suspicion bordering on contempt for – many international institutions. Treaties deemed injurious to the national interest were disregarded or abandoned (the Anti-Ballistic Missile Treaty) or left to work as best they could without the participation of the US (Kyoto, the International Criminal Court). Supranational entities were either treated with mild disdain (the UN), received mixed embraces according to their utility to US interests (the World Trade Organization, G8) or became increasingly problematic and largely politically symbolic vehicles for the expression of multilateral commitments by the US (North Atlantic Treaty Organization). Bush's world view was premised from the start on the need to resist unduly burdensome constraints – from international laws to allies – in order to ensure America's security and to change the global status quo to deal with security threats. While the extent to which the administration has consistently ignored international obligations has been widely overstated, the tilt of US policy towards a more unilateral approach was initiated in January, not September, 2001.

Yet many of these themes were more familiar than new to American foreign policy elites. The Cold War's end occasioned a voluminous amount of literature on foreign policy, the principal feature of which was the lack of agreement among its leading cohorts on the nature of the international system, the key threats posed America and its allies and the optimal strategic and tactical responses to these. In this sense, 9/11 offered a particular coalition of operatives within the Republican Party a series of enticing opportunities to advance objectives, priorities and strategies and tactics that they had long held dear. Conceiving of themselves as the functional equivalents of the Truman administration at the outset of the Cold War, the main foreign policy players in the administration envisaged the post-9/11 world – and America's place and role within it – to be at an historic turning point of epochal dimensions. It was this milieu that gave rise to the enunciation of the Bush Doctrine during 2001–02.

These were not, however, exclusively the infamous 'neo-conservatives' that have attracted so much attention as the infamous drivers – or, more commonly, 'hijackers' – of American policy. To be sure, certain self-consciously neo-conservative operatives occupied positions of notable influence in the administration (Paul Wolfowitz as the Deputy Secretary for Defense, Lewis Libby as Dick Cheney's Chief of Staff, Richard Perle as Chairman of the Defense Advisory Board and Elliot Abrams as Assistant Secretary for Middle East Affairs). But, as other commentators have noted, none of the central players – Bush, Cheney, Rice, Rumsfeld and Powell – were neo-conservatives. All of these were traditional conservatives or American nationalists, heavily influenced by realist conceptions of America's vital interests, sceptical of idealistic blueprints for the world and attentive to power politics and the use of force. Outside the administration, moreover, few neo-conservatives could even be identified – much less viewed as influential – in the precincts of Congress. Finally, those neo-conservatives who regularly found expression in print and television outlets were themselves frequently divided over both strategy and tactics.[3]

Central to the response to 9/11, and relatively neglected in most analyses of the Bush foreign policy, are three important developments. First, the American two-party system has, since the end of the 1960s, witnessed a steady but inexorable polarization that has exerted a profound influence on foreign policy. The Republican majorities' hold on the House and Senate from 1994 to 2006 (barring the period from June 2001 to January 2003 when the Democrats held the latter) was not only significant in itself but also, because the types of Republican officeholders were increasingly conservative, ideologically and increasingly secure electorally. While many were largely untroubled by foreign policy concerns, most held relatively hawkish views on the US role in the world, the significance of military might and the pusillanimous nature of the Clinton administration, erstwhile allies and institutions such as the UN. Second, the Cold War's end had lessened still further the American public's interest in international affairs, but this had not altered the nature of its views on military interventions or elite disagreements over them. If anything, the partisan conflicts over foreign policy that bedevilled Clinton from 1993 to 2001 confirmed that the Constitution's 'invitation to struggle' over control of foreign affairs was now rarely refused by either party. Third, to the extent that 9/11 represented a grievous failure of epic dimensions in established US policy, decision-makers in Washington had few sources to turn to for innovation other than conservative groups. The fact that terrorism had not figured as a priority on the Project for a New American Century's founding mattered less than that the group's members had been lobbying for a more aggressive and self-confident foreign policy since 1997. With Democrats facing the return of national security to the first rank of issue concerns, the resistance to Bush's declaration of a war on terror was minimal. The resistance to his framing of Iraq as a second front in that war, not a distraction from it, was only marginally less so in 2002. Through commission and omission, then, bipartisanship returned to the central organizing principle in US foreign policy for the first time since 1968.

The partial embrace of neo-conservative tenets was therefore a development that was powerfully advanced by 9/11 and the imperative that this forced on the administration to act with both urgency and commitment to confronting the existential threats – traditional and 'new' – to American national security. Four events during 2001–2 outlined the key elements of the Bush Doctrine before they were more or less concisely crystallized in the NSS. First, Bush took the strategic decision immediately following the attacks to declare this a 'war' rather than a criminal act and to cast states that harboured or assisted terrorists as *de facto* terrorists themselves (the initial reference to terrorists 'of global reach' was subsequently, and quietly, abandoned). This framing of the new era not only facilitated the targeting of Afghanistan – as the 'host' state of al-Qaeda (albeit that the latter arguably had as much control as the Taleban) – but also opened the possibility for broader American actions against states from Pakistan and Iran to Iraq and Syria. But it simultaneously raised the issue of who 'the enemy' was and how best to prevail over them. As George Friedman notes:

> The war that began on September 11, 2001, might be called the Fourth Global War, the US–Jihadist War, the US–al Qaeda War, or the US–Islamist war. Some would argue that it isn't a war at all but an isolated act of terrorism that has been manufactured into a war. Nothing tells us more about the extraordinarily ambiguous and divisive nature of the war than the fact that three years into it, we do not even have a name for it.
> (Friedman 2004: ix)

Second, the world was divided into a simple and binary 'us versus them' division on the basis of states' positions on the war on terrorism – at once providing clear threats to 'rogue states' such as Iraq, Iran and North Korea (compounded by their representation in the 2002 State of the Union address as an 'axis of evil') but also providing opportunities for potential US rivals such as Russia and China to side with 'democracy' against terror. Third, the threat served to legitimize Bush at home and unify the nation against a shared enemy, albeit one that shifted from a tactic alone (terrorism) to a potential pooling of terrorist activities and chemical, biological or nuclear threats. Fourth, the Doctrine assumed what its critics viewed as an openly messianic form in identifying the spread of a 'balance of power that favours freedom' as the ultimate solution to the growth of 'superterrorism'. Although the real focus of the anti-terror campaign was not directly cited as radical Islamists – the central 'swamp' that needed to be 'drowned' – the main, although not the only, source of the Islamist terrorists was clearly the Middle East. With growing conviction, the administration's key players thus embraced democratization as the surest path to a securer region and, thereby, a securer America and world.

For its supporters, the Bush Doctrine represented a shrewd, timely and pro-active foreign policy that distilled the best of American traditions together. In one of the earliest and most succinct expressions of the post-9/11 neo-conservative world view, Lawrence Kaplan and William Kristol (2003: 63) argued that, during the post-Cold War era, liberals and realists had approached the world from markedly different intellectual premises but reached the shared destination of a 'minimalist approach to foreign policy – one because the very concept of self-interest provokes discomfort, and the other because it defines the national interest far too narrowly'. By rejecting both the 'narrow realism' of George H.W. Bush's administration and the 'wishful liberalism' of the Clinton years, George W. Bush instead championed a 'distinctly American internationalism' and a maximalist foreign policy. In similar vein, Charles Krauthammer (2004) characterized the Bush approach as less one of neo-conservatism than 'democratic realism'. Metaphorically, Jacksonianism and Wilsonianism had been melded into a new hybrid, one unafraid to project American power or American values – indeed, one that saw the combination as inextricably linked for the preservation of American security. In this regard, the traditional biases of foreign policy approaches were subverted. The Bush Doctrine embraced liberal idealists' faith in (American) values, agreeing that the form of domestic regimes bore directly on their foreign policies and that 'democratic peace' proponents had it right. But the Doctrine evinced a much more tepid faith in international law and multilateralism as promising instruments to ensure liberty's advance in the new era. Wilsonian ends were thus married to hardheaded, realist means to yield idealism without illusions. The combination emphatically confirmed that, under the Bush Doctrine, the US was no longer a 'status quo power'.

To the extent that all public policies – and foreign policies in particular – are in part inherited rather than invented, three elements distinguished the new approach in the eyes of both its proponents and its critics. First, and most notable, was the openly positive embrace of what has commonly been termed 'pre-emptive action' but is more accurately known as 'preventive' war. Facing – in radical Islamists committed to catastrophic terrorism – implacable and determined enemies whose eschatology renders them undeterrable, in an era of WMD proliferation, the 'crossroads of radicalism and technology' precluded the notion that the conventional deterrent strategies of the Cold War could suffice any longer. 9/11 not merely legitimized but necessitated 'worst-case scenario' thinking. As Arthur Schlesinger (2004: 23) notes:

> Given the disrepute attached to the idea of 'preventive' war, the Bush administration prefers to talk about 'pre-emptive war', and too many have followed its example. The distinction between 'pre-emptive' and

'preventive' is well worth preserving. It is the distinction between legality and illegality. 'Pre-emptive' war refers to a direct, immediate, specific threat that must be crushed at once; in the words of the Department of Defense manual, 'an attack initiated on the basis of incontrovertible evidence that an enemy attack is imminent'. 'Preventive' war refers to potential, future, therefore speculative threats.

In this regard, while it remains unclear as to whether the leading administration figures' references to pre-emption were deliberate or inadvertent (and likewise why so many commentators referred to pre-emptive war without reference to the important distinction), the Iraq war was as clear an instance of preventive war – illegal under the UN Charter – as possible. As Lawrence Freedman (2004: 86) notes:

> Prevention is cold-blooded: it intends to deal with a problem before it becomes a crisis, while pre-emption is a more desperate strategy employed in the heat of crisis. Prevention can be seen as pre-emption in slow motion, more anticipatory or forward thinking, perhaps even looking beyond the target's current intentions to those that might be acquired along with greatly enhanced capabilities.

Like many of Bush's critics, Freedman is wrong to suggest that the collapse of Soviet power combined with the rise of superterrorism 'together suggested that deterrence was no longer relevant' as a strategy (Freedman 2004: 85). Just as national missile defence (NMD) is designed to supplement, not supplant, conventional defences, so preventive war is designed to add to traditional deterrent strategies rather than replace them. Iraq, however, was intended to be the first, but not necessarily the last, exercise of such an approach.

Second, the refusal to allow peaceful coexistence with rogue states prioritized regime change and recognized that America's national interests were best pursued by spreading democratic forms of governance: in stark contrast to the tenets of most realist theory, 'the character of regimes – not diplomatic agreements or multilateral institutions – are the key to peace and stability' (Kaplan and Kristol 2003: 105). As people should not be governed without their own consent, an unfree people would – explicitly or tacitly – consent to US government intervention to help bring about their freedom. To characterize this as imposing 'democracy by gunpoint' is an unfair caricature of the administration's policy, not least because the methods by which this administration – like its predecessors – has sought to encourage democratization range from economic incentives and aid conditionality to public diplomacy. What is clear is that Bush personally, with seemingly increasing conviction, adopted the tenet that the spread of American values is a fundamental public good. Robert Jervis (2005: 80) quotes Bush declaring to the Air Force graduating class in June 2004:

> Some who call themselves 'realists' question whether the spread of de-
> mocracy in the Middle East should be any concern of ours. But the real-
> ists in this case have lost contact with a fundamental reality. America has
> always been less secure when freedom is in retreat. America is always
> more secure when freedom is on the march.

Freedom, democracy and free markets represent, as the NSS puts it, 'the
single sustainable model for national success'.

Third, these and other second-order goals required the US vigorously to
preserve and enhance its global military pre-eminence as the surest route
to maintaining – depending on the author – its 'primacy', 'hegemony' and
'empire'. A humane global future requires a combative US foreign policy
that is 'unapologetic, idealistic, assertive and well funded', as the alternative 'is a chaotic, Hobbesian world where there is no authority to thwart aggression, ensure peace and security or enforce international norms' (Kaplan
and Kristol 2003: 120–1). A demonstration of an implacable willingness to
sustain and increase military primacy would help to foster a peaceful world
by making the logic and price of military competition unfeasibly high for all
other states, whether friend or foe. As Bush put it in his West Point address of
2002, 'America has, and intends to keep, military strengths beyond challenge
– thereby making the destabilizing arms races of other eras pointless, and
limiting rivalries to trade and other pursuits of peace'. This was not merely
a matter of sustaining such a level of expenditures that no other state or
group of states would seek to challenge the US, but also a declaration that
others would rely on the US to use force to defend them from threats. While
Madeleine Albright had previously antagonized some Europeans by referring to the US as the 'indispensable' nation, the Bush administration's open
commitment to maintaining an enduring and unassailable military primacy
fuelled fears of an excessively belligerent US approach to the world – not so
much indispensable as inescapable.

If the enthusiasm of long-standing conservative activists and intellectuals such as Kristol, Richard Perle and David Frum was predictable enough,
the Doctrine also won selective plaudits from some more surprising quarters
(Frum and Perle 2003).[4] In turning to what many heralded as a similarly
epochal moment, the pre-eminent scholar of the Cold War, John Lewis Gaddis, offered a qualified defence of the Bush 'grand strategy' as rational, reasonable and far more intellectually coherent than that of Clinton previously
(Gaddis 2002). Philip Zelikow, who went on to assist the 9/11 Commission's
investigation into September 11, also advanced the case that the new dangers,
structures and conditions of the post-9/11 world necessitated fresh thinking
and innovative policies (Zelikow 2003). Perhaps most remarkably, even some
intellectuals whose loathing of Bush's domestic policies bordered on vitriolic
embraced his presidency on foreign policy with equal enthusiasm. Most notably, berating his 'fellow travellers' on the Left, Christopher Hitchens (2003)
even touted Bush as exactly the type of president equipped – through faith,

conviction and certainty – to wage a global campaign against 'Islamo-fascists' intent upon their own version of global *jihad* (although, as Niall Ferguson (2005: 75) rightly notes, al-Qaeda is more appropriately regarded as 'Islamo-Bolshevist', 'committed to revolution and a reordering of the world along anti-capitalist lines').

If some new bedfellows were thereby acquired, it was no less surprising that previous partners in the conservative coalition now experienced considerable discomfort. The distinctive new approach generated fissures both between and within traditional foreign policy camps. Among traditionalist conservatives, several noteworthy figures were clearly ill at ease with the articulation of a global strategy that forsook subtlety, case-by-case analysis and clear-headed pragmatism regarding both objectives and instruments for an ideologically driven prescription of a 'one-size-fits-all' character. The cautionary op-eds of key operatives in the George H.W. Bush administration, such as Brent Scowcroft, James Baker and Lawrence Eagleburger, were mirrored within the George W. Bush administration by well-publicized spats between Powell – reluctant even to travel internationally for fear of being bested in Washington power politics – and Rumsfeld and Cheney. 'Palaeo-conservatives' such as Pat Buchanan, meanwhile, railed against the threat posed to the republic by openly imperial projects of global transformation. Within the American conservative coalition, however, such reservations occasioned memories of the 1980s, when another idealistic president had proved the supposedly wiser, more learned and sceptical counsels of Nixon and Henry Kissinger wrong. Reagan's death in 2004 added poignancy to the echoing fissures among conservatives.[5]

Among liberals, however, the embrace of a values-laden foreign policy exposed the fundamental strategic and tactical dilemmas confronting post-Cold War American leadership. That is, if the promotion of democratic forms of governance and America's ability to intervene to prevent genocide was contingent on the prior approval of other states and the concurrence of the civilian and military leadership in the Pentagon, such occurrences would probably be rare, inconsistent and ill-effective. For Democrats no less than Republicans, the painful memories of the Somalia, Haiti, Bosnia, Rwanda and Kosovo interventions during the 1990s cautioned against too strong and unqualified an embrace of multilateral institutions. That the post-9/11 threats to the US should be 'clear and present' dangers only compounded the political dilemma confronting sceptics of the Bush policy. With the notable exception of former Vermont Governor Howard Dean, the main presidential aspirants for the Democratic Party's presidential nomination in 2004 – including Kerry, John Edwards, Joe Lieberman and Richard Gephardt – had voted in 2002 for the authorization to use force against Iraq. Critics of Bush therefore focused on three key problems they identified in the new Doctrine.

First, and despite its commonsense logic, preventive war posed more problems than it solved. Not only did the Doctrine risk forfeiting the legitimacy of American action through its manifestly unilateral character, but it also risked spreading wars through its wider appropriation. The notion that states from Israel and India to Russia and China might be able to justify such action on the US precedent suggested that the entire edifice of international law – whose central premise was the unacceptability of wars not authorized by the UN Security Council – was now crumbling. Moreover, neither the standards of evidence nor the identity of the judge scrutinizing the imminence or inevitability of a particular threat seemed clear. The combination of the 9/11 attacks and the anthrax scare that immediately followed created a sufficiently broad and serious climate of fear in the US that the Bush administration's framing found resonance, with prior 'soccer moms' now morphing into 'security moms'. Who, after all, would wish to witness a 9/11 with WMD? Who could question acting first if such an event were likely? But that prospect occluded in many minds the more basic question of capabilities. That al-Qaeda would launch such an attack if it could was clear. That Iraq or Iran might wish to was less so. That they possessed the weapons to do so was even more open to question.

Second, regime change raised profound questions about the limits of state sovereignty that neither Bosnia nor Kosovo in the 1990s, nor Iraq in the 2000s, resolved. The US attacks on Afghanistan occasioned relatively little dissent from the political mainstream in America or elsewhere. But no broad-based or enduring international consensus had yet developed about the conditions under which a state lost its sovereign status – either because of its domestic repression or genocide or because of its supporting terrorists or engaging in WMD proliferation – or, if so, the mechanisms by which intervention should then occur. As the lamentable failure of both the UN and the 'international community' over the genocide in Darfur, Sudan, in 2004–5 once more illustrated, the history of multilateralism working in practice to address profound breaches in human rights was far from unblemished (see Power 2002; Polman 2003).

Third, the embrace of American pre-eminence was deemed problematic. For some critics, this was simply the 'arrogance' thereby implied. For others, the case was one of both 'overstretch' and excessive demands that could more plausibly be met by a more equitable international balance of power. For the majority of critics, however, the central flaw in this notion was less the basic goal than the overly narrow conception of power and the excessively limited range of instruments employed to achieve American goals. Joseph Nye, arguably the most prominent exponent of this viewpoint, strongly disagreed with the militaristic definition of power so beloved by the Bush hawks and the downgrading of 'soft power' – the ability to attract by example – that he claimed had been so vital over previous decades (Nye 2003a, 2005). But more conservative voices also rejected 'a risky and adventurous policy that utilizes military power as the instrument of first resort for a wide range of policy challenges' (Halper and Clarke 2004: 4). In Kaganite terms (Kagan 2003), in either neglecting or ignoring the multifaceted nature of 'hard' and 'soft' power, the 'Martian' administration not only alienated existing and potential allies but also squandered the 'Venusian' opportunities for maximizing its global influence – ironically, on this conception, the maximalist policy espoused by Kaplan and Kristol yielded minimalist results and those 'democratic imperialists' so enamoured of the rise of American empire pursued precisely the goals that were most likely to bring about its immediate failure and ultimate fall.

The Bush Doctrine and the legacies of Iraq

As the focal point for the Bush Doctrine's central tenet of confronting threats before they could strike, the stark contrast between the rapid military victory in May 2003 and the abject failure of post-war planning in Iraq over 2003–4 suggested to many observers that the Doctrine was an aberrant and temporary hiccup in post-1945 American foreign policy. The failure of the Rumsfeld approach, emphasizing light and mobile forces over large numbers of ground troops, suggested that the Powell Doctrine was less an exercise in timidity than an object lesson in judicious calculation – while the anti-American animus stoked by the intervention promised to bring the White House painfully back to recognizing the limits of unilateral action and the benefits of multilateral support. The practical politics for all concerned once again raised the spectre of Vietnam, occasioning echoes of long-familiar laments about Americans being unwilling to pay the 'blood price' to achieve stated ends. Far from its vindication, to many inside and outside the US, Iraq discredited the Doctrine only two years after its promulgation. The 'end of the neo-conservative moment' also represented the demise of the 'unipolar moment' – a fleeting and mercifully brief departure from multilateral reality, international legality and diplomatic moderation (Ikenberry 2004).

But declarations of the Doctrine's demise are decidedly premature, for reasons deriving from both domestic American politics and the current configuration of the international system. In certain critical senses, the attention devoted to Iraq over 2002–4 – while entirely justified – has rather obscured the extent to which 9/11 has not only altered the lenses by which a notoriously insular American public views the world but also reconfigured the terms of engagement for all parties in the international system. Let us take each in turn.

International relations scholars are often dismissive of the significance of domestic politics to foreign policy outcomes, but the US case is the least convincing in this regard. From the complex constitutional design and fragmentation of the state through the heterogeneity of its social base and hyperpluralism of its interest group universe to its Byzantine bureaucracy, American government – and hence public policies – is a porous entity subject to immense and conflicting pressures. In foreign policy, the importance of the public's insularity is not that this is unusual but that, because America is so powerful, it matters much more than the insularity of Belgians or New Zealanders. The steadily declining approval rating for Bush among the American people, from its peak in the high 80 per cent range in the months following 9/11 to barely 50 per cent throughout most of 2004, reflected not only the pronounced discontent with the outcome of the conflict, the continued violence and the controversy of Abu Ghraib but also substantial doubts about the terms of its original 'sale'. The failure to discover WMD, combined with the stream of charges of inadequate, unreliable and politicized intelligence, eroded support for the war (although less so than in the UK, where the Blair government had focused more consistently on WMD alone as the justification rather than on regime change, democratization and links to al-Qaeda).

More stark, however, was the continued agreement by the vast majority of Americans on the goals of US foreign policy and the broad bipartisanship on the war on terror. In July 2004, for example, the Democratic Party's national convention platform on foreign policy emphasized three priorities: fighting the war on terrorism; halting the proliferation of WMD; and spreading democracy around the globe. Shorn of the appeals for regaining America's 'respect' in the world, the three elements could have been lifted straight from the NSS. The broad bipartisan consensus on the war on terrorism predated and outlasted the dissensus over Iraq, however intense and partisan the latter undoubtedly became. Indeed, the Kerry campaign's evident discomfort over Iraq ('I voted for the appropriation before I voted against it') was a telling indication of the continued salience of fundamental security concerns to the American electorate.

In this respect, and notwithstanding its razor edge outcome in the popular vote, Bush's re-election in November 2004 put the lie to the notion that neo-conservatives had somehow hijacked American foreign policy after 2001. Or at least, it suggested that the concerns of that tendency extended far beyond the narrow confines of the American Enterprise Institute and were, in fact, deeply rooted in America's revolutionary history. But it was less the victory than the vexing problems that remained in the international system that suggested that the days of the Bush Doctrine were anything but numbered. Indeed, had 2 per cent of Ohio voters changed their minds, a Kerry White House would in all probability have faced similarly vexing international problems, similarly limited policy options and similarly unanticipated events – however much more syntactically correct and complete sentences would have finally reappeared in presidential addresses. The basic continuity of the Doctrine stems therefore from the deep continuity that its principal themes have with American values, interests and capabilities. While it remained the case that, even prior to Iraq, the administration's approach was not in sync with the more multilateral inclinations of the American public, a strong case can be made that – on international as well as domestic matters – the US remains closely, but not deeply, divided.[6]

Parmar is correct that the radicalism of the policy shift that occurred after 9/11 was not matched by automatic or permanent shifts in American public opinion. Opposition to the Iraq war was substantial. Even those supporting the invasion had reservations over the administration's case, and it is clear that support and opposition rested in part on the sources of information about the 'threat' (see, in particular, Kull *et al.* 2003–4). According to exit polls, almost 80 per cent of those listing Iraq as the key issue in their presidential vote in 2004 cast their ballots for Kerry.[7] But this should not obscure the broader support for the war on terror. Moreover, it is important to note that presidential elections are more the exception than the rule. Only rarely do elections to the House and Senate turn on foreign policy issues, allowing substantial autonomy to elected officials to pursue their own preferences. As such, the imprecise fit between the Bush administration's unilateralist tilt and the more multilateral tendencies of the American public may plausibly continue rather than falter.

If domestic factors point to its persistence, the Doctrine's continued salience also rests on six intractable features of the post-9/11 international system. First, American military primacy is unlikely to face serious challenge – either as a bipartisan cornerstone of policy or in terms of the military capacities of other leading powers. As such, any intervention in the world requiring large-scale military forces will be unable to occur without the US. Moreover, the fundamental logic of maintaining American supremacy remains sound. Iraq revealed a profound failure of planning for the occupation. But it also confirmed the lessons of the first Gulf War, Kosovo and Afghanistan, namely that no state with a rational leadership would actively seek a conventional military confrontation with the US. That the US spends more on defence than all other powers combined, at just 4 per cent of its gross domestic product (GDP), is merely suggestive of the distance. The technological superiority of the US – such that even established allies such as the UK find it difficult to overcome problems of 'interoperability' to work with US forces in coalitions – remains remarkable.

Second, the fact of US primacy reinforces two troubling consequences. As the logistical difficulties of working with allies compound the political ones, the inclination in Washington to go it alone will be reinforced. At the same time, the incentives for allies both to free ride on America's security guarantees and to distance themselves from its dealings with the world's most difficult states, threats and crises will probably grow apace. While Timothy Garton Ash's (2004) analysis of the interests that America and Europe share in working together to achieve a 'free world' remains fundamentally sound, the incentives by which both overcome their recent differences remain opaque. For America's adversaries, meanwhile, the costs of conventional war provide additional incentives either to acquire WMD to deter a US attack (or launch their own) or to engage in asymmetric warfare. If it is therefore deeply ironic, but essentially unavoidable, that the very preponderance of American power provides such incentives, it is nonetheless naïve to imagine that a reduction in such power would yield a preferable alternative.

Because of the above logic, the third constant in US policy is that the principle of prevention will remain on the table, however much the practice of state-building in Iraq will temper the political enthusiasm and severely constrain the resources for this in the medium term. The implicit admission by the administration in 2005 that, in seeking to end Iran's pursuit of a nuclear arsenal, a direct invasion was not feasible was the most obvious indicator of this. But the fact that the UN itself has had to consider how its Charter should be revised to take account of the possible legitimacy of preventive war is a powerful reflection of the changed conditions in the post-9/11 world. Perhaps the most serious long-term consequence of the campaigns to convince sceptical mass publics of the merits of preventive war in Iraq and the subsequent absence of WMD is that the bar has been raised much higher than in 2002–3 for the next instance of such an intervention. An American public already cynical about government and politicians has been confirmed in its cynicism. The evidential standards demanded for such preventive action in the future may well be not only much more demanding but impossible to meet without compromising intelligence operatives or the actual mission. A government that presses ahead regardless would be unlikely to survive long.

Fourth, whether or not anti-Americanism and the pool of *jihadist* terrorists would both have been swelled without the Iraq war, there seems little doubt that Iraq advanced both phenomena. The National Intelligence Estimate of 2005 confirmed that the situation in Iraq was likely to continue to worsen for years ahead. As such, continued terrorist attacks are inevitable, and the next 9/11 remains a matter of when and where, not whether. But European critics of Bush need to reason carefully as to these existential threats. Many of the *jihadists* – from 9/11 through the Madrid bombings to the Iraqi occupation – were recruited in or returned to Europe, and the strengthening of US homeland security is likely to impede al-Qaeda's dedicated efforts to strike again in the US. There is good reason to believe that it is Europe that faces the most serious threat of further superterrorist successes. As such, continued cooperation with the Bush administration on counterintelligence, combating money laundering and the other instruments of undermining terrorist cells worldwide remains central in the self-interest of all European governments and peoples.

Fifth, no serious comprehensive or compelling alternatives to the Bush Doctrine have yet been advanced beyond either a return to the partial multilateralism of the Cold War and post-Cold War/pre-9/11 eras or more utopian schemes for global government and the global redistribution of resources. The agenda of reform of the UN is one that will probably increase, not diminish, the prospect for international actions legitimized by a UN imprimatur while simultaneously decreasing the prospects of Security Council agreement to such actions. To add major powers will only increase the prospects for inaction, be this in regard to traditional security threats or instances of ethnic cleansing such as Kosovo and Darfur. The conditions and evidentiary standards for preventive war will likewise become more numerous and less feasible to meet. At the same time, the EU remains a military pygmy, riven by internal dissensus – not least over its fledgling constitution – and unable to exert meaningful influence globally other than through mechanisms of diplomacy and offers of financial assistance. Soft power, moreover, is not a power that is easily deployed by government and one of dubious utility when – for many radical Islamists – it is precisely what America is, not simply what it does, that is the problem. For all their vociferousness, many if not most critics of Bush have been silent on an alternative grand strategy that would prove both more acceptable internationally and more effective in achieving a secure America and secure world.

Sixth, and finally, the charge of unilateralism is likely to remain a familiar and, to non-Americans at least, a telling one. To Kyoto, the ICC, the biological weapons convention, the Anti-Ballistic Missile (ABM) treaty and Iraq, there will no doubt be many more to come. Unilateralism, however, is not synonymous with 'isolationism' but, rather, is a form of internationalism and, as such, represents 'the oldest doctrine' of all in American foreign policy (see Schlesinger 2004). Moreover, as a compelling analysis of President Bush notes, the reality is far more complex than crude caricatures of the 'cowboy' loner suggest. Bush is not averse to engaging with other governments. Indeed, he is a rather unusual unilateralist inasmuch as he places extraordinary – arguably too much – faith in his personal relationships with foreign leaders, be they favourable (Blair, Howard, Putin) or unfavourable (Arafat, Chirac, Schröder), such that they can even compromise the narrow pursuit of US interests (the relationship with Saudi Arabia being the most obvious example). As Stanley Renshon (2004: 71) argues:

> Criticisms that Mr Bush is a unilateralist and has alienated 'traditional allies' never really confront the questions that the president must answer. How much of America's security should he be willing to put into the hands of the French or Germans, whose national interests are not synonymous with those of the United States? How much of America's national security should be placed in the hands of the United Nations, given its track record on a number of international security matters? Until critics are willing to answer these questions, their critiques cannot be taken seriously.

The rise of the US as the world's only major superpower has prompted other states to recalibrate their own calculations of national interest accordingly and, thereby, to usher in a new system of US alliances with long-lasting allies (the UK, Australia, Japan, Israel), new ones (Poland, Thailand), strategic partners (Russia, Pakistan, India, Egypt), unreliable and partial allies (France), strategic competitors where selective common ground can sometimes be found (China), neutral allies aligned with the US in theory but often not in practice (Germany, Canada) and enemies (North Korea). The forging of 'coalitions of the willing' in pursuit of discrete, specific goals – whether the Iraq coalition, the six-party talks on North Korea or the Proliferation Security Initiative – represents an enterprise that is increasingly part and parcel of the Bush approach. But it is one that any occupant of the Oval Office would probably be forced to adopt given the nature of the international system. International collegiality, however desirable, has rarely been a product of nations pursuing their distinct interests (and, as Renshon notes, collegiality is not synonymous with good judgement and can be a key element of groupthink; the fact that an intervention may be unilateral does not of necessity mean it is wrong).

If domestic and international factors therefore suggest that the Bush Doctrine is not yet an aberration, at the start of Bush's second term, the principal constraints on the employment of its most controversial feature – preventive war – are also both domestic and international in nature. To take the latter, the prospect of Bush assembling a coalition is minimal. Even the UK is unlikely to participate in another military intervention on the scale, or pretexts, of Iraq. That does not preclude the prospect of more bellicosity from Washington or, for example, special operations or air strikes on states such as Iran and Syria – but it does suggest that sabre rattling will entail more selective means than massive ground forces.

But the most powerful constraint is likely to be domestic. From profoundly different perspectives, Nye and Ferguson have rightly argued that the American public's support for a *Pax Americana* is strictly limited in breadth and depth. The threefold deficits of economics, manpower and attention span are supremely immovable objects in the American political system, rendering presidential leadership difficult for even the most skilled of politicians equipped with a clear and far-reaching 'mandate' (Ferguson 2004). Admittedly, the evidence suggests that 9/11 raised the bar on the acceptability of military casualties (although public support has long rested more on the objectives of the mission and its prospects for success than casualties), and the Pentagon's prohibition on photographs of returning dead servicemen and women no doubt assisted in limiting the most heart-rending images of American fatalities. But more large-scale deployments are not only politically but also militarily infeasible with US forces currently stretched to their limits. The main mechanisms for addressing these key deficits – increased taxes, a partial return to the draft – are politically off the agenda, while the scepticism that will attend any campaign for preventive action (without a compelling level of credible intelligence) will be formidable. Furthermore, in one of the many ironies that the Bush approach has yielded, the more time that mainland America goes without a second 9/11, the less purchase on the public calls for preventive war will be likely to exert.

One final variable – perhaps the most significant and least predictable of all – is Bush himself. For the most powerful politician in the world, subject to constant scrutiny, Bush still remains a somewhat enigmatic figure after more than four years in office. In 2005, the academic debate over his genuine political colours remains as animated as most popular commentaries are heated and hostile. Is Bush a transformational leader, a political revolutionary who is willing to do whatever it takes to secure the goals he sees as necessary and desirable at home and abroad? Or is he a more FDR-style pragmatist, exploiting opportunities where he can but bereft of an overarching vision beyond opportunism? Is he a 'compassionate conservative' who seeks to use government to instil virtue and responsibility in American citizens or a hard-right ideologue whose secret agenda is the dismantling of American liberalism? Has Bush – as his generous and repeated praise for Natan Sharansky's *The Case For Democracy* in 2004 suggested – genuinely embraced democratic imperialism or is his instinctive realism the real George W. Bush? That such questions can legitimately be raised so far into such a controversial presidency, and after his re-election, may perhaps be indicative of how little we know about the American president even now.

Melvyn Leffler (2004), among others, has argued persuasively that Bush's radicalism has been powerfully overstated. In comparative and historical terms, patterns more familiar than unfamiliar are readily identifiable in Bush's approach since 2001: embracing a world order based on freedom, self-determination and open markets; accepting as legitimate anticipatory action couched in the rhetoric of liberty; desiring coalitions but lacking able and willing partners; approaching international affairs through a new prism because of the dawn of a new threat; stoking anti-American sentiment; and even preventive action. The extent of the confusion over Bush is partly an artefact of the exigencies of modern American politics and partly a function of the dynamics of intellectual life, with both supporters and opponents of the Bush approach exaggerating the extent of its break with historical precedent. Leffler's case is that Bush is vulnerable to criticism not because he has departed from prior policies but because the 'goals are unachievable because the means and ends are out of sync. . . . Only when ends are reconciled with means can moral clarity and military power add up to a winning strategy' (Leffler 2004: 28). Democratization of the Middle East, for example, rests uneasily with preventive war and supporting authoritarian regimes. Democracies may also be necessary, but not sufficient, conditions for ending terrorism. The challenge of the second Bush term is to achieve such a reconciliation of ends and means. Many of the key elements shaping the success of the Doctrine rely on forces beyond Washington's control but, if Bush has demonstrated one constant, it is that his critics all too often 'misunderestimate' a leader at once more resourceful, complex and authoritative than they typically concede.

Conclusion

History only rarely proffers the gift of accurate analysis upon presentist or 'in-time' critiques of momentous events and shifts in public policies. Few would have predicted in 1952, for example, that the incumbent president – declining to run for re-election in the face of a stalemate in the Korean War, McCarthyite accusations of widespread communist subversion in the counsels of government and massive public disenchantment at home – would

40 years later be lauded as a 'near great' president. Few, similarly, would have predicted that some 37,000 US troops would remain on the peninsula until 2004 and that their partial removal would then be deemed productive to the resolution of the ongoing conflict. Few, similarly, would have anticipated in 1981 the remarkable wave of American public sympathy and positive (re)appraisals that accompanied Reagan's funeral in 2004.

If there appears to be little reason to anticipate a change in doctrine in the Bush second term, there may nonetheless be cause to expect a change in practice, for four reasons. First, the burdens of Iraq, the less militarist approach to Iran and North Korea and the partial return to multilateralism over Syria indicate an appreciation by the administration of the limits of unilateral action. Second, the limited popular approval ratings of Bush and the continued human and financial costs of war pose severe political constraints on further military campaigns. Third, Bush's ambitious domestic agenda – featuring social security reform, tort reform, tax cuts and controversial Supreme Court nominees – combined with the growing national debt may plausibly limit both the political and the financial capital available to spend on further controversial projects abroad. Fourth, as ever in American politics, the ambitions of elected politicians – to return to Congress in the 2006 midterms and to advance to the White House in 2008 – invariably temper support for risk-laden presidential undertakings.

Rarely has a presidential foreign policy received so much opprobrium from so many quarters as that of George W. Bush. While it would be decidedly premature amid the voluminous amount of highly critical scholarly books, articles and anti-Bush polemics to speculate about the likelihood of revisionist works on the Bush presidency, a cautionary note is perhaps worthwhile. Bush's instinctive foreign policy approach has remained clear both prior to and since 9/11. Indeed, it exhibits more continuity than change with the sweep of US foreign relations through 200 years. What 9/11 primarily did was to alter the lenses through which he and key personnel in his administration viewed the world and America's role and place therein. That glaring, tragic and unnecessary errors of tactics, presentation and implementation occurred that characterized the Iraq occupation cannot be denied. The short-term consequences – for America's standing in the world, the spread of anti-Americanisms and perceptions of an existing or inevitable 'clash of civilizations' – have been immense and are likely to shape international politics for a generation. Whether the character of the analysis of the Bush Doctrine is more penetrating and prescient than misguided and malign, however, remains a matter upon which only the full course of Bush's second term and many more years of careful reflection will be able to judge.

Notes

1 The most cogent arguments for the revolutionary nature of the Bush Doctrine are Daalder and Lindsay (2003); Halper and Clarke (2004); and, in support of

the Doctrine, Kaplan and Kristol (2003). The most cogent attempt to locate continuity with prior US historical precedents is Gaddis (2004).

2 On the phenomenon of anti-Americanism and its relationship to US foreign policy, competing interpretations abound in: Hollander (2004); O'Connor and Griffith (2005); Revel (2002); and Ross and Ross (2004).

3 The most comprehensive and balanced analysis of the neo-conservative movement and ideas is Stelzer (2004).

4 Frum and Perle (2003), however, are decidedly more aggressive than Bush on US relations with Saudi Arabia and other authoritarian Middle Eastern states.

5 The clearest and most forceful conservative critique of Bush that rejects any comparison with Reagan is Halper and Clarke (2004).

6 This case is made with particular force in regard to domestic US politics by Fiorina (2005).

7 For the evolving American public support for the war, see the polls at http://www.pipa.org/

3 Western Europe

M. Donald Hancock and Brandon Valeriano

The American-led march to war in Iraq prompted what none other than Henry Kissinger proclaimed the 'worst estrangement' in transatlantic relations since the end of World War II.[1] Responses to the Bush strategy of preventive warfare varied widely at both governmental and citizen levels throughout Western Europe, prompting regional and domestic cleavages that mirrored political divisions within American society as well. The longer term consequences of regime change in Iraq, and potentially other countries in the Middle East, pose a formidable challenge to leaders and publics on both sides of the Atlantic. Can the transatlantic alliance be reconstituted on the basis of diplomacy and shared responsibilities in promoting American international priorities, as Bush administration spokesmen would have it? Or will Europe – acting through the European Union (EU) – eventually emerge as a counterforce to the American hegemon?

Fundamentally different perspectives on regional and international affairs underlie these choices. America continues to epitomize what Robert Cooper (2003: 22) has depicted as the 'modern' world, one based on the primacy of the nation-state and the use of force as 'the ultimate guarantor of peace'.[2] In contrast, most member states of the EU – now extended to include much of Central and Eastern Europe – constitute a 'post-modern' world characterized by the collapse of the traditional nation-state system into 'greater order rather than disorder' (Cooper 2003: 26). In Cooper's view, the chief tenets of the EU include political openness, shared sovereignty and the rejection of force by most of its members as a 'way of settling disputes' (ibid.: 30). The latter principle translates into a broadly consensual European policy embrace of what Mary Hampton (1966: 9) defines as a key tenet of 'the Wilsonian impulse': a preference for 'a jointly managed or regulated international system . . .' entailing 'the domestication and routinization of international politics'.[3]

The West European response to the Iraqi crisis divided governments and their domestic constituencies. One group of nations – led by the United Kingdom (UK) – joined the American effort to achieve regime change. A second group – dominated by Germany and France – voiced determined opposition to the Iraqi invasion. A third group of nations also voiced opposition, but in less strident language of internationalism. The purpose of this chapter is to explore these contrasting responses as a basis for assessing future prospects of transatlantic relations (including European efforts to achieve a viable regional foreign and security policy).

Divergent West European responses

Like most members of the international community, Europeans on both the elite and the mass levels of politics had vehemently condemned the attacks of 9/11. Similarly, West European officials had demonstrated strong support within North Atlantic Treaty Organization (NATO) for subsequent American military action against the Taleban regime in Afghanistan. But fissures began to surface within the transatlantic partnership during the summer of 2002 when the Bush administration declared its determination to launch a unilateral attack against Iraq to oust Saddam Hussein and destroy his alleged weapons of mass destruction (WMD).

Alongside Italy and Spain, Prime Minister Tony Blair announced his government's early support for an American-led pre-emptive strike. In contrast, most other EU member states – including several crucial NATO allies – favoured a diplomatic approach to the escalating crisis, advocating the resumption of UN weapons inspections in Iraq. In their view, military intervention to ensure the destruction of possible WMD should be considered a measure only of last resort – one that should necessarily be sanctioned by the UN Security Council.[4] On 4 September 2002, Chancellor Gerhard Schröder openly declared Germany's opposition to the American position on the grounds that a pre-emptive attack 'would amount to "submission" to US policy goals'.[5] Schröder's announcement signalled an open split within the Atlantic alliance between opponents and proponents of the Bush Doctrine. This cleavage carried over into the highest policy counsels of the EU, whose leaders proved unable at an emergency summit meeting in Brussels in February 2003 to forge a joint position on the Iraqi crisis in the context of the EU's common foreign and security policy.

The special case of Britain

The resumption of UN weapons inspections, the Bush administration's rejection of the team's findings and a threatened veto by France, Russia and China of a proposed British–American Security Council resolution sanctioning the use of military means to enforce Iraqi compliance with disarmament constituted a rapidly spiralling prelude to the American-led invasion of Iraq on 20 March 2003. Britain joined the American side as the most visible member of an ad hoc 'coalition of the willing'. Other West European contingents – in descending order of the number of troops they eventually deployed to Iraq – included Italy, Spain (until 2004), the

Netherlands, Denmark, Norway and Portugal. Ireland lent verbal, but no material, support to the Anglo-American position.[6]

In the UK's case, the historically based 'special relationship' between Britain and the US proved of primary significance in Tony Blair's early moves to ally himself with the Bush administration. Just as both countries had supported each other in most twentieth-century international conflicts,[7] it followed that they would join forces once again. Other considerations influenced Blair's decision as well. One of them was Britain's long-standing rivalry with Iraq and its guarantee of an independent Kuwait, which helped prod the US to take action against Iraq in the Gulf War of 1991. In addition, Britain has been the only European country consistently to support the Bush administration's policies against international terrorism in general and the Middle East in particular. Blair endorsed the invasion of Iraq as a 'just cause', just as he subsequently supported American strategies of post-war reconstruction and democratization.

Moreover, alliances come in many forms, and one such form is a restraining alliance (Schröder 1976: 227–62). A partial explanation for Britain's active engagement in NATO is that it serves as a counterweight to perceived American militarism. Blair also presumably believed that Britain could assert a moderating influence on the course of the war, its intermediate aftermath and possible future applications of the Bush Doctrine.

Continental and Nordic support

In the absence of a special relationship with the US comparable to Britain's, domestic political factors proved the over-riding motivation in decisions by various continental and Nordic governments to support the 'coalition of the willing' – and later, in the case of one of them, to prompt a dramatic policy reversal. The decisive variable was governance by centre-right coalitions whose leaders intuitively sympathized with American policy.

National elections prior to the Iraqi invasion had yielded conservative victories in all six of the West European countries that joined Britain in contributing forces to the Iraqi operation. Spain's Popular Party – comparable ideologically to Christian Democratic parties elsewhere on the continent – easily won re-election in March 2000 after serving four years in office. Both the Socialists and the separatist Basque Party suffered major losses as the Popular Party rode an economic boom to gain an absolute majority of seats in the lower house of parliament. Its leader, José María Aznar, was reappointed Spain's premier for another four-year term.

The Italian election of May 2001 yielded a similar ideological tilt to the right, albeit under the conditions of a more fragmented multiparty system. Silvio Berlusconi, chair of the maverick *Forza Italia!* populist movement, led a centre–right coalition of parties to victory over the previously governing 'Olive Tree' coalition of centre-left parties dominated by the (post-communist) Socialists.[8] Centre-right parties scored equivalent victories in Denmark and Norway that same year and in Portugal in March 2002, while a Christian Democratic-dominated coalition assumed power in the Netherlands following a close election in January 2003.

Together, these six countries contributed the approximate equivalent of two-thirds of the military forces deployed by Britain by the spring of 2004, as indicated in Table 3.1. Italian, Spanish and Dutch troops comprised relatively meaningful contingents, while Danish, Norwegian and Portuguese troops were at best token members of the 'coalition of the willing'.

Public opinion was sharply divided among members of the coalition about whether the Iraq war was worth the eventual loss of lives and other costs. According to opinion surveys conducted in 2003 by the German Marshall Fund, the highest level of support was in Britain where 45 per cent of respondents supported the war effort compared with 55 per cent who were opposed. Corresponding figures were 41 per cent in favour and 59 per cent opposed in the Netherlands and only 28 per cent in favour and 73 per cent opposed in Italy (Asmus *et al*. 2004: 8).[9] Governance rather than public opinion was thus decisive in determining West European support for American actions.

The primacy of domestic politics in determining continental West European responses to the application of the Bush Doctrine to Iraq was dramatically underlined in the immediate aftermath of a terrorist train attack that killed more than 200 people on 11 March 2004 in the Spanish capital of Madrid. The Christian Democratic-led government initially blamed Basque separatists for the carnage, discounting evidence that al-Qaeda operatives had executed the onslaught. The opposition Socialist party rode the wave of a voters' backlash against the governing coalition's misinformation to score a decisive victory in a parliamentary election three days later. After the Socialist victory, Premier-elect José Luís Rodríguez Zapatero sharply criticized the Anglo-American leaders of the war effort: 'Mr Bush and Mr Blair must do some reflection and self-criticism. You can't organize a war with lies'. He characterized the Iraqi invasion and subsequent occupation as 'a disaster. It

Table 3.1 American and West European troops in Iraq, March 2004

Country	Number of troops
United States	130,000
United Kingdom	9,000
Italy	3,000
Spain	1,300
Netherlands	1,100
Denmark	420
Norway	179
Portugal	128

Source: PWHCE (Perspectives on World History and Current Events), 'Coalition of the Willing', www.electablog.com, 13 November 2004.

hasn't generated anything but more violence and hate.'[10] True to his campaign promises, Zapatero subsequently withdrew Spanish troops from Iraq and vowed to move Spain 'closer to Europe'.

The March bombings and their political aftermath thus diminished by one country the official pro-American alignment within Western Europe. Romano Prodi, president of the European Commission, praised the Zapatero cabinet for Spain's policy reversal. 'With this decision', Prodi declared, 'Spain has fallen into line with [the position of most members of the EU]. The divide that prevented Europe from having a common position is being overcome.'[11]

German–French opposition

Western Europe's most outspoken critics of the Iraqi invasion – and by extension the Bush Doctrine – were Germany and France. Chancellor Schröder had voiced his government's opposition to American policies as early as August 2002 when he described an invasion of Iraq as 'an adventure' that 'could destroy the international alliance against terror' assembled by the US after 9/11.[12] President Chirac and other officials were initially more ambivalent in their response to the escalating crisis, indicating that France might join in military intervention if the UN Security Council determined that Iraq had blatantly violated Security Council resolution 1441 with regard to the existence of WMD. France shortly joined the Germans, however, in condemning Anglo-American determination to engage in pre-emptive action.[13] These nuanced positions reflected contrasting national calculations based on a combination of domestic politics and EU sensibilities.

Schröder's immediate partisan concern was the fate of his governing coalition, made up of the Social Democrats (SPD) and the Greens. Following elections in 1998, the Social Democrats and Greens had displaced a Christian Democratic–Free Democratic coalition that had governed Germany since 1982. National elections scheduled in September 2002 would determine whether or not the SPD–Green coalition would continue in office for another four years. Opinion surveys indicated massive citizen opposition to the impending Iraq war, which Schröder and other SPD–Green party stalwarts seized upon to mobilize electoral support on the government's behalf. In a larger sense, Schröder's anti-war campaign rhetoric expressed deeply felt beliefs among most adult Germans that war unsanctioned by UN Security Council resolution was not a legitimate policy option. These beliefs are rooted in a fundamental transformation of German political culture from historical patterns of militarism associated with the Imperial and Nazi eras to entrenched mass attitudes affirming a mixture of pacifism and Wilsonian principles in the conduct of German (and European) foreign policy.

Opposition candidates in the Christian Democratic and Free Democratic parties tacitly endorsed the government's declaration that Germany would not support a war effort against Iraq while attempting to transform the electoral campaign into a national referendum on Germany's sluggish economic performance and high unemployment rate. In the end, the SPD–Green strategy prevailed. Despite a modest increase in electoral support for the Christian Democrats, the SPD and Greens won a combined majority of 47.1 per cent of the popular vote and a sufficient number of seats in the lower house of parliament to reconstitute the governing coalition. Schröder felt personally and politically vindicated by his defiance of American policies. President Bush churlishly returned the 'favour' by undiplomatically refusing to call Schröder to congratulate him on his re-election.

The French position largely paralleled that of Germany, albeit for different political reasons. After first considering and then rejecting possible French participation in a military campaign against the Hussein regime, Chirac joined Schröder in issuing a joint statement in Paris on 22 January 2003, opposing immediate military action. Chirac asserted: 'France and Germany have the same point of view on this crisis. Any decision belongs to the Security Council and the Security Council alone.'[14] More stridently, Chirac instructed his foreign minister, Dominique de Villepin, to declare at a meeting of the UN Security Council in New York that 'nothing today justifies envisaging military action'.[15]

Chirac's principal motivation was France's long-standing claim to assert political leadership in Europe. This vision had prompted the French initiative in helping to launch the European integration movement in the early 1950s, former President Charles de Gaulle's imperious decision to quit the military arm of NATO and create an autonomous nuclear *force de frappe* in the mid-1960s and an ongoing French–German alliance on behalf of strategic initiatives to dominate political discourse and policy outcomes within the EU. Chirac's calculation was that, by opposing the Anglo-American campaign, France – with the support of Germany and other EU members – could transform Europe into a political hegemon in its own right.

The middle position

Between the extremes of British-led support for military action against Iraq and adamant German–French opposition, a number of West European countries embraced an internationalist position on the conflict. These included Sweden, Finland and Austria (all of which are officially non-aligned) as well as NATO members Luxembourg and Greece.

Representative of an explicitly 'post-modern' stance on the conflict was a declaration by the Swedish Foreign Ministry in March 2003: 'It is deeply regrettable that war has now broken out. The US and its allies are attacking Iraq without a mandate from the UN and are therefore violating international law.' The Swedish government readily conceded that the Hussein regime was a 'danger against international peace and security', but it could justify military action against the regime only as 'a final recourse if Iraq refused to cooperate with the UN's Security Council in conformity with resolution 1441 and if Iraq continued to develop or maintained WMD. Only the Security

Council – *not a country acting unilaterally* – has the authority to pass judgement on Iraq's behaviour and to decide whether to use military force against it'.[16]

West European attitudes in the aftermath of war

A key question for Western Europe is 'what did its leaders and citizens learn from the attacks of 9/11?' As the Bush Doctrine states, 'The events of September 11, 2001, taught us that weak states, like Afghanistan, can pose as great a danger to our national interests as strong states.'[17] Did Europe draw the same conclusion? Not entirely. Clearly leaders from London to Paris and Berlin recognize international terrorism as a serious threat to their own national security. Yet most West Europeans – emphatically including a majority of Spaniards, who have thus far experienced the closest equivalent to 9/11 – reject the American rationale for pre-emptive strikes. With notable exceptions such as the Blair administration, much of Western Europe continues to espouse Wilsonian and post-modern principles of internationalism and collective security.

In the short run, the Iraq war sharply eroded European confidence in American global leadership. According to Eurobarometer surveys conducted in October–November 2004, aggregate public belief in the 15 West European member states of the EU that the US 'positively contributes' to world peace declined from 30 to 21 per cent from the previous year. The corresponding percentage of those who held a negative attitude towards the US role jumped from 42 to 61 per cent.[18] Among the larger West European states, the most negative opinions were predictably voiced in France, Germany and Spain. Public attitudes towards the US in Italy and the UK were somewhat more balanced, although negative opinions outweighed positive ones in both countries (Table 3.2).[19]

West European attitudes towards the role of the US in combating international terrorism were relatively more supportive, although negative opinions continue to dominate in the countries that most vehemently opposed the Iraqi invasion. Again, public attitudes in the UK and Italy were more favourable (Table 3.3).

Table 3.2   Percentage responses within the EU to the question: 'In your opinion, would you say that the United States tends to play a positive role, a negative role or neither regarding peace in the world?'

Responses	*EU 15*	*France*	*Germany*	*Spain*	*Italy*	*UK*
Positive	21	10	17	17	30	32
Negative	61	74	69	67	48	44
Neither positive nor neutral	14	12	12	9	16	19
Don't know	4	4	2	6	7	5

Source: Eurobarometer 62 (December 2004). Rounding errors in Eurobarometer 62 have resulted in some columns adding up to 99 or 101.

Table 3.3   Percentage responses within the EU to the question 'In your opinion, would you say that the United States tends to play a positive role, a negative role or neither regarding the fight against terrorism?'

Responses	France	Germany	Spain	Italy	UK
Positive	27	36	23	37	55
Negative	55	45	58	42	27
Neither positive nor neutral	13	15	13	15	13
Don't know	5	4	6	6	4

Source: Eurobarometer 62 (December 2004).

Partly as a consequence of widespread scepticism towards US foreign policy in the aftermath of the war, a majority of West European citizens expressed increased confidence in the EU as an international political actor. According to Eurobarometer data released in December 2004, 61 per cent of respondents viewed the EU as making a positive contribution to peace in the world (compared with 11 per cent who considered its role as negative and 22 per cent who had no opinion). A nearly identical 59 per cent accorded the EU a positive role in the international fight against terrorism.[20]

An even greater number of West Europeans affirmed their support for a Common Defence and Security Policy (CDSP) as a security extension of the EU and therefore conceivably a potential counterweight to America's role in world affairs.[21] Reflecting regional European cleavages during the war, French and German respondents expressed the strongest endorsement of a CDSP. Somewhat narrower majorities expressed support in Italy and Spain. Less than two-thirds were in favour of CDSP in the UK (Table 3.4).

Intermediate transatlantic responses

Public attitudes constitute an important source of support for and constraints on policy choices, but actions by national elites – in the absence of revolutionary or quasi-revolutionary popular upheavals against their authority – determine both immediate and intermediate political outcomes. Reconciling themselves to Bush's re-election in 2004 and the extension of his presidency for another

Table 3.4   Percentage responses within the EU to the question 'Are you for or against a Common Defence and Security Policy among EU member states?'

Responses	EU 15	Germany	France	Italy	Spain	UK
For	77	87	81	79	78	60
Against	15	10	12	12	11	27
Don't know	8	3	7	9	11	14

Source: Eurobarometer 62 (December 2004).

four years, West European leaders proved publicly responsive to initial efforts to reconstitute the transatlantic alliance (especially in the aftermath of democratic elections in Iraq in January 2005). They listened attentively to Secretary of State Condoleezza Rice's call for Europe to join the US in a joint effort to promote peace and expand democracy in the Middle East. In a speech at the Institute of Political Studies in Paris, Rice declared to a generally receptive audience of French luminaries: 'America has everything to gain from having a stronger Europe as a partner in building a safer and even a better world. So let each of us bring to the table ideas, experience and resources, and let us discuss and decide, together, how best to employ them for democratic change.'[22]

President Bush's own trip to Europe several weeks later underlined his administration's rhetorical commitment to strengthening transatlantic ties weakened by American unilateralism against Iraq. As Bush declared in mid-February in Brussels, 'The alliance of Europe and North America is the main pillar of our security in a new century. Our strong friendship is essential to peace and prosperity across the globe – and no temporary debate, no passing disagreement of governments, no power on earth will ever divide us.'[23]

Despite expressions of personal warmth by Chirac and studied cordiality by Schröder during Bush's European visit, important EU–American differences continue to confront the Atlantic alliance. Iraq remains a foremost conundrum. A formidable sceptic of US policies is the EU's High Representative for Common Foreign and Security Policy (CFSP), Javier Solana, who critically reflected in an interview whether the January 2005 election to an Iraqi national assembly was 'a vindication when you count how many billions of dollars have been spent, how many people have been killed, how many soldiers have died? It is a little too early to say.' Solana then added: 'Iraq is not over . . . Think about it. What kind of regime will emerge? It is too early to say. You don't know what is going to happen in Iraq . . . Will it be a government of theologians or engineers?'[24]

Other divisive issues include a transatlantic dispute over the resumption of European arms sales to China and possible US military intervention against Iran and other 'rogue nations' in the name of the Bush Doctrine. Assessing these conflicts extends beyond the scope of this chapter but, collectively, they underline the significance of different strategic choices confronting member states of the North Atlantic community.

Alternative strategic choices

One response is for West European leaders to take the second Bush administration at its word, as most of them did in early 2005, and join the US in a coordinated strategy of nation-building in Iraq and democratization beyond.[25] For all of his criticism of the Iraqi invasion, Schröder has declared: 'As Europe expands and deepens as a result of the integration process, its unity will become increasingly apparent in issues of foreign and defense policy, and this united Europe must be a partner of the United States, a partner of equal standing.'[26]

An early expression of transatlantic acquiescence in Bush's international security strategy was the European response to the first application of the (as yet unnamed) Bush Doctrine in the war against the Taleban regime in Afghanistan. Whereas President Bush was widely perceived as 'an ill-informed cowboy' upon his election in 2000, Gordon and Shapiro (2004) note that he 'surprised the Europeans with his patient, careful, and proportionate action in Afghanistan. In turn, Europeans also broke with stereotypes, strongly supporting military action not only against the al-Qaeda network but also against its Taleban hosts.'

Contrasting European responses to the Afghanistan and Iraqi operations reveal different levels of acceptance of the Bush Doctrine. West Europeans support action against terrorism largely because of their own vulnerability to such attacks, but most reject the corollary application of the Bush Doctrine against sovereign states. Accordingly, a unilateral invasion of another independent nation-state – for example, Iran or Syria – would be likely to encourage an alternative West European response. Specifically, such an act might prompt at least some European leaders to seek to forge a regional political and military counterweight to the American hegemon. Opinion polls cited above reveal widespread public support for a stronger CDSP under EU aegis. To be effective, such a response would have to be backed by forceful common EU positions on international issues and the deployment of operational military forces.

Yet how realistic is this prospect? Not very, at least in the foreseeable future. A key reason is that member states – even those most critical of the Bush Doctrine – remain reluctant to transfer national sovereignty over security issues to intergovernmental, much less supranational, institutions. As Roger Cohen has noted, 'the Iraq war posed an intra-European crisis that was as acute as the transatlantic crisis. The EU was split . . . [S]o deep was the division that no serious attempt to reach a united EU position was made.'[27] Underlining this difficulty is that Europe does not currently have a strategic doctrine beyond a preference shared by France and a number of other countries to include the UN Security Council in important security decisions.

Conclusion

From a more abstract perspective, while Europe has always been the test case for models of realist action (including power politics and balance of power), rarely has Europe adopted the concept of traditional realism in the way that American academics have readily accepted the theory. Consistent with the EU's status as a post-modern system, most Europeans do not consider power the ultimate rationale for international action. Nor do they embrace concepts such as the 'defence of national interest' (at least in the post-Gaullist era) unless they express a deep concern for the territorial integrity of Europe.

Instead, as Kaplan suggests, 'Europe, because of its unique historical experience in the past half-century . . . has developed a set of ideals and principles regarding the utility and morality of power different from the ideals and principles of Americans, who have not shared that experience' (Gordon and Shapiro 2004: 215).

A European theoretical outlook on warfare will therefore remain largely an institutionalist statement on the efficacy of international regimes. European leaders place greater faith in the UN, EU and NATO than their American counterparts. As the divergent European responses to the Iraqi war revealed, most of Western Europe rejected the Bush Doctrine's rationale for unilateral military action in favour of diplomacy and a combination of economic incentives and sanctions to encourage the peaceful resolution of international crises.[28]

This conflict over values and interests is likely to shape the course of transatlantic relations for years to come. As Kaplan (2002: 211–44) has observed, 'the reasons for the transatlantic divide are deep, long in development, and likely to endure'. One cannot understand the current situation without reference to the past and the evolution of strategic doctrines within each country. Concomitantly, one also cannot assume that the differences are a result of power considerations (Europe is now weak and America is strong). Instead, they are the result of real philosophical differences regarding the use and morality of force in the international system.

To conclude on a sobering note, the Bush Doctrine and its 'successful' application against the Hussein regime in Iraq establishes a disquieting precedent for other modern states to resort to pre-emptive measures against enemies of their own. This very prospect should encourage post-modern systems to redouble their efforts to reassert the dual primacy of diplomacy and international law.

Notes

1 Henry Kissinger. 'Role reversal and alliance realities'. *Washington Post*, 27 March 2003. Cited in Pond (2004: ix).
2 Cooper also distinguishes a 'pre-modern' world of nations characterized by 'pre-state, post-imperial chaos', citing as examples Somalia, Afghanistan, Liberia and Chechnia (p. 16).
3 Another crucial tenet of Wilsonianism was, of course, a willingness to go to war to 'make the world safe for democracy'.
4 This position was supported at the time by 65 per cent of American public opinion and 60 per cent of the Europeans.
5 Facts on File, World News Digest, 'US President Bush vows to seek support from Congress, allies on Iraq attack'. 5 September 2002 (www.facts.com).
6 A number of Central and East European countries eventually contributed troops as well: Poland, Ukraine, Romania, Bulgaria, Hungary, Azerbaijan, Latvia, Lithuania, Slovakia, the Czech Republic, Albania, Georgia, Moldova, Macedonia and Estonia. See Chapter 2 for details.
7 An obvious exception was American condemnation of the French–British invasion of the Suez Canal zone in 1956.

8 The winning coalition consisted of Berlusconi's *Forza Italia!* ('Go Italy!'), the pro-market Northern League and the post-fascist National Alliance.

9 The survey reports no opinion data from Spain, Denmark, Norway or Portugal.

10 Facts on File, World News Digest, 'Socialists win Spanish elections in aftermath of Madrid bombings'. 18 March 2004, p. 2.

11 *New York Times*, 19 April 2004.

12 Facts on File, World News Digest, 'Germany: Chancellor rejects US war on Iraq', 22 August 2002. Germany had previously demonstrated its support for the international anti-terrorist campaign by committing 4,000 troops to Afghanistan.

13 The governments of Belgium and Greece also joined Germany and France in opposing the Anglo-American invasion.

14 Facts on File, World News Digest, 'France, Germany oppose military action against Iraq'. 23 January 2003, pp. 2–3.

15 Ibid.

16 Utrikesdepartementet (Swedish Foreign Ministry), 'Svensk uppfattning i Irak-frågan' (Stockholm, 21 March 2003). Author's translation. Italics added for emphasis.

17 *National Security Strategy of the United States of America*, p. 2.

18 Eurobarometer 62 (December 2004).

19 A 7 per cent increase in negative attitudes in Italy presumably contributed to Premier Berlusconi's declaration in March 2005 that his government would begin withdrawing troops prior to the 2006 national election.

20 Eurobarometer 62 (December 2004). Eleven per cent held negative views towards the EU's role in combating terrorism and 23 per cent said they did not know.

21 The European Union's existing CFSP has its roots in a long tradition of European Political Cooperation (EPC) launched during the early decades of European integration. It was formally institutionalized in the Treaty of European Union of 1992. The CFSP is an intergovernmental extension of the EU and largely rests on unanimous decisions among the member states on whether to endorse a collective position on external conflicts and engage in collective security operations. Useful assessments of CFSP include Duke (2000), Hoffmann (2000), Ginsberg (2001), White (2001) and Smith (2004).

22 *New York Times*, 9 February 2005.

23 *New York Times*, 21 February 2005.

24 *International Herald Tribune*, 21 February 2005.

25 An empirical measure of such support was an agreement among most NATO member states to help train Iraqi security forces, albeit in the case of France and Germany not on Iraqi soil.

26 *New York Times*, 21 May 2004. A core uncertainty in Schröder's prescription is whether the US will accept his call for equal partnership. The evidence is that it will not.

27 *International Herald Tribune*, 9 June 2004.

28 A key example is the West European effort to discourage the government of Iran from diverting the country's nuclear energy resources into military weapons.

4   Poland and Central Europe[1]

George Blazyca

When, on 31 December 2004, Polish President Aleksander Kwaśniewski made his traditional and final New Year address, a subtle shift in emphasis could be detected. Europe and European matters figured very strongly while other international issues were deftly sidestepped. Iraq was mentioned as the President was duty bound to send a message to his troops in 'Camp Babilon', the headquarters of the Polish zone of occupation. But those thanks to the military personnel serving in Iraq were almost a footnote alongside the usual presidential reminder to keep in our thoughts at this emotional time of year all those separated from their families for whatever reason.[2] There was certainly none of the hubris of the earlier period in mid- to late 2003 when presidential advisers trumpeted the enormous international success and prestige earned by Poland through its brave decision unhesitatingly to side with the first Bush administration in joining the 'coalition of the willing' with a military presence in Iraq. Poland did so along with other Central European countries, most of which committed relatively small numbers and from specialists units (such as anti-chemical warfare). They included Hungary, the Czech Republic, Slovakia, Ukraine, Romania, Bulgaria and the Baltic states of Lithuania, Latvia and Estonia – in other words, the key countries in the region with no known cases of outright refusal to participate.

It may be that we are witnessing, in the case of Poland, the start of a major foreign policy shift, one that may also exist in other new EU members in Central Europe and the Baltics, where, after the 'diversion' of the Iraq adventure in 2003–4, from 2005, we may see a rebalancing of foreign policy and international relationships away from excessive and uncritical 'Atlanticism' towards more intense engagement with Europe and EU developments. Evidence from the Polish case suggests this. Given that Poland has been the major Central European player in the 'coalition of the willing', it makes some sense to explore the Polish reaction to the Bush Doctrine in greater detail, touching meanwhile on the contrasts, where they exist, between Poland and some other countries in the region.

This chapter analyses the response in Poland to the build-up from the beginning of 2003 to the US-led military action 'Operation Iraqi Freedom' as illustrative of developments in Central and East European Countries (CEEC), making some comparative observations. It summarizes the rationale as far as it can be detected for the various, more or less similar, foreign policy decisions made by Central European countries that led them to be labelled, provocatively, by the US Secretary of State for Defense, Donald Rumsfeld, as the trusted 'new Europe' unlike the disloyal 'old Europe' of France and Germany. It also explores the exceedingly limited domestic discussions regarding the Bush Doctrine and the situation in Iraq, and finds a change of tone in 2004 with stronger criticisms appearing in the media of the earlier decisions of the Polish authorities. As the Pentagon's confident predictions on the welcome that coalition forces would find on the streets of Baghdad were found to be seriously wanting, this change is perhaps no great surprise. The more vigorous engagement of the CEEC with European and particularly EU developments will also demand a greater commitment, sensitivity and understanding on the part of some, if not all, of the older EU members.

Central Europe and its post-communist foreign policy

After the revolutions of 1989, the foreign policy objectives of the former Soviet bloc countries in Central Europe quickly became focused, in most cases, on the twin objectives of achieving EU and NATO membership – the one offering economic and the other political security. In contrast to the early thinking on the major reconfigurations taking place on the geo-political scene, the latter proved easier to manage (for some at least) than the former. Poland, Hungary and the Czech Republic were admitted to NATO in March 1999 in the final period of the Clinton White House. EU membership was a much longer haul, with association agreements put into place in the early 1990s followed by a lengthy period of rumbustious toing and froing, laced with sometimes bitter argument and dispute between Brussels and individual candidates, before the EU agreed on a 'big bang' enlargement that would see ten countries (eight of them post-communist)[3] being admitted in May 2004.

While EU membership had a very strong material aspect, joining NATO was probably viewed by politicians in the post-communist region largely as an emblem, one that would demand little commitment but huge reward as CEEC sheltered under the security umbrella of the sole remaining superpower, the US. The last thing on the minds of either politicians or citizens was that it might lead to a situation in which foreign troop deployments might have to be made and a 'blood price' paid in far-off countries. That, however, was for the future; in the late 1990s, getting into the key international economic and political organizations was the priority. Russia's leaders, viewing NATO expansion as a threat to security, were displeased by these developments but, given Russia's enfeebled state, could not prevent them. And while doubts existed even in the west on the role of NATO in a completely transformed post-Soviet world, these were not allowed to dampen the celebratory mood as the organization gathered new members. Even much later, Ukraine's President Leonid Kuchma saw NATO as a prize for which it was worth sending troops to Iraq. The Slovak authorities took a similar view, notwithstanding the fact that Slovak society was less certain and becoming more sceptical on the matter. In October 2002, some 50 per cent of the population was reported to be in favour of NATO membership, compared with 57 per cent in March of that year.[4] The worsening international situation as the build-up to war in Iraq was taking place was echoed in public opinion in Slovakia, as in other European countries.

The deteriorating international political scene could hardly have come at a worse moment from the viewpoint of those CEEC countries about to join the EU. Membership was at last finally agreed – grudgingly, as it seemed to some of the candidates – by the existing member governments at the Copenhagen summit in December 2003. The long march under the banner 'return to Europe' that started under the first Solidarity government in Poland in September 1989 and was quickly followed by the collapse of the Berlin Wall in November 1989 was about to reach its destination with much to be done to make enlargement a success. Just as European unity was about to be celebrated through this historic EU enlargement, it suited US diplomacy to sharpen the divide among EU countries that had emerged in attitudes towards the Bush Doctrine and war in Iraq.

Old and new Europes: the world according to Donald Rumsfeld

A particularly important development was the idea, originally conceived at the *Wall Street Journal* (WSJ), that an endorsement of the Bush Doctrine from a cross-section of European leaders would be helpful to the US administration. This led to the orchestration of the now famous 'letter of the eight' (seven prime ministers plus one president) published by the WSJ and other leading papers on 30 January 2003. The letter was signed by the prime ministers of Spain, Portugal, Italy, UK, Denmark, Hungary and Poland as well as by Václav Havel in his final hours as Czech President. It immediately caused a furore across Europe as Jacques Chirac and Gerhard Schröder as well as the Greek EU presidency and the EU's Minister for Foreign Affairs, Javier Solana, had had absolutely no idea of what was coming. According to a well-informed report, Mr Solana, who had a few days earlier managed to secure agreement across the EU 15 for a common foreign policy position on Iraq, first heard about the letter on the radio on the day of its publication.[5] A close colleague noted that 'he was furious and disappointed'. The report continued, 'he felt betrayed – both by the EU members who had signed and by the candidate countries'. 'Solana was not only stabbed in the back', added his colleague, but 'our common foreign and security policy was now a shambles. It was awful. And no minister had had the nerve to inform us beforehand of their intention.'[6]

These developments chimed well with the Rumsfeld view that France and Germany could be brushed aside as 'old Europe' while a 'new Europe', its 'centre of gravity moving east', understood better the new geo-politics around the

Bush Doctrine. 'New Europe' was ready to give the US its unstinting support as the 'letter of eight' and later military assistance showed. A few days later, on 3 February, a second letter of support for US policies appeared, generated (with help) by the ten NATO candidates in Europe, the so-called 'Vilnius 10'. The rift among European countries that had already been opened became wider. It was bound to make the new enlarged EU (if matters got that far) much more difficult to manage. French president Jacques Chirac famously scolded the candidates for 'missing a good opportunity to shut up' while they in turn shouted back that they had not just shaken off one oppressive regime just to be told by Paris and Berlin how to behave.[7] The Chirac intervention played very badly, especially in Warsaw, where it was not difficult, says Tomasz Zarycki, a Warsaw University academic, to find the sentiment, 'It took you 15 years after we toppled communism to offer us EU membership. You think you can treat us like rubbish? Now we've shown you!'[8]

New Europe's 'Atlanticism'

Why did Hungary, Poland and the Czech Republic, all NATO members and all on the threshold of an historic EU membership, act in the way they did? Why did the Vilnius 10 join in so enthusiastically? Why was the 'transatlantic' choice so easy to make? How were the decisions taken uncritically to go along with the Bush Doctrine on Iraq – especially in view of the solid 'anti-war' positions of most citizens across the CEEC region?

The first observation is that, if Poland is in any way typical, there was very little attempt in the region by established politicians or political parties to encourage wider debate of the issues at stake: the situation in Iraq, the Bush Doctrine or the legal and moral modalities. There is no evidence to show that any of the leaders, so determinedly clear on the policy option they were about to take, thought it important to engage with society on the matter. Of course, political leaders across the region knew that there was a critical public opinion. Alongside this was the vivid post-communist legacy, which revealed decidedly strong anti-war sentiments finding it impossible to transform, bottom-up, those views into any kind of reasonable-scale anti-war movement or even to force politicians to account for their actions. Political leaders across the region marched to war while their citizens sulked off in the opposite direction.

The Polish media did virtually nothing to fill that gap.[9] For reasons that are not entirely clear, they were happy to be co-opted or to volunteer to ensure that no serious domestic debate on international affairs was stimulated. This is not to say that from 2002 to 2004 no critical voices appeared in the media, but they were rare. In 2004, however, there was a more critical disposition, reflecting the fact that Operation Iraqi Freedom was not going to plan. But to the extent that a rethink of basic questions became increasingly unavoidable, the serious media played a marginal role.

In Poland, the decision to commit troops to the 'coalition of the willing' was made mainly by the president and premier in consultation with the ministers for foreign affairs and defence.[10] There was no wider cabinet discussion and no parliamentary debate.[11] While the Foreign Minister, Włodzimierz Cimoszewicz, explained that the decision was not easy, it was reached remarkably quickly. It seems likely, too, that its rationale was based on factors some of which also figured in the similar decisions made by Hungary, the Czech Republic and other countries in the region. In Poland, three issues seem to have been critical in shaping foreign policy decision-making: first, loyalty to the US, perhaps combined with an element of 'EU accession resentment'; second, the idea that engaging in a major international military operation would enhance Polish 'prestige' on the international stage; and third, the lure of lucrative contracts in rebuilding post-war Iraq.

Polish governmental loyalty to the US, like other countries in the 'new Europe' – especially the newly independent Baltic states that had once been part of the Soviet Union – was unquestioned in 2003. Its principal source was and is fear of Russia. Polish and other CEEC leaders are by no means naïve, realizing full well that the EU is a long way from developing any effective military/security muscle, but its membership is desired for plainly long-term material reasons. The EU accession process was onerous, quarrelsome, tiresome and lengthy, with genuine EU affection probably running at a low ebb. There is also a growing awareness that NATO is not as effective as it once was, leaving the world's only superpower as the real guarantor of security in the CEEC region. It is a bizarre curiosity that the government of the Democratic Left Alliance (SLD) that was so quick in Poland to back the Bush line was a government dominated by post-communist personalities. Although once loyal to Moscow, they had no trouble in transferring affections across the ocean to Washington. Nevertheless, they also reflected a deep current running through virtually all of CEEC society that the US was a committed ally, a long-standing friend and should not be let down.

This meant, too, that the Washington rationale for going to war was accepted uncritically. The Polish authorities, like others in the region, accepted the Bush/Blair view that Saddam Hussein possessed weapons of mass destruction (WMD) that were a real and imminent threat. They were even ready for war on the premise that regime change was cause enough to act – legally weak in international law. They accepted without demur the controversial view that Saddam was in league with terrorists, with al-Qaeda, and ready to pass on weapons support. After reviewing such matters in a lengthy piece in *Rzeczpospolita* in August 2003, a leading presidential aide, Marek Siwiec, was starkly clear on his position, 'The US is driven by motives that are therefore justified and that I fully share.'[12] Polish President Kwaśniewski must have concurred. However, it is perhaps revealing of the sensitive awareness of public opinion's resistance to sending soldiers to Iraq that political figures such as Marek Siwiec tried to persuade the Polish people that the Iraq commitment was little different from the peace-keeping 'blue beret' operations that Polish forces have taken part in throughout the history of the UN.

The matter of Polish 'prestige' on the international scene was one alluded to, at least throughout 2003, by many Polish politicians. Foreign Minister

Włodzimierz Cimoszewicz, in one of the few semi-public debates that took place (sponsored by a charitable institution and not widely reported) in early 2003, had 'no doubt that (thanks to the Iraq issue and EU accession) the position of Poland in international relations has grown stronger'.[13] There was great delight in Warsaw as the payback for siding with the US seemed to come so soon after the 'letter of eight' had been dispatched. In May, President Bush began his trip to Europe in Kraków. Tony Blair also paid a visit to Warsaw, both events demonstrating – according to *Rzeczpospolita*'s leader writers – that Poland was at the top table, a serious partner, by no means a vassal or satellite of the US, and certainly no 'Trojan donkey' as the German press had it. All of this vindicated, said the paper, decisions made on Iraq.[14] By September 2003, the Polish Defence Minister, Jerzy Szmajdziński, felt able to declare that, by taking command of a zone of occupation (always carefully referred to in official discussions as 'zone of stabilization'), 'we strengthened our position in the international arena'. He went on, 'we are viewed as a trustworthy ally and active participant in international undertakings' and 'it maintains at a high level our strategic partnership with the US and good relations with other NATO members'.[15]

Another feature of the Polish presence in Iraq was the idea that it was 'good business' to be there. Polish firms, especially in construction and defence, had long experience of working in Iraq, and it was fervently hoped that Poland would, as trusted ally, do particularly well in the share-out of contracts for the post-war reconstruction. Indeed, Marek Belka, a previous Polish finance minister and soon to be elevated by President Kwaśniewski to the position of prime minister, was appointed as Director of Economic Affairs in the first US administration in Iraq headed by Paul Bremmer.

Governments other than Poland's from the CEEC region that joined the 'coalition of the willing' drew especially on loyalty to the US as justification for their actions. Yet their citizens tended to share with Polish society deep doubts as to the wisdom of direct military involvement in Iraq.[16] As in Poland, however, they found it impossible to translate doubts into wider public protest or even debate. Meanwhile, political leaders had little interest in engaging with the public on these matters. Loyalty to the USA was viewed by some in Slovakia and in Ukraine as a passport to NATO membership.

As Table 4.1 shows, Poland was by far the most important contributor of CEEC forces in Iraq, both in numbers and in significance of the role played. Poland was given responsibility for an occupation zone in which the military from the countries listed participated. In some cases, the contribution was 'token' only, of special anti-chemical weapons forces and the like.

Doubts creep in?

As the Polish authorities rushed to embrace the Bush Doctrine in early 2003, very few voices counselled caution. The best known was that of Poland's first post-communist Prime Minister, Tadeusz Mazowiecki. Mazowiecki expressed early doubts about signing up so quickly and 'without sufficient reflection'

Table 4.1   Central European participation in the 'coalition of the willing' (troop commitments in Iraq at 9 December 2003)

Poland	2,400
Ukraine	1,650
Romania	800
Czech Republic	700
Bulgaria	480
Hungary	300
Latvia	142
Lithuania	105
Albania	100
Slovakia	80
Estonia	32
Macedonia	28

Sources: *Rocznik Strategiczny 2003–04*, Fundacja Studiów Międzynarodowych (Wydawnictwo Naukowe Scholar, Warszawa, 2004), p. 239; Estonia – personal communication; the figure for Ukraine is for June 2004, as reported in *Washington Times*, 22 June 2004.

to the 'letter of the eight'.[17] He was joined by one *Gazeta Wyborcza* columnist, Leopold Unger, who wondered, like Mazowiecki, whether it was necessary to sign up to a document that would 'offend Europe so sharply'.[18] But these were lone voices. Nevertheless, the former Solidarity premier was one of a tiny band who would continue to put Poland's political leaders on the spot, demanding justification for the government's decision on military engagement in Iraq. Mazowiecki wanted, among others, to examine publicly what was entailed by the 'stabilization' mandate that Poland was about to pick up. It was crazy, he told the daily newspaper *Gazeta Wyborcza*, to accept such a mandate without the widest possible public discussion and full knowledge of what was entailed. He noted too, with a hint of sadness, that this was an issue that, for the first time since the collapse of the old system in 1989, split asunder the consensus that had existed in Polish society on foreign policy objectives. The world had certainly changed, Mazowiecki admitted, and key questions now demanded clear answers: 'First – unilateralism or pluralism in the world order. Second – relations between Europe and America. Third – how Poland should fit in all this'. He continued, 'on those fundamental questions we have slipped into a new order as if it demanded no reflection!'[19] He also noted that the Iraqi operation would have to be a success over the longer term for Poland to make any gains in 'prestige by association'.

The idea that it could turn out otherwise was rarely entertained. One commentator, however, Bartłomiej Sienkiewicz, saw Poland's political leaders as 'hostage' to the US military. Sienkiewicz, writing in March 2003 in *Rzeczpospolita*, hoped only that the decision to engage in Iraq, 'taken somewhere between the presidential palace and the cabinet was made under the calculation of such significant benefits that our country would obtain from its brotherly defence with the US in the case of decisive victory'. He continued, 'I can only hope that the effective hostages made of the authorities in Poland by the American generals know what they are doing . . . otherwise we face trouble . . .'[20]

When he had the chance to press the government and especially Foreign Minister Cimoszewicz yet again in May 2003 in the discussion organized by the Stefan Batory Foundation, Mazowiecki went on the offensive. 'The minister said', Mazowiecki noted, 'that Polish–US relations have improved. I'm afraid we are deluded . . . our importance is illusory, a bubble inflated by our special transatlantic relations.'[21] How could, he went on, a country with such a weak domestic situation as Poland's hope to make any serious impact on the international stage? It was a consideration that others would return to in due course.

For Mazowiecki, another deeply troubling issue, as for Sienkiewicz, was the manner in which the decision to go to war had been taken. Mazowiecki told the Batory conference that:

> . . . as an observer and participant of public debate in Poland, I remain unaware of the mechanisms used to make key decisions in Poland. Little is known of the very difficult debates of the government and President concerning key Iraq questions . . . the general public has the impression that the decisions were made automatically. I criticized it publicly and I still believe that the decisions were automatic while the present situation requires at least a moment of reflection . . . I am not a supporter of the decision for Poland to run the occupation zone in Iraq. But you can't discuss this issue publicly at all. Everyone is ecstatic about it, any moment now we will set up the Colonial League! I said that in an interview for *Gazeta Wyborcza* but it seems that the Polish media are bowing to a kind of political correctness, so the decision cannot be criticized.

It is striking that the daily diet served up for most television news viewers as well as in the press, both popular and more serious, is very frequently focused on '*skandale i afery*' on the domestic scene. And Poland has certainly generated a huge volume of 'scandal and affairs'. These are usually at the interface of politics and business, in recent times involving mainly the transgressions of the (until May 2004) party of government, the SLD. Once considered as a supremely professional or at least slick and disciplined political party, the SLD was exposed as highly corrupt as one after another of its '*baronowie*' (barons), local leaders or members of parliament were forced out of office or subject to investigative scrutiny of one sort or another – parliamentary or criminal. Commissions of enquiry were established to probe doubtful privatization decisions such as that of the PZU insurance company, or how business and politics had become too intertwined as in the investigation of links between Poland's richest businessman, Jan Kulczyk, the Polish president, the prime minister and Polish and Russian oil interests, or as in the 'Rywingate' affair where the *Gazeta Wyborcza* group, *Agora*, was offered media law concessions that would allow it to expand its interests in return for a $17.5m payment to Lew Rywin, said to be an intermediary to the highest level of government.[22] Added to this was another tributary of scandal via allegations that leading personalities on the political scene worked at one time or another for the security services of the communist regime. Thus, the media had rich pickings on the domestic scene with little need to look too closely at questions regarding the reshaping of the international order.

One must ask whether a country with such a wide range of domestic difficulties in state and institution building can really make a strong contribution to state-building elsewhere? Can a country with what appears to be a deeply unhealthy domestic politics–business set-up, where corruption is a familiar day-to-day affair, really project enhanced prestige on the international scene simply because it is a willing partner in an *ad hoc* coalition led by the US?

One writer who was keen to draw attention to such questions was Roman Kuźniar, a leading foreign affairs academic, in a scathing contribution hidden away in the relatively obscure *Strategic Yearbook 2003–04*, published by the Foundation for International Studies, set up in 1993 as an offshoot of the Institute for International Relations at Warsaw University.[23] Like other critics, Kuźniar notes the 'complete lack of debate on the reasons for our participation in the war in Iraq' and worse still, this even after the justifications given for war were undermined as no WMD were found and US and British administrations conceded that Saddam had no links with al-Qaeda. Whereas in America and Britain this gave rise to demands for commissions of enquiry, in Poland, Kuźniar heard 'silence'. For Kuźniar, the 'exotic' Iraq adventure meant taking the eyes off the real challenge facing Poland – how to build a modern and effective state able to engage with the EU. It exposed, too, the 'mixed up geo-political instincts of the Polish political class'. One consequence of this was, for example, that Poland became distracted from the real role it could play in helping to shape a more active 'eastern policy' for the EU, a policy towards Russia, Belarus and Ukraine – 'a sphere of strategic significance for Poland' – but one that was overlooked because of the existing 'geo-political disorder' affecting the minds of Warsaw's politicians. It might be argued that the 'orange revolution' in Ukraine in November 2004 helped to jolt those politicians from Baghdad to Kiev. Certainly, Kwaśniewski was keen to offer his services to any European politicians keen to come to him for a better understanding of Ukraine and played a positive role, alongside others, in resolving the crisis by helping to persuade political personalities in that country of the merits of a rerun of the contested presidential vote.

In early 2004, those doubts that had been expressed quietly in the odd rather obscure article or conference began to gain, albeit very slowly, a greater currency and momentum. Although few people were talking about it publicly, the lack of evidence of WMD or Saddam's terrorist links – as well as a small but growing Polish casualty list in the field – was deeply troubling. Bold claims about Poland's growing international prestige evaporated as evidence mounted on the use of torture by US forces in Iraq and Guantánamo Bay. Whether, as a loyal partner, perhaps listened to by the US, the Polish authorities quietly commented on these developments is not known; what is clear, however, is that beyond immediate items of news they were not allowed to upset the media's generally low-key coverage of Iraq-related events or to reach any wider public. 'Did our government react? . . . public opinion knows nothing about this' commented one observer in August 2004.[24]

Material benefits were also decidedly slow to appear. In a visit to Warsaw in late 2003, the US Trade Secretary, Donald Evans, was reported to have discussed with president, premier and economy minister the possibility that the Polish defence contractor, Bumar, would earn contracts of $500m. In fact, in 2004, the company's Iraqi military business was worth only $54m, although a $131m helicopter contract was said to be close to signing by the end of the year.[25]

Perhaps the most hurtful of all the blows to Polish sensibilities was the White House refusal to ease visa requirements on Poles travelling to the US. One observer, Piotr Semka, writing in April 2004, noted that the White House had a very poor understanding of Polish politics, barely picking up on the fact that the Kwaśniewski–Miller leadership that had opted for war was on its last legs.[26] Prime Minister Miller was about to resign after taking Poland into the EU on 1 May, and Kwaśniewski, whose presidency would end in October 2005, was already 'distancing himself from "Uncle Sam"'. In mid-March 2004, the President, inadvertently it is presumed, caused a minor furore between Washington and Warsaw when he appeared to admit that 'we were deceived' on the issue of WMD. In summary, said Semka, Poland was far from winning the prizes that should have come from its alliance with the US, yet had no choice now but to stick things out.

By late 2004, it became reasonable to ask, 'when will we pull out of Iraq?'. Even the Defence Minister, Jerzy Szmajdziński, put the question, answering it himself with the end of 2005 as the key date, before being quickly slapped down by the Prime Minister, Marek Belka, who reminded his colleague that Poles will be in Iraq until 'our mission' there is completed. Meanwhile, throwing his view into the ring, Foreign Minister Cimoszewicz explained that Poland would like to withdraw soon after Iraqi elections, adding for good measure – although somewhat disingenuously (this at the end of 2004) – that 'we never accepted the way Mr Rumsfeld tried to divide Europe into the old and new parts'.[27]

One important feature that emerges from Poland's commitment to the Bush Doctrine is the enormous gap, noted earlier, that opened up between people, politicians and political leaders. Yet none of the Central European capitals saw major popular anti-war demonstrations or movements develop, as happened in the west. It is tempting to suggest that this is one of the consequences of post-communism and the difficulties encountered across the region in building strong and lively 'civil society'. Societies that generated revolutions 15 years ago appear to have turned away from conventional political activity, politics and politicians. This comes after the genuinely ex-hausting 1990s efforts in system transformation when energies were focused on private, individual or family-based adjustment to new situations that left no time, energy or inclination to get involved in protest or debate. It is also interesting that few political parties tried to capitalize on exceedingly strong anti-war sentiment. In the Polish case, the war was supported by the govern-ing party (the SLD) and by the leading opposition party, the centre-right Citizens' Platform (PO). The anti-war argument was left with the Polish Peasant Party (PSL) and the Farmers' Self-Defence Party (Samoobrona), and neither bothered very much with it, finding that, whenever they did, they simply attracted accusations of 'populism'. In the election year of 2005 in Poland, that may change but, in the early months, it looked very much as if a domestic agenda would dominate political debate.

Polish responses to the Bush Doctrine and the conflict in Iraq, also visible across the CEEC region, can be summarized as follows. First, a loyalty to the superpower, the US, as ultimate guarantor of security, able to keep Russia in its place, was paramount. Second, governments and political leaders could ignore with impunity the very strong anti-war sentiments of their citizens – knowing full well that underlying pro-US sentiment was generally strong and would probably hold up. Third, there was virtually no attempt across the region from any source – politicians in government or opposition – to stimu-late debate and discussion on the big issues being raised. Fourth, the media were happy to be co-opted by governments in all of this and, even as the original (WMD, terrorism) rationale for war vanished, no Central European leadership was called to account. Fifth, such calculations as were carried out to justify actions were highly pragmatic and materialistic – either to achieve international security goals such as NATO membership (Slovakia, Ukraine) or to do business in post-war Iraq (Poland). Sixth, for those countries about to join the EU, the Bush Doctrine and the Iraqi war were serious and, as some have said, 'exotic' diversions, the full consequences of which remain to work themselves out.

Conclusion

As the largest of the new members of the EU, with potentially most to offer in the development of an 'eastern policy', Poland has been especially neglectful of its non-EU neighbours: Russia, Belarus and Ukraine. Political developments in Ukraine in November 2004 brought Poland back to a more sensible disposition, tugging it away from the 'disordered geo-political instinct of the Polish political class', as Roman Kuźniar put it. Perhaps this useful corrective will encourage whichever parties and president come to office in Poland after elections in 2005 to rebalance foreign policy thinking? Unless this happens, it seems hard to believe that Poland and other countries in the region will make a long-term success of EU membership. After lengthy efforts across the region to achieve two clear foreign policy objectives in the first post-communist period – NATO and EU membership – the test for the future will be to figure out what NATO is for and to make the enlarged EU work effectively, bridging the gap between those members that live under strong fears of Russia and those where such fears are absent.

The old/new Europe rift that opened as the Bush Doctrine unfolded will take some time to close. Meanwhile, the new EU of 25 is about to enter a particularly turbulent period and will by no means be easy to manage. There is little doubt that older EU members need to give enlargement more serious thought than has been the case so far. We may also be witnessing the start of a new period of rebalancing of foreign policy where making a success of EU membership becomes a genuine policy priority, especially for the organizations' new members. On the other hand, this may be no more than wishful thinking, reflecting a desire to find order and a new commitment to Europe where little exists.

Notes

1 My thanks are due to Professors Józef Niżnik, Tadeusz Kowalik, Ludmila Malik-ova, Ryszard Rapacki and Leonidas Donskis, also to Drs Tomasz Zarycki, Václav Žák, Kasia Wolczuk, Robert Geisler, John Fells, Jan Čulik and Ms Kadri Liik for helpful criticism, and Wendy Blazyca for advice and support.

2 Available in English from the President's web address at http://www.prezydent.pl.

3 Poland, Hungary, Czech Republic, Slovakia, Latvia, Lithuania, Estonia, Slovenia, Malta and Cyprus.

4 From Matúš Korba, 'Slovakia and the Iraqi crisis' (mimeo), Institute of International Relations, Prague/Centre for Security Studies, Bratislava, 2003. Slovakia was admitted to NATO alongside six other former communist countries (Slovenia, Bulgaria, Romania, Estonia, Latvia and Lithuania) in April 2004.

5 'The rift that turns nasty: the plot that split old and new Europe asunder', *Financial Times*, 28 May 2003, p.19.

6 Ibid.

7 This spat with the French was to get very much worse when the Polish army claimed that it had discovered French 'Roland 2' rockets in Iraq and accused the French of sanction busting.

8 Personal communication.

9 Our review is of the press titles frequently reckoned to be the most influential in Polish policy-making circles, the dailies *Gazeta Wyborcza* and *Rzeczpospolita* combined with selective viewing of the main news bulletin broadcast each evening at 19.30 (*Wiadomości*) by the principal channel, the state-owned *Telewizja Polska*. The daily *Trybuna* did strike a more critical pose and, among weeklies, Jerzy Urban's magazine *Nie* and the left-leaning *Przegląd* were no friends of the Iraq adventure.

10 A very small Polish contingent (200) of special forces (GROM) participated in the initial March assault but, when Poland was invited by the US to supervise a zone of occupation alongside the US and UK in July 2003, its troop commitment rose to 2,400, the third largest in Iraq although very much smaller than the US and UK.

11 The then Polish finance minister, Grzegorz Kołodko, confirmed at a private dinner that the decision was taken by Miller and Kwaśniewski, Premier and President, with no full cabinet discussion. Some speculate too that Kwaśniewski was

particularly persuaded by the strong pro-war arguments of Adam Michnik, the chief editor of the newspaper, *Gazeta Wyborcza*.

12 'Dlaczego do Iraku', Marek Siwiec, *Rzeczpospolita*, 12 August 2003, p. 7. Siwiec outlines one of the clearest and fullest statements of support for the Bush Doctrine; he notes, 'Defending ourselves from hostile risks means changing our philosophy of action. Above all we must locate the enemy, not waiting for the enemy to find us. Secondly he must be neutralised before he grows strong . . .'

13 Włodzimierz Cimoszewicz in his address to the Stefan Batory Foundation discussion held on 9 May 2003 on 'Poland in the world: challenges, achievements, threats', Warsaw, 30 June 2003, available at http://www.batory.org.pl/english/pub/index.htm.

14 'Polska w roli partnera', *Rzeczpospolita*, 31 May–1 June 2003, p. 2.

15 'W imieniu cywilizowanego świata', Jerzy Szmajdziński, *Rzeczpospolita*, 3 September 2003, p. 8.

16 Throughout 2004, the proportion of Polish citizens declaring that they did not support the Polish military engagement in Iraq was rarely below 60 per cent with fewer than 30 per cent in favour. In December 2004, 68 per cent were against and 27 per cent for. CBOS data reported in *Rzeczpospolita*, 18–19 December 2004, p. 3.

17 See the quarterly, *Polish Foreign Affairs Digest*, t. 3 (91), 2003, p. 10. This gathers English-language versions of papers published in Polish journals such as *Polski Przegląd Dyplomatyczny*.

18 Leopold Unger, 'Polska bez Churchilla', *Gazeta Wyborcza*, 31 January 2003.

19 'Bez mandatu nie jedźmy', interview with Tadeusz Mazowiecki, *Gazeta Wyborcza*, 9 May 2003, p. 20.

20 'Polska w roli zakładnika', Bartłomiej Sienkiewicz, *Rzeczpospolita*, 31 March 2003, p. 10.

21 'Poland in the World: Challenges, Achievements, Threats', op. cit.

22 Lew Rywin lost his appeal against conviction on fraud charges in December 2004. The appeal court also ruled that Rywin had not acted alone, endorsing the commission of enquiry view that Rywin was an intermediary to a 'group in authority' that was no fiction. See 'Była grupa trzymająca władzę', *Rzeczpospolita*, 11–12 December 2004. Meanwhile, the commission of enquiry into what became known as 'Orlengate' was occupied with questions regarding political pressures on Orlen's top management as well as alleged offers made by Jan Kulczyk to smooth the way, via political contacts at the highest level, to give Russian oil business access to Orlen's privatization. Questions have also been raised regarding the earlier first stage of privatization of the PZU insurance company that may lead to yet another commission of enquiry being set up.

23 See the introduction (wprowadzenie) to *Rocznik Strategiczny* 2003–04, Fundacja Studiów Międzynarodowych (Wydawnictwo Naukowe Scholar, Warszawa, 2004).

24 Piotr Winczorek, 'Po co tam pojechaliśmy', *Rzeczpospolita*, 12 August 2004, p. 7.

25 See reports in the *Rzeczpospolita* business section on 18 December 2003 and 15 December 2004.

26 Piotr Semka, 'Polskie prawo do krytyki', *Rzeczpospolita*, 27 April 2004, p. 10.

27 Daniel Dombey and Guy Dinmore, 'US and Europe say they want close ties. Can they overcome their differences?', *Financial Times*, 15 November 2004, p. 17.

5 Reactions in the Russian Federation and security in Central Asia

Mary Buckley

In his rhetoric about terrorism, President Vladimir Putin has shared much with US President George W. Bush, even though the constellation of domestic, international and historical pressures on him have differed hugely from those on his US counterpart. While they have a shared interest in the global war on terror and some common aims, Putin and his government have been less enthusiastic about the wide remit of the Bush Doctrine and its criteria for permissible use of force against other states, notably Iraq.

This chapter examines responses from president, government ministers and public opinion to the Bush Doctrine and more widely to American foreign policy, of which the doctrine is one inter-related part. It also examines Russian reactions to questions of security in Central Asia. All these have to be understood against the historical backdrop of the Russian context and recent terrorist acts inside the Russian Federation as well as global developments.

Recent presidential rhetoric on terrorism

In February 2004, President Putin reiterated his position that 'Russia does not conduct talks with terrorists, Russia destroys them'.[1] This statement was made after a bomb exploded on a metro train leaving Moscow's Avtozavodskaia station, killing over 40 and injuring over 120.[2] Then, in a special television address on Saturday 4 September 2004, a grave Putin now warned that 'the direct intervention of international terror against Russia, with total and full-scale war' meant 'an attack against all of us'. Putin alleged that, as well as trying to 'tear off a big chunk' of Russia, the terrorists were in fact being assisted by countries who found Russian nuclear power still a threat.[3]

This emotional broadcast was in response to the seizure on 1 September of School Number 1 in the town of Beslan in North Ossetia and the 52-hour hostage crisis that followed.[4] Over 1,000 were taken captive, 70 per cent of whom were children (although the regime covered up these high figures at the time), and more than 400 died. Before this tragedy occurred, two incidents had already contributed to a tense atmosphere in Moscow: the coordinated explosion of two aircraft over Russia; and another bomb blast at a metro station. On 25 August, flights leaving Domodedevo airport bound for Volgograd and Sochi came down over Tula and Rostovoblasts. All passengers and crew on both died – a total of 89.[5] Then, on 31 August, an explosion at Rizhskaia metro station left nine dead and 44 injured.[6] Beslan came fast on its heels, leaving many in Russia reeling from an onslaught of different attacks that created a widespread sense of unease and insecurity. Psychological crisis telephone lines were opened to the public.

In the days that followed Putin's speech, the Patriarch of the Russian Orthodox Church drew parallels with Russia's plight during the Great Patriotic War and called for unity in adversity. Press articles echoed this. Accompanying *Literaturnaia gazeta*'s headline of 'People's War' was the well-known 1940s image of a vulnerable mother, shawl on her head and wide-eyed with fear, clutching her child with the enemy's bayonet threatening her. The menacing Nazi had been replaced by a bearded terrorist, looking like Shamil Basaev, former Chechen Prime Minister turned radical field commander. The appeal to the Red Army to save remained.[7] Putin now promised firm new measures to combat terrorism in the wake of his regime's failure to protect the country. He painted a new official picture of a 'weak' Russia that had been 'unprepared' for many changes after the collapse of the USSR. Since 'the weak are beaten', it was imperative that the 'new security and defence needs' were met by a package of new 'measures'.[8] The Russian budget in 2005 was to allocate an extra $5.1 billion to the war against terrorism. Igor Ivanov, as Secretary of the Security Council, announced that just as Russia had a mobilization plan in the event of war, now Russia would be drafting a mobilization plan for the war on terror.[9]

Russian leaders have used 9/11, the war on terrorism and recent terrorist acts inside Russia, particularly the Moscow theatre siege in 2002 and the hostage crisis in Beslan, to claim that international terrorism has been behind events in Chechnia, thereby seeking legitimacy for their own military actions and for stepping up wider policies of 'securitization'. Putin has constructed as bedfellows the demand for Chechen independence and global terrorism. In the emotional and tense aftermath of Beslan, he promised Russian citizens action from law enforcement agencies 'adequate in level and scale to the new threats'.[10]

The theme of international terrorism at play in Chechnia, North Ossetia and Moscow has been combined with that of 'securitization', in what amounts to a rhetorical 'information war'.[11] Critics of this linkage inside Russia, such as Boris Kagarlitsky, have observed that joining in Bush's war against terrorism Putin has tried to craft credibility into the need for Russian troops in Chechnia as well as to bolster the notion that Russia is not acting alone but is part of a much wider world struggle for freedom from arbitrary terrorist acts.[12] This has not, however, meant a wholesale Russian acceptance of the

Bush Doctrine. Rather, the Russian presidential administration has acquiesced with those parts of the doctrine that best suit its interests.

The Russian context

Russian reactions to the Bush Doctrine must be understood in the wider context of Putin wanting Russia in 2002 to be seen to be a great power by Western leaders, after disagreements in 1999 over NATO intervention in Kosovo and subsequent discomfort at NATO expansion eastwards, topped in 2004 with reluctant acceptance of the accession on 1 May of Estonia, Latvia, Lithuania, Hungary, the Czech Republic, Poland, Slovakia and Slovenia to the European Union (EU). These humiliations, pragmatically swallowed by Putin, occurred against the backdrop of a geo-politically weakened Russia after the collapse in 1989 of the Soviet Union's East European empire and the implosion of the Soviet state in 1991, followed by an unstable period of Yeltsin's leadership of the Russian Federation up to 2002 when Putin became president (Buckley 2001: 156–75; Buckley 2003: 221–38). The serious disquiet of some commentators at the use of military bases in Kyrgyzstan, Tajikistan and Uzbekistan by Western forces in the US 'war on terrorism' in Afghanistan highlighted the sensitivity in Russia to penetration into what was perceived as its own security space just south of its border in the 'near abroad'.

Having suffered a serious identity crisis – domestically and internationally – Russian leaders wanted in 2001 and, more pressingly, in 2002 (due to bomb explosions inside Russia) to be a 'partner' of the US in the global war against terrorism, thereby underscoring and promoting Russia's own importance as a global power. Yet, while advocating a common security space in Europe, Russian leaders simultaneously insisted upon defending and reasserting their own national interests on the world stage, particularly as domestic nationalist pressures grew.

Elections in December 2003 to the State Duma returned a more nationalist parliament, now shed of the liberals *Soiuz Pravykh Sil* (SPS) and *Yabloko* (Apple). Victory on the party list over the 5 per cent hurdle for *Edinaia Rossiia* (United Russia), the Communist Party of the Russian Federation (KPRF), the bloc *Rodina* (Motherland) and Vladimir Zhirinovsky's LDPR strengthened the arguments of the *derzhavniki* – those who asserted Russia to be a great power.[13] The move towards centrism in the Duma blended with Russian nationalism was at the expense of the tiny amount of pro-westernism that had graced the legislature of January 2000–December 2003. Putin's expressed concerns for the 'erosion' of Russian interests in the near abroad were now more warmly welcomed in the parliament. Putin's reactions to the Bush Doctrine also met sympathetic agreement in the Duma and were also largely shared by SPS and Yabloko outside it. Moreover, most Russian politicians abhorred the bombing of Iraq just as they had objected to NATO intervention in Kosovo in 1989. Thus, there was little dissent from Putin's responses, albeit some criticism that he should be more forceful.

Terrorism inside Russia

What Russian leaders branded as 'terrorism' inside Russia, rather than as 'freedom fighting' for an independent Chechnia, further reinforced the sentiment that global action against terrorism was crucial and that Russia had an important role to play in this, shoulder to shoulder with the US. Necessary background is that, in November 1992, the democratically elected Chechen parliament had proclaimed independence from Russia, prompting Yeltsin to declare a state of emergency and dispatch troops but then in June to withdraw. From December 1994 to August 1996, however, Russian troops waged war there in an attempt to crush those bent on independence (Lieven 1998). The troops then returned to Chechnia in October 1999 after bomb explosions in a Moscow apartment building killed 300, which critics dubbed as a mere excuse for further fighting. The consistent Moscow line was that separatists were bandits and terrorists.

The first terrorist attack outside Chechnia in the new millennium occurred in Kaspiisk, Daghestan, on 9 May 2002 when an explosion rocked a Victory Day parade, leaving 42 dead and over 130 wounded. Putin pronounced that 'scum' were behind it and stressed the importance of unity against international terrorism.[14] Anxiety about terrorism rose sharply on 23 October 2002 when 50 armed Chechens took over 800 hostages in the Moscow Dubrovka theatre siege, demanding independence for Chechnia. The theatre was eventually stormed by crack troops after gas had been released that killed 129. Putin afterwards insisted that the attack had been prepared in 'foreign terrorist centres', likened it to al-Qaeda's destruction of the Twin Towers in New York and dubbed it 'Russia's September 11'.[15] The message for Russia was that 9/11 and 23 October 'set the global vector of development for the entire international community'.[16] Terrorism in the Russian capital rather than in distant Daghestan fed public unease and made explicit the seriousness of Chechen frustrations. In response, Putin demanded a revision of the National Security Concept.[17]

The momentum built further on 27 December 2002 when a car bomb assault blew up the Chechen administration in the capital Grozny, killing 80,[18] and, in May 2003, a truck bomb smashed into a government building in Znamenskoye, north of Grozny, killing 60.[19] A Russian military bus became a target in North Ossetia in June 2003 followed by a Moscow rock concert the next month.[20] Soon after, in September, a bomb exploded on a crowded commuter train in Kislovodsk and another in December on a train near Yessentuki in Stavropol krai, killing seven and over 30 respectively.[21] A new Chechen constitution adopted in March 2003 had failed to bring the 'normalization' that Moscow was seeking. Embittered women who had lost their husbands in what they perceive as a senseless war became suicide bombers known as 'black widows' to draw attention to the situation in Chechnia.

In 2004, the aforementioned bomb blasts at Avtozavodskaia and Rizhskaia metro stations, the coordinated plane crashes and events in Beslan were part of this wider sequence of spiralling attacks and with ever tightly spaced timings. The siege at Beslan was also distinct for provocatively targeting innocent and vulnerable children, prompting global revulsion. Putin's response to Beslan was to deny any link between that horror and his own policy in Chechnia. Negotiation even with milder nationalists in Chechnia, as advocated by his critics including Mikhail Gorbachev, was ruled out.[22] Instead, he announced an end to the election of regional governors, the appointment of Dmitri Kozak as plenipotentiary to the Southern Federal District and a new crisis management system. The critical newspaper *Novaia gazeta* adopted the headline 'the president is using the tragedy in Beslan as an excuse for ending the democratic experiment in Russia'.[23] Despite a more cowed media under Putin due to what critics viewed as a growing authoritarianism emanating from his policy of what Putin called firming up the 'power vertical', there was some discussion of the chaotic handling of the crisis on the ground and much questioning of how the school seizure had even been possible. After initially refusing an enquiry into the crisis, Putin finally gave in to pressure.[24] Debates in the media included whether the death penalty should be reinstated, how schools should best be protected and what life-long psychological impacts the incidents would have on child victims.[25] Officially organized demonstrations against terrorism on 7 October in Moscow, Petersburg, Omsk and elsewhere smacked of the way such events had been organized under Soviet power, although much of the emotional outpouring on the part of citizens was genuine.[26] The day of mourning on 6 October (*den' traur*) was used, in the words of Moscow mayor, Iurii Luzkov, to reiterate the call to 'be together'.[27] The dire need for unity was the message from the top. Although a case can be made that the regime fuelled and structured an outpouring of fear to suit its own end of stepping up security, it must be stressed that much anxiety in the population was real due to the unpredictability of attacks and the perceived inability of guarding against them.

By September 2004, Putin's resolve to quash terrorism was as high as George Bush's when he formulated his doctrine. Both, however, focused more on waging war against it than in coming to grips with its causes or tackling the roots of its proliferation.

Immediately after the declaration of the Bush Doctrine

Although Russia did not issue a detailed response to the US announcement of its National Security Strategy (NSS) on 17 September 2002, Russian leaders' reactions to its content can be inferred by their actions on its key points. In the immediate aftermath of the publication of the Bush Doctrine, Putin was especially preoccupied with three issues: the Pankisi Gorge in Georgia; weapons inspectors in Iraq; and NATO expansion.

In September, Putin was embroiled in disagreement with Georgia and argued that Eduard Shevardnadze was failing to prevent terrorist attacks from the Pankisi Gorge into Russia.[28] Defence Minister Sergei Ivanov went so far as to tell journalists in Washington that Russia would launch a pre-emptive strike against Georgia if 'bandits' were seen within 10–15 kilometres of the border.[29] Russia insisted that terrorists from Chechnia, as well as from some Muslim states, gathered here, some with alleged links to al-Qaeda. In response, US leaders urged patience and negotiation with Georgia.[30] Later in the month, Ivanov stressed that the issues of Iraq and the Pankisi Gorge had to be kept separate and that the latter was of much greater interest to Russia.[31]

United with his Foreign Minister Igor Ivanov and Defence Minister Sergei Ivanov, Putin advocated the return of weapons inspectors to Iraq in order to establish whether or not weapons of mass destruction (WMD) existed.[32] Russian thinking among the top leadership held that, if there were no weapons, then there was no justification for war. In their view, war amounted to a violation of the UN Charter because the Security Council had not authorized it or backed the overthrow of a leader of a sovereign state.[33] Thus, Bush's insistence on the use of 'hard power' according to the Russian president and his top ministers was inappropriate in this instance, although it had been acceptable in Afghanistan. A clear difference prevailed between Putin and Bush. However, Putin and both Ivanovs all insisted in the weeks after 17 September that disagreement with the US over Iraq would not mean an end to the strategic partnership that existed between them. Putin's constant emphasis was that the issue of Iraq should be solved by political and diplomatic means. Sergei Karaganov, Chair of the Council on Foreign and Defence Policy, however, was explicit that the US did not need Russia's backing to act against Iraq and could do it alone. He, too, nonetheless, added that, even if the US and Russia differed seriously on Iraq, it would not culminate in a significant worsening of relations. There would be business as usual.[34]

Although Putin welcomed Bush to Moscow and Petersburg, his emphasis was different from Karaganov's. Putin warned the US not to go it alone against Iraq and, together with France and Germany, urged 'positive results' by working through the UN and by staying within the remit of Security Council Resolution 1441 in an attempt to get Iraq to disarm.[35] The issue for Putin at this point was not really a conceptual one of whether the US justified itself by acting in preventive or pre-emptive fashion. Rather, it was about the lack of evidence concerning WMD together with a deeply rooted Russian resistance to American interference in the domestic affairs of other states, dating back to the Soviet past and, more recently, to intervention in Kosovo.

The issue of NATO expansion had been smouldering in 2001. Defence Minister Sergei Ivanov was especially preoccupied with what it meant for Russia's role in NATO and for US withdrawal from the 1972 Anti-Ballistic Missile (ABM) treaty.[36] Initially, both Moscow and Beijing had reacted negatively to the latter and to the US intent to build a National Missile Defence (NMD) system (Buckley 2003: 222–7). After 9/11, however, Putin commented that Russian opposition to NATO expansion could be reassessed in view of the need for a global anti-terrorism coalition. He linked the issue of tackling terrorism in Afghanistan with Russia's priority to deal with it in Chechnia.[37] Sergei Ivanov maintained his more openly critical stand when expressing his hostility in February 2002 to Bush's notion of an 'axis of evil' embracing North Korea, Iran and Iraq.[38]

Leaders nonetheless attempted to show pragmatism and cooperation, although Defence Minister Ivanov was keen to stress that membership of the Baltic states was especially worrying for Russia given that they had not signed the treaty on Conventional Armed Forces in Europe (CFE). In his view, as Russia had agreed to limit its presence in north-west Europe, then the Baltic states should do likewise.[39]

Throughout arguments about NATO, Foreign Minister Igor Ivanov played a predictably diplomatic role, ever concerned to press for joint approaches between NATO and Russia and for an equality of relations in matters of se-curity. In February 2002, the new NATO–Russia Council (NRC) replaced the NATO–Russia Permanent Joint Council (PJC), in part an acknowledgement of Russian concerns to be better consulted. A NATO liaison office opened in Moscow in May 2002. The NRC did not herald smooth relations between NATO and Russia on all issues (Buckley 2003: 223–6). The new Foreign Min-ister since March 2004, Sergei Lavrov, grumbled in June 2004 at a NATO summit in Istanbul that NATO's military explorations in its new members would increase NATO's presence near Russia's borders.[40]

The Iraq war

After the declaration of war on Iraq on 18 March 2003, Igor Ivanov pointed out that the US and Britain were violating the UN Charter. He insisted that Bush and Blair had no authorization for war or for the overthrow of the leader of a sovereign state. The official Russian position was that there were no grounds for stopping the work of the weapons inspectors. Putin branded US and British policy as 'a big political mistake'.[41]

Parties across the spectrum generally concurred with Putin's anti-war po-sition, even if the level of vitriol against the US varied. The KPRF declared that 'Bush is a new Hitler' and Vladimir Zhirinovsky of the LDPR argued that the war 'means the collapse of the entire geo-political world model' and 'the demise of the United Nations'.[42] Both thought that Putin was too gentle in his dealings with the US. More calmly, Irina Khakamada, former co-leader of SPS, condemned the war too, but spoke out against any fuel-ling of 'anti-American hysteria'. She wanted Russia to initiate discussions on post-war reconstruction and on how to prevent similar operations in Iran and elsewhere. Unlike the KPRF and LDPR, Khakamada called for compro-mise and constructive talks with the USA on a 'new international security framework'.[43] From SPS and *Yabloko* outside the parliament to *Edinaia Rossiia*, *Rodina* and deputies groups such as Russia's Regions and the Agro-Industrial group inside it, the overwhelming feeling was that Saddam gave Bush no grounds for aggression.[44]

The Russian executive accepted parts of the Bush Doctrine and rejected others. With Bush, Putin was outspoken against terrorism and the destruction and chaos that it wrought. Putin was also committed to using intelligence, homeland defence and military power to defeat it, as the doctrine proclaimed. Russian backing of military action in Afghanistan in 2001, its own support for the Northern Alliance and the participation of Russian troops and special forces confirmed this. Putin also liked the NSS's description of Russia as 'a partner in the war on terror' and frequently named the US as such too. And just as the doctrine refused to make concessions to terrorist demands or to 'strike deals' with them, so too did Putin.

Where Bush and Putin differed was over the nature of what constituted 'good offence'. The NSS argues that 'our best defence is good offence'.[45] While Putin and his ministers may have concurred with this general principle regarding Chechnia, they did not find adequate grounds for offence in Iraq and consistently argued against it. Chechnia, after all, was part of the Russian Federation in Putin's eyes, and Iraq a sovereign state. Controversial in Moscow was the NSS statement that 'We must be prepared to stop rogue states and their terrorist clients before they are able to threaten or use weapons of mass destruction against the United States and our allies and friends'.[46] First, the concept of 'rogue state' was contested in Russia; second, concerns were expressed about the speed of action against Iraq and the lack of evidence for the existence of WMD there; and third, heavy emphasis was placed on the pivotal role the UN should play in world affairs. It was not sufficient for Russia that according to customary international law it was accepted that preventive force was permissible in self-defence (Arend 2003: 90).[47] In Iraq's case, Putin and his government consistently hammered the position that the UN charter had to be followed. Accordingly, if there was no imminent threat, a unilateral attack – whether 'preventive' or 'pre-emptive' – was unlawful. In the view of the Russian leaders, there was no impending threat in this case. It was not a question of opposition to invasion in general, but rather opposition in this instance.[48]

Partly in response to the more frequent usage of the notion of 'pre-emptive strike', in a pragmatically assertive mode in October 2003, Putin told journalists that Russia too 'retains the right to launch a pre-emptive strike'.[49] This was, in fact, a way of stressing that, if other states advocated pre-emptive strikes, then Russia as a great power inevitably would as well. Putin qualified his observation with 'if this practice continues to be used around the world'.[50] First, this pandered to nationalist sentiments inside Russia; second, it sent a message to the international community that, if the US could advocate this, then Russia would not exclude herself from this option; third, it was part of a broader policy to reassert Russia's might and came after remarks earlier that month about possibly taking SS-19 missiles, 'our most menacing missiles', out of storage.[51] Putin wanted Russia to be seen as more grandiose and as a military force with whom to reckon. Forthcoming elections to the State Duma in December 2003 and to the presidency in the following year contributed to the force of his point. Defence Minister Ivanov, speaking in Reykjavík, reiterated that Russia would use pre-emptive force if a threat were 'visible, clear and unavoidable'.[52] Publication of Russia's new military doctrine in *Krasnaia zvezda* included the observation that penetration of Russia's borders and 'military threats to security' were possible. Russia's national interests required that the armed forces 'neutralize' these.[53] Central Asia was named as a problem area and as 'potentially dangerous'.[54]

After his meeting in July 2004 with Jack Straw, British Foreign Minister, Sergei Lavrov, in his capacity as Russian Foreign Minister, stressed that Britain and Russia had common views on most issues concerning terrorism, the non-proliferation of WMD, regional conflicts and the UN's role. He advocated denuclearization of the Middle East and the establishment of nuclear-free zones in all regions.[55] Former Foreign Minister Igor Ivanov, now Secretary of the Security Council, similarly stressed the extent of common thinking.[56]

Russia's main interest in the Middle East, however, was trade. Lavrov emphasized this later in July when he insisted that Russia would not dispatch troops to Iraq to join the US-led force but would contribute to the situation there by developing trade and easing debt burdens. Pragmatically following Russia's own interests, Lavrov wanted to move ahead with securing oil contracts, consistent with the history of Russia's dealings with Iraq.[57] In 2002, Saddam Hussein had cancelled a $3.7 billion deal with Russia's Lukoil on the grounds that it had not met its obligations to start work. Lukoil argues that this deal is still valid and that UN sanctions had prevented work previously. Lukoil wanted to produce oil in 2005 from the West Qurna field.[58]

Scandal, however, hung over Russia's business dealings with Iraq. The Central Intelligence Agency (CIA) had confirmed the findings of the US-led Iraq Survey Groups that Iraq had granted special vouchers to Russian oligarchs, political parties and officials to buy oil at knockdown prices. Allegedly, Russia had received 32 per cent of all oil-for-food (OFF) contracts.[59] The UN Security Council had established the OFF programme in 1995, and serious irregularities were found in its administration.[60] 'Saddamgate' broke in January 2004 with the exposé of bribery of individuals and companies by Saddam with free oil in exchange for political support and for payment of items forbidden under the prewar embargo of Iraq. The charge was that Russia, China and France had benefited. Russia, however, denied such corruption. When, in November 2004, the Russian government pledged to write off some of Iraq's debt, reversing an earlier position, two likely consequences were aired in the press: first, that fresh scrutiny of Russian companies named in the OFF scandal should take place; and, second, that Putin now expected benefits from the rebuilding of Iraq, particularly oil deals.[61]

Public opinion

Since the collapse of the Soviet state, perceptions in Russia of US foreign policy and the situation in the Middle East have fluctuated. The firm 98 per cent against intervention in Kosovo had softened by the end of 1999, with 52 per cent predicting a normalization of relations with NATO (Buckley 2001: 165–8). In late September 2001, a solid 80 per cent of Russian citizens believed that the attacks of 11 September concerned everyone, but only 9 per cent soon after favoured Russian military involvement should any conflict break out between NATO and a part of the Muslim world (namely Afghanistan, Iran and Iraq). Nationwide polls in 2002 saw Russian attitudes altering from a low of 17 per cent who saw the US as 'friendly' to an improved 37 per cent who valued the US as an 'ally' to 55 per cent who felt 'basically good' about it. However, in March 2002, support for Russian participation in attempts to topple Saddam was seriously wanting. Only 1 per cent backed action alongside the US in March 2002. Although 42 per cent were content for Russia to be in an anti-terrorism coalition, the overwhelming preference was to be on the sidelines when it came to military involvement (Buckley 2003: 229–31).

Nine months after the US and Britain went to war, a nationwide survey in Russia of December 2003 recorded divided views. Only 5 per cent of Russians felt 'completely positive' about the US but 53 per cent were 'mainly positive,' 23 per cent 'mainly negative,' 8 per cent 'completely negative' and 11 per cent did not know. Questioning the same sample revealed that just 2 per cent, however, were 'completely positive' about the temporary occupation of Iraq by US troops, a mere 7 per cent 'mainly positive' about it, and a much higher 39 and 35 per cent were, respectively, 'mainly negative' and 'completely negative,' while 17 per cent did not know. Thus, feelings about the US in general were far more positive than attitudes to the Iraq occupation. Just eight months earlier, however, in April 2003, 80 per cent of Russians had expressed 'indignation' at the US military campaign in Iraq, 11 per cent had 'no particular feelings,' only 3 per cent showed approval, 4 per cent commented that they did not know enough about it and 2 per cent did not know. The campaign itself, then, was seriously opposed from the beginning, with only a small amount of warming to it months later. When asked what the Americans had brought to Iraq, only 10 per cent of Russians thought 'freedom'. Forty-five per cent responded 'anarchy,' 19 per cent saw 'a regime more cruel than Saddam' and 26 per cent did not know.[62]

When asked about what the US purpose was in entering Iraq, a high 49 per cent believed it was to gain control over Iraq's oil, 27 per cent thought the US wanted to 'show everyone who is boss in the world' and 8 per cent named the desire to boost the US economy with military orders. Only 7 per cent responded that it was to 'destroy terrorist bases' and just 6 per cent thought it was about stopping Iraq from producing WMD. Another 6 per cent suggested it was to divert attention from a crisis in the US economy. Fourteen per cent did not know.[63] Putin's actions, in contrast, won more approval. In April 2003, 39 per cent of Russians saw him 'staying on the sidelines', 52 per cent believed he had 'criticized US actions', only 2 per cent declared he had supported the US and 7 per cent did not know.[64] In another poll in the same month, a solid 45 per cent praised Putin for his 'reasonable and correct' actions compared with 38 per cent who maintained he 'should have opposed the US more decisively'. Fourteen per cent did not know.[65]

When asked about their responses about Middle Eastern countries in January 2004, Russians revealed a pragmatic approach. Eighteen per cent said that the statement 'Syria, Iraq and Libya are Russia's historical allies' was closest to their own view. Just 9 per cent could relate to 'we should support Western sanctions against Libya and Iraq'. The majority, 43 per cent, believed 'we should try to get advantage from Western conflict with the Arab world' and 30 per cent did not know.[66]

After the hostage taking in Beslan, a nationwide survey in September showed that 31 per cent of Russians believed there was probably a worldwide conspiracy against Russia, 14 per cent thought there definitely was, whereas 30 per cent considered that there probably was not but only 9 per cent held that there definitely was not. Sixteen per cent claimed not to know.[67] Conspiracy theories have long thrived in Russia, fuelled in the past by the closed system and the power of rumour in it. By October 2004, over 68 per cent felt that enemies abroad could attack Russia and one in four believed the US was the most likely state to do so.[68] Terrorist attacks inside Russia have contributed to the sense of vulnerability and possible attack from others. Putin's comments to the effect that other countries are ready to assist terrorists have, if anything, stirred apprehensions about other states rather than cultivated friendship for them. Moreover, suspicion of the US has deep historical roots, evident particularly among the elderly who oppose market reforms, hanker for the social protections of state socialism and have lived through the Cold War.

Security in Central Asia

The republics of Central Asia did not strive for independence from the Soviet Union, as did others with keen nationalist movements such as Lithuania, Georgia and Ukraine. As newly independent states, Kazakhstan, Kyrgyzstan, Uzbekistan, Tajikistan and Turkmenistan were loosely held together with other former Soviet states, excluding the three Baltic states and initially Georgia, in the Commonwealth of Independent States (CIS). This has proved to be little more than an institution that facilitated the mopping up of outstanding issues left over from the Soviet state concerning property, troops and fleet. Yet, despite numerous predictions of its imminent death, it has survived and been one forum through which Russia has periodically tried to push its dominance and to foster greater integration (Webber 1997).

Since 9/11, Putin has used the discourse of anti-terrorism in attempts to reassert a Russian presence in Central Asia and to establish hegemony. Results have been mixed. The Collective Security Treaty Organization (CSTO) of May 2002 included Russia, Kazakhstan, Kyrgyzstan, Tajikistan, Belarus and Armenia. Crucially, however, Uzbekistan and Turkmenistan refused to join. Differences and disagreements across the Central Asian states have made for centrifugal tendencies and a tepid striving for coordinated actions. Weak state capacities here also make for ineffective and highly selective commitments. At best, Central Asian leaders adopt a 'mix and match' approach to regional projects, as Roy Allison has characterized it.[69]

Nonetheless, some coordination has occurred. On 2 August, the already planned initial preparatory stage of joint military exercises of the states of the CSTO began in Kazakhstan. Commanders from Russia, Kazakhstan, Kyrgysztan and Tadjikistan carried out procedures for multinational counterinsurgency operations inside the CSTO.[70] Manoeuvres began on 3 August in Kyrgysztan, involving over 2,000 troops from the four states who together make up the CSTO's Collective Rapid Deployment Forces. Defence ministers from Russia, Tadjikistan and Kazakhstan attended and met with Kyrgyz President Askar Akaev.[71]

This did not, however, preclude US overtures and positive reactions to them at the same time. US General John Abizaid, Head of the Central Command, toured the region in July and August, visiting leaders in Kyrgyzstan, Tajikistan, Uzbekistan and Kazakhstan. When he met Kazakh President Nursultan Nazarbaev and his Defence Minister, on the agenda were Kazakh plans for closer cooperation with NATO and the US priority for expanded US–Kazakh military and security relations. Abizaid thanked Nazarbaev for sending Kazakh troops to Iraq.[72]

Russia's role in Central Asia has been further complicated by the US presence in the region after 9/11. Both the US and France were turning the airport at Bishkek into a main airbase with the agreement of Kyrgyzstan and Uzbekistan. There were over 10,000 Western troops in Tajikistan, Uzbekistan and Kyrgyzstan, and the Pentagon was intending to rent for 25 years an old aerodrome in Uzbekistan, with over 1,500 Americans already stationed there (Buckley 2002: 35; Cummings 2003: 239–51). Putin ultimately accepted these developments as necessary to the war in Afghanistan, but he and Igor Ivanov repeatedly commented that they were temporary. His critics, however, accused Putin of acquiescing in the geo-political weakening of Russia. Politicians in the Duma and in the Federation Council wrote how the US presence in the near abroad was 'alarming' and 'negative'.[73] Boris Usviatsov declared that it meant that the US could thereby 'throttle' Russia and that Russia should adopt a policy of 'strict pragmatism'.[74]

In reality, there was little Putin could do to stop the US presence. Russia no longer commanded sufficient power and influence globally or in the region to prevent it and, in any case, the Central Asian states welcomed US cash injections and saw an advantage in having another power to check Russian ambitions. The presence of two large powers in any region also always gives the weaker states the chance to play them off against each other for maximum benefit. The same pattern applied in the 1970s in African states, such as Angola, when newly independent states played the superpowers off against each other in their competition for influence (Donaldson 1981). In the circumstances, Putin was as pragmatic as he could be, just as General Secretary Leonid Brezhnev had to be then.

Recent violence in Uzbekistan in March 2004 that left 47 dead, however, resulted in talks between President Karimov and Putin, partly due to a cooling of Uzbek–US relations and US criticisms of human rights abuses.[75] Then, on 30 July 2004 in Tashkent, there were three coordinated suicide bombings that targeted the US and Israeli embassies and the office of the Prosecutor-General. Three died and eight were injured. These attacks occurred following the start of a trial of 15 Islamic militants who were allegedly associated with the banned group Hizb ut-Tahrir and were accused of carrying out the March bombings. President Karimov insisted that Hizb ut-Tahrir was responsible for events in March and July, although the group denied this and another called the 'Islamic Holy War Group in Uzbekistan' declared itself behind the July attacks.[76] In response, Kyrgyzstan, Kazakhstan and Tajikistan temporarily tightened internal and border security. Then, in May 2005, violence against protesters in Andijan in Uzbekistan sparked further international alarm at serious human rights abuses.[77]

Russia's main concerns about the US presence in the region include unease at diminished Russian clout due to partial displacement. This has implications for influence, political stability, trade, domestic politics and status. Moreover, this regional power shift contributed to a perception of encroachment and encirclement: first from the West due to NATO expansion and now from the underbelly. The new Russian airbase at Kant in Kyrgyzstan since October 2003 can be interpreted as part of Russia's attempt to limit Western influence in the region.[78] Similarly, in August 2004, a Russian diplomat in Dushanbe commented that Russia was hoping for a military base for its presence in Tajikistan, sealed in June in a new bilateral military cooperation agreement.[79] In Georgia in the Transcaucasus, however, limiting US influence is harder to do. Tensions with the former Soviet republic over Abkhazia and South Ossetia topped with US military aid to Georgia rankle, despite Putin's insistence in August 2004 that Russia was not taking sides and was ready to be a mediator.[80] The US is especially interested in Georgia and its conflicts because of the construction of the Baku–Ceyhan oil pipeline that runs from Azerbaijan to Turkey.[81]

Surprising to many were events in Kyrgyzstan in March 2005, dubbed the 'tulip revolution'. Protestors expressed mounting defiance at the results of parliamentary elections in February and the second round in March, eventually storming the main administration building in Bishkek in their thousands, with widespread looting thereafter.[82] The opposition declared Kurmanbek Bakiev acting president and Akaev fled to Russia, later resigning.[83] Lavrov accused the OSCE's assessments of the elections as 'destabilizing' and expressed concern in Russia at the political situation in the CIS.[84] Preoccupation with the themes of order and stability in the region prompted renewed debates about the 'failures' of the CIS, the role of Western influence, whether a revolution could happen inside Russia in the aftermath of upheavals in

Georgia, Ukraine and now Kyrgyzstan, and whether a ripple effect would destabilize Kyrgyzstan's neighbours too or trigger ethnic conflict between Kyrgyz and Uzbeks, as had occurred in 1990. Putin quickly called for calm and subsequently pledged aid to Kyrgyzstan as an ally to help reconstruction and spring sowing, seeking to promote normalcy and to maintain Russian influence, but without the interference he had shown in the upheavals in Ukraine.[85] Sergei Ivanov also insisted that scheduled joint military exercises of signatories of the Collective Security Treaty would go ahead with the planned participation of Kyrgyz units.[86]

There was, however, serious worry in the Kremlin about destabilizing implications for Russia itself, despite protestations to the contrary. So much so that Vladislav Surkov, deputy head of the presidential administration, held a meeting in March with Russian rock stars and requested that they refrain from becoming involved in any events that could contribute to a Ukrainian-style 'orange revolution' in Russia.[87]

Conclusion

Russian reactions to the Bush Doctrine can best be understand alongside a package of responses to wider global and geo-political issues of which they are only one part. Together, these responses are shaped by the current priorities of Russian foreign policy, contemporary perceptions of what constitutes terrorism and how it should best be dealt with and contributing domestic pressures. Understanding Russian reactions to the doctrine cannot be separated from these; indeed, it is filtered through them. Above all, Russian leaders' concerns are to pursue Russian interests in the first place and to reap maximum benefits from 'partnership' with the US but not at the cost of sacrificing Russia's geo-political presence and influence, nor at the cost of building ties with other states such as China. Pursuing a 'multi-vector' foreign policy remains a priority and building a 'strategic partnership' with China included in 2005 joint military exercises on Chinese soil.[88]

While Putin has pragmatically accepted many recent global economic, political and military realignments that he has been powerless to prevent, including Bush's withdrawal from the ABM treaty and US commitment to NMD, he remains keen to assert Russian leadership in areas where it is not yet a spent force, particularly in Central Asia.[89] Konstantin Kosachev, Duma Foreign Relations Committee Chairman, has stressed that Russia does not wish to see US moves towards permanent military bases in Georgia, Azerbaijan or Kazakhstan.[90]

The consequences of Russian reactions for Russia itself are so far propitious. Criticism of the US and British invasion of Iraq has not seriously jeopardized relations with these states. Even though Bush threatened to punish states that did not come on board, Russia has benefited from regular high-level talks with the US. In August 2004, for instance, Donald Rumsfeld and Sergei Ivanov discussed bilateral military cooperation along with questions concerning Iraq, Afghanistan and South Ossetia. They also prided them-selves on 20 joint drills scheduled for September and on Russian willingness to cooperate in the development of an anti-missile defence system.[91] Russia also won huge global sympathy after the seizure in Beslan.

Nationalists in Russia, however, were not overjoyed at Bush's announce-ment on 16 August that thousands of US troops would be redeployed and that, as a result, many could potentially move closer to the Russian border.[92] The argument that this would enable the US to respond better to global ter-rorism received some degree of support in Russia, but there was still unease about relocations to the Baltic states and Poland.[93] This amounted in many Russian eyes to one more visible extension of US hegemony into states once part of the Soviet empire. It was bad enough that Russian power had gone but, up to 2004, there had been no threat of a US military presence to em-phasize Russia's waned clout.

In this wider context of reduced regional power, lost superpower status and overwhelming US military might, Russian leaders have pragmatically not condemned the Bush Doctrine outright. Rather, they have agreed with many of its points where they suit Russian interests. While the doctrine's ap-plication to Iraq was opposed, it does not follow that Russia would necessarily oppose another war or incursion against another state, depending upon its location and the wider context. Leaders would most probably argue against hostilities against Iran and North Korea without proof of serious terrorist activities there, but might threaten attacks on Georgia on the grounds that terrorists who were a threat to Russia were being harboured. In December 2004, the Russian Air Force Commander General Vladimir Mikhailov kept up this rhetoric with the statement that 'long-range highly precise cruise missiles and aerial bombs' would be used against terrorists outside Russia's borders if necessary.[94]

Nor did Russian leaders bemoan Bush's re-election in November 2004, despite their criticism of the Iraq war. Instead, Putin criticized Osama bin Laden for trying negatively to influence Bush's chances and praised the American people for not being frightened by terrorists from taking an 'ad-visable' decision.[95] There was, moreover, a strong view in Moscow that, had Kerry become president, it would have meant more US questioning about authoritarianism in Russia and the fate of democratization, human rights and the war in Chechnia. Bush's triumph was ironically believed to suit Rus-sian interests better.[96]

Partnership as global leaders in the war against terrorism had bound Putin and Bush. Strong initial disagreement at the end of 2004 between Moscow and Washington over the outcome of the presidential election in Ukraine, resulting in pragmatic agreement that fresh elections should be held, is testi-mony to this. Putin may not have liked developments in Ukraine, but he was not going to let them jeopardize good working relations with America. The cost for Russia would be too great. Similarly, Russia's authoritarian tenden-cies were not sufficient for Bush to halt US–Russian cooperation, although he insisted upon criticizing the lack of a free press and an end to gubernatorial elections and stressed the need for the rule of law and a political opposition. Although both Putin and Sergei Ivanov reacted in February 2005 to Rice's and Bush's admonishments about democratic backsliding, with Ivanov graphically arguing that 'democracy is not a potato which can be transplanted from one soil to another', they, like Bush, had no interest in letting this disagreement jeopardize the global coalition against terrorism.[97] By then, however, Putin's popularity in Russia had plummeted to 42 per cent from highs of over 70 per cent, partly because of the way he attempted to make changes to social benefits, whereas a survey reported that 62 per cent of Russians felt 'good' about the US, 32 per cent 'bad' with just 6 per cent not knowing.[98] Thus, the US, still occupying Iraq but after elections there, was more popular in Russia for a short time than Putin, until he modified his policy on benefits.[99]

Notes

1 *Izvestiia*, 6 February 2004.
2 Ibid. For Iurii Luzhkov's comment on casualties, see Radio Free Europe, Radio Liberty (RFE/RL), *Newsline*, 8 (27), part I, 11 February 2004, p. 3.
3 *Rossiiskaia gazeta*, 7 September 2004, p. 1.
4 *Nezavisimaia gazeta*, 2 September 2004, p. 1; *Rossiiskaia gazeta*, 3 September 2004, p. 1; *Rossiiskaia gazeta*, 4 September 2004, pp. 1–2; *Rossiiskaia gazeta*, 7 September 2004, p. 1.
5 *Rossiiskaia gazeta*, 26 August 2004, p. 1; ibid., 27 August 2004, pp. 1–2.
6 Ibid., 2 September 2004, pp. 1 and 3.
7 *Literaturnaia gazeta*, 8–14 September 2004, p. 1.
8 *Rossiiskaia gazeta*, 7 September 2004, p. 1.
9 RFE/RL, *Newsline*, 8 (176), part I, 15 September 2004, p. 1.
10 *Rossiiskaia gazeta*, 7 September 2004, p. 1.
11 This is what Graeme P. Herd dubs 'soft war'. See Herd (2002).
12 http://www.rferl.org/nca/features/2002/11/05112002161104.asp.
13 For full details see: http://www.rferl.org/specials/russianelection/archives/0712203.asp.
14 RFE/RL, *Newsline*, 6 (86), part I, 9 May 2002, p. 1; ibid., no. 87, 10 May 2002, p. 1.
15 *Izvestiia*, 25 October 2002; *Itogi*, 5 November 2002; RFE/RL, *Newsline* 6 (202), part I, 25 October 2002.
16 *Itogi*, 5 November 2002.
17 RFE/RL, *Newsline*, 6 (205), part I, 30 October 2002.
18 *Izvestiia*, 29 December 2002, p. 1.
19 http://www.rferl.org/reports/corruptionwatch/2003/05/18-220503.asp; for a useful overview of these and other attacks, see *Independent on Sunday*, 6 July 2003.
20 *Izvestiia*, 6 July 2003, p. 1.
21 See *Izvestiia* on 3, 7 and 10 September 2003; and RFE/RL, *Newsline*, 7 (228), part I, 5 December 2003.
22 For responses from former presidents Mikhail Gorbachev and Boris Yeltsin, see *Moskovskie novosti*, 17–23 September 2003, p. 10.
23 *Novaia gazeta*, no. 68, 16 September 2004, p. 1.
24 *Moskovskie novosti*, 13 September 2004, p. 1.
25 *Vechernee vremia*, 10 September 2004, pp. 1–3; *Komsomol'skaia pravda*, 4 September 2004; *Nezavisimaia gazeta*, 2 September 2004, pp. 2–3.

26 *Moscow Times*, 8 September 2004, p. 1.
27 '*Sobytiia*', 10 pm.
28 RFE/RL, *Newsline*, 6 (176), part I, 18 September 2002.
29 Ibid., no. 177, 19 September 2002.
30 Ibid., no. 178, 20 September 2002.
31 Ibid., no. 179, 23 September 2002.
32 Ibid., vol. 7, no. 50, 17 March 2003.
33 Ibid., vol.7, no. 53, 20 March 2003.
34 Ibid., vol. 6., no. 178, 20 September 2002.
35 Ibid., no. 195, 16 October 2002.
36 Ibid., vol. 5, no. 229, 5 December 2001.
37 http://www.RFE/RL,org/nca/features/2001/11/221122084257.asp. For fuller dis-
    cussion of reactions to the US reneging on the ABM treaty, see Buckley (2003).
38 RFE/RL, *Newsline*, vol. 6, no. 23, part I, 5 February 2002.
39 Ibid., vol. 6, no. 177, 19 September 2002; ibid., vol. 6, no. 197, 18 October 2002.
40 RFE/RL, *Newsline*, vol. 8, no. 122, 29 June 2004.
41 *Rossiiskaia gazeta*, 21 March 2003, p.1.
42 http://www.cdi.org/russia/249-6.cfm and http://www.top.Rbc.ru/english/index.
    shtml?/news/english/2003/03/20/2012081bodshtml.
43 http://www.cdi.org/russia/johnson/7126-7.cfm.
44 *Pravda*, 20 March 2003.
45 http://www.whitehouse.gov/nsc/print/nssall.html, p. 4.
46 Ibid., p. 7.
47 Thanks to Rob Singh for drawing this article to my attention.
48 For further views across political parties, see *Rossiiskaia Federatsiia Sevodnia*, no. 7,
    April 2003, pp. 5–7.
49 RFE/RL, *Newsline*, vol. 7, no. 194, part I, 10 October 2003, p. 1.
50 Ibid.
51 *Krasnaia zvezda*, 11 October 2003; www.globalsecurity.org/military/library/
    news/2003/10/mil-031014-rferl-17115.htm; www.citeglobalsecurity.org/military/
    library/news/2003/10/mil-031003-shape02.htm.
52 *Krasnaia zvezda*, ibid.
53 Ibid., 10 November 2003, p. 7; see also www.redstar.ru/2003/10/11_10/3_
    01.html.
54 *Krasnaia zvezda*, ibid., p. 9.
55 http://www.newsfromrussia.com/main/2004/07/0754831.html.
56 Ibid.
57 http://www.mosnews.com/news/20004/07/26/iraqaid.shtml.
58 Ibid.
59 http://www.mosnews.com/news/2004/10/08/Iraq.shtml.
60 For details, see http://www.un.org/Depts/oip and http://www.globalsecurity.org/
    wmd/library/news/iraq/2004/10/iraq-041011-rferl01.htm.
61 http://www.globalsecuritynews.com/showArticle3.cfm?articleid=10500&topicID
    =30.
62 http://www.RussiaVotes.org.
63 Ibid.
64 Ibid.
65 Ibid.
66 Ibid.
67 Ibid.
68 RFE/RL, *Newsline*, vol. 8, no. 193, part 1, 12 October 2004, p. 2.
69 Roy Allison, 'Introduction', *International Affairs* 80 (3), May 2004, p. 426.
70 RFE/RL, *Newsline*, vol. 8, no. 145, part 1, 2 August 2004.
71 Ibid., vol. 8, no. 148, 5 August, p. 6.

72   Ibid., vol. 8, no. 146, 3 August, p. 6.
73   'Tochka zreniia na problemy chlenov Soveta Federatsii i deputatov Gosudarst-vennoi Dumy', *Rossiiskaia Federatsiia Segodnia*, no. 5, 2002, pp. 58–60.
74   Boris Uviatsov. 'Ob'iatiia po-Amerikanskii', *Rossiiskaia Federatsiia Segodnia*, ibid.
75   RFE/RL, *Newsline,* vol. 8, no. 71, part 1, 16 April 2004, p. 1.
76   Ibid., vol. 8, no. 145, part 1, 2 August 2004, p. 7.
77   Both the 'tulip revolution' in Kyrgyzstan and the events in May 2005 in Andigan are not discussed fully here as they occurred after this chapter had been completed. For commentary on human rights in Uzbekistan, refer to Macfarlane (2005).
78   Ibid., vol. 7, no. 181, part 1, 23 September 2003, p.1.
79   Ibid., vol. 8, no. 150, 9 August 2004, p. 6.
80   *Izvestiia*, 19 August 2004; *Krasnaia zvezda*, 18 August 2004.
81   RFE/RL, *Newsline*, vol. 8, no. 149, part 1, 6 August 2004, p. 5.
82   *Slovo Kyrgyzstana*, no. 21, 1 March 2005; ibid, no. 25, 11 March; ibid., no. 29, 23 March; ibid., no. 26, 15 March.
83   Ibid., no. 34, 5 April 2005.
84   RFE/RL, *Newsline*, vol. 9, no. 60, part 1, 31 March 2005, p. 1.
85   *Slovo Kyrgyzstana*, no. 32, 31 March 2005; RFE/RL, *Newsline*, vol. 9, no. 58, part 1, 29 March 2005, p. 1.
86   RFE/RL, *Newsline,* ibid.
87   Ibid., vol. 9, no. 60, part 1, 31 March 2005, pp. 2–3.
88   Ibid., vol. 8, no. 242, part 1, 30 December 2004, p. 2. Joint exercises were also planned in 2005 with France and Italy as well as naval exercises with the US.
89   Buckley (2003: 223–7); http://www.brook.edu/comm/transcripts/20010502.htm.
90   RFE/RL, *Newsline*, vol. 8, no. 156, part 1, 17 August 2004, p. 2. For statements from Washington that the US would not ratify the amended Treaty on Conventional Forces in Europe until Russia honoured the 1999 OSCE Istanbul Resolution by removing troops from Moldova and reaching agreement with Georgia about Russian presence there, see ibid., vol. 8, no. 229, part 1, 8 December 2004, p. 2.
91   Ibid., vol. 8, no. 155, 16 August 2004.
92   *Krasnaia zvezda*, 17 August 2004; *Nezavisimaia gazeta*, 16 August 2004; *Izvestiia*, 16 August 2004.
93   RFE/RL, *Newsline*, vol. 8, no. 156, part 1, 17 August 2004, p. 2.
94   Ibid., vol. 8, no. 227, part 1, 6 December 2004, p. 3.
95   *Rossiiskaia gazeta*, 4 November 2004; http://www.rian.ru/rian/intro.cfm?nws_id=724509.
96   *Kommersant*, 4 November 2004; *Nezavisimaia gazeta*, 4 November 2004.
97   *Izvestiia*, 14 February 2005.
98   http://www.RussiaVotes.org.
99   Most of this chapter was written in the autumn of 2004 with minor updating additions early in 2005 up to 6 April.

6 North-East Asia

Rex Li

The United States (US) has a long-standing interest in North-East Asia,[1] where it has a military presence and strong defence ties with several countries. Japan and South Korea are US allies, and Taiwan has a close, albeit informal, security relationship with Washington. At the same time, the Bush administration is facing considerable challenge from an increasingly powerful China. This chapter will consider the impact of the Bush administration's foreign policy on North-East Asian security. In particular, it will examine the reactions of China and Japan to the Bush Doctrine and the US-led invasion of Iraq. It will also analyse the strategic relations among the three great powers in the region. Special attention is paid to the two major regional security issues, the North Korean nuclear crisis and Taiwan.

China's response to the Bush Doctrine and the Iraq war

Since the end of the Cold War, Chinese leaders and policy elites have been suspicious of US intentions of shaping the structure of the international system according to American values and interests (see the analysis in Li 1999a). Despite talk of a 'strategic partnership' during the Clinton administration, US–China relations remained rather unstable throughout the 1990s. When George W. Bush was elected president in 2000, Chinese leaders were convinced that China would become a 'strategic competitor' of the US.

The events of 9/11 provided an opportunity for the two countries to improve their relations through anti-terrorist cooperation. Chinese leaders, however, were alarmed by the rapid expansion of American influence across the world. They were particularly concerned about US entry into the oil-rich area of Central Asia, which was seen as a serious challenge to China's energy and military security. To the Chinese, the swift removal of the Taleban regime in Afghanistan demonstrated unambiguously US determination and capability of using its superior military power to eradicate any threat to American security interests (Li 2003a). Chinese leaders were increasingly worried that the Bush administration would exploit the post-9/11 security situation to enhance America's global position. This was why former Chinese Foreign Minister Tang Jiaxuan warned at the UN in September 2002 that 'efforts should be made to prevent the arbitrary expansion' of the war on terror.[2]

From China's perspective, the publication of the US National Security Strategy (NSS)[3] confirmed its view that the Americans were actively seeking to utilize their formidable power to achieve absolute security and global dominance. The emphasis on preventing potential adversaries from challenging American power was seen as a clear indication of US hegemonic ambitions. Unsurprisingly, America's intention of leading the cause of promoting democracy, development, free markets and free trade throughout the world was viewed with great suspicion (Su 2003; Guo 2003).

What worried Chinese leaders most was the inclusion of the Bush administration's new strategic doctrine in an official document, which signified a fundamental shift from the Cold War strategy of deterrence to a new doctrine supporting pre-emptive strikes against terrorist groups and any states sheltering them and/or possessing weapons of mass destruction (WMD). The Bush Doctrine, they fear, could be used to justify any military actions in the name of self-defence and anti-terrorism. Chinese analysts such as Su Ge and Guo Xianggang argue that it is against international law and the UN Charter to launch pre-emptive attacks on other countries that, in their judgement, would seriously undermine international stability and world order (Su 2003; Guo 2003).

Chinese leaders consistently urged America to handle the Iraq crisis through the UN. China voted along with other permanent Security Council members on resolution 1441 in November 2002 in the hope that the US could be dissuaded from tackling the crisis unilaterally. As Zhang Qiyue, Foreign Ministry spokeswoman of the People's Republic of China (PRC), put it: 'I think our position is extremely close to that of France.'[4] In a telephone conversation with President Jacques Chirac, former Chinese President Jiang Zemin reportedly said that 'the Iraq issue should be resolved through political and diplomatic means within the framework of the UN'.[5]

Although Chinese scholars and commentators were critical of US approaches to Iraq, the official media had by and large refrained from publishing reports that expressed strong anti-American sentiments. However, from January 2003 onwards, Chinese analysts became much more outspoken, and there were noticeably more articles criticizing US policy. When two UN arms inspectors, Drs Hans Blix and Mohamed Bharadei, informed the Security Council that they were unable to find evidence of WMD in Iraq (Blix 2004: 175–8), Tang Jiaxuan joined his French and Russian colleagues in pressing for continued UN inspection. He argued that 'to intensify inspections for the purpose of seeking a peaceful solution to the Iraqi issue, we are obliged to try our best and use all possible means to avert war'.[6]

In the build-up to war, the Chinese Communist Party's Leading Group on National Security (LGNS)[7] met regularly to discuss how China should respond to the situation. The LGNS was deeply concerned about the tendency of 'US unilateralism' and America's global ambitions and their implications for Chinese security interests.[8] After President Bush asserted that it would no longer be possible to disarm Saddam Hussein peacefully, Chinese officials, including Premier Wen Jiabao and Foreign Minister Li Zhaoxing, continued to express their opposition to military attack on Iraq without UN approval[9] but did not wish to confront Washington directly. When the US and Britain decided to withdraw their application for a second resolution, PRC leaders were relieved that they did not have to vote on it.

Critical of the US-led military actions, Chinese officials called for an end to the war, emphasizing the consequences of civilian casualties and humanitarian catastrophe. The invasion had, in the words of Li Zhaoxing, 'trampled upon the UN Constitution and international law'. The war was also condemned by China's parliament, the National People's Congress and the advisory Chinese People's Political Consultative Conference. Chinese leaders were warned by their advisers that America could become more assertive in Asia in pursuing its interests following a successful operation in Iraq.[10] A group of Chinese intellectuals was permitted to organize a conference that condemned US 'hegemonism'.[11] Meanwhile, numerous articles were published in the state media that vehemently criticized the US invasion. Most Chinese writers asserted that the war had seriously damaged the world order and that the philosophy of 'might makes right' could now prevail in international affairs (Li 2003).

This anti-war sentiment seemed to be shared by some Chinese intellectuals, academics and students who tried to organize demonstrations in Beijing. Three thousand people were reported to have signed an anti-war petition, according to one western report. China's official news agency Xinhua claimed that 'cadres and masses in different parts of the country have expressed their support for the government's stand on the Iraqi issue and they appeal for an end to the war'. However, the activities of anti-war supporters were closely monitored and curtailed by the Chinese authorities.[12] PRC leaders were worried that widespread anti-American demonstrations might put pressure on them to take tougher actions against Washington, thus destabilizing Sino-US relations. Even before the war, there had been demands for public protests, but the government invariably rejected these. Nevertheless, Chinese academics were allowed to gather over 900 signatures for an open letter opposing America's invasion of Iraq. It is also interesting to note that a small number of intellectuals were able to issue public statements on the Internet showing their support for the US military operations in removing Saddam's regime.[13]

Some Chinese analysts argue that the Iraq war represents the beginning of a process whereby the US attempts to reshape the world order based on its new security strategy. The doctrine of pre-emption, they predict, may well be applied to other countries, making certain states vulnerable. To the Chinese, America's 'pre-emptive strike' on Iraq reflects its unilateral position, total disregard of world opinion and contempt for the UN. According to Chinese analysis, Iraq posed no imminent threat to America nor did it possess any WMD. The real motive behind the invasion, it was argued, was to fortify US economic, political and military dominance in the world (Wang 2003).

Chinese policy elites predict that the Bush administration will become more conservative and hawkish in its foreign policy after the success of US military occupation of Iraq. They maintain that most members of the administration are neo-conservatives who believe that American interest is best served by military expansion and worldwide democratization. The establishment of a 'democratic' Iraqi regime is seen as the first step towards their goal of 'democratization of the Middle East', closely linked to America's anti-terrorist strategy. This would also help to enhance US economic and strategic interests in the region which, combined with America's growing influence in other areas, would ensure its global dominance in the post-9/11 world (Li 2003).

Japan's response to the Bush Doctrine and the Iraq war

Throughout the Cold War years, Japan was a staunch US ally in its battle against communism in Asia. The American 'security umbrella' enabled Japan to develop its economy rapidly and to achieve the status of an economic superpower. Despite occasional trade frictions, the two countries remained close allies in the post-Cold War era. The 1996 'US–Japan Joint Declaration on Security Alliance for the 21st Century' and the revised 'Guidelines for US–Japan Defence Cooperation' further strengthened their security relationship (Hook *et al.* 2001: ch. 6). In the meantime, there has been a greater demand from Japanese elites and public that Japan should seek to adopt a higher profile in both regional and global affairs. A solid security relationship with Washington is therefore essential to Japan's quest for a more significant role in the world.

Following 9/11, the Japanese government offered firm support for America in its global 'war on terrorism'. On 19 September, Prime Minister Junichiro Koizumi announced a seven-point assistance plan, which was followed by the passage of counter-terrorism legislation by the Diet in October. Although the legislation had a two-year limit, it allowed the Self-Defence Forces (SDF) to provide logistical, rear-echelon support to the American and British forces in the Indian Ocean. Meanwhile, the government approved the dispatch of Japanese C-130 transport planes to provide relief supplies to Afghan refugees in Pakistan. In November, Tokyo decided to send two destroyers and a supply ship to the Indian Ocean. A year later, the Koizumi administration decided to offer further surveillance and logistical support to American and British naval forces by sending an AEGIS-equipped destroyer to the area.[14]

Mindful of the accusation of lack of alliance commitment to the US operations in the 1991 Iraq war, the Japanese government responded to 9/11 decisively. It also expressed its willingness to back America if it were to attack Iraq. However, Japan was constrained by Article 9 of its constitution, which would prevent the SDF from taking part in US military operations. Initially, the Japanese government was in favour of finding a peaceful solution to the Iraq crisis. After America, Britain and Spain set a deadline for disarming Iraq through diplomatic channels, Koizumi announced Japan's support. He expressed his regret for the UN's failure to deal with the crisis peacefully, but noted that military operations could be legitimized by past UN Security Council resolutions.[15]

Nevertheless, Koizumi did not hide the fact that his government backed the US invasion because of the necessity of maintaining the US–Japan security alliance. 'To lose trust in the Japan–US security relationships', as he explained in March 2003, 'would be against Japan's national interests'.[16] This was particularly true when nuclear development in North Korea was considered as an escalating threat to Japan. The Japanese government may have had some reservations over Washington's strategy of military pre-emption in tackling regional issues, but it stood shoulder to shoulder with the Bush administration in its decision to attack Iraq.

Clearly, Koizumi acted against public opinion in his country. According to an opinion poll conducted by the Japanese broadcasting station NHK on 7–9 March 2003, 70 per cent of respondents did not support a US military attack on Iraq even with UN approval, and 80 per cent of them opposed the war without a UN resolution. The results of other opinion polls were remarkably similar.[17] For example, a poll conducted by the Japanese newspaper *Mainichi Shimbun* on 1–2 March showed that 84 per cent of the Japanese people were against an attack on Iraq.[18] Another poll in *Asahi Shimbun* conducted on 23–24 February also revealed that 78 per cent of the respondents opposed the war. Apart from negative public opinion, the Koizumi government faced opposition from the leaders of its coalition partners, the new Conservative Party and the new Komei Party, as well as members of its own party, the Liberal Democratic Party.

Koizumi, however, promised that Japanese forces would not take part in the US-led invasion of Iraq. Instead, they would contribute to the rebuilding of post-war Iraq, made possible by the passage of a law by the Diet in July 2003. In December, the Koizumi government approved a plan to dispatch several hundred non-combat troops to Iraq for a period of one year. Even though the main task of the troops was to provide humanitarian assistance, it aroused intense debate as the move was widely seen as a violation of Japan's pacifist constitution. Only 9 per cent of the population showed their support for the plan. Critics pointed to the dangerous situation in Iraq and the possibility of the troops being drawn into combat.[19]

While Japanese troops did not suffer any casualties in Iraq in 2004, Japanese civilians became the targets of Iraqi militants who demanded the withdrawal of the 550-strong Japanese troops in southern Iraq. A number of Japanese nationals were abducted and one of them was killed. Two Japanese freelance journalists were also shot dead. One Japanese tourist was abducted and beheaded after Japan refused to concede to the demands of Iraqi insurgents.[20]

Despite these shocking incidents, the government decided in December 2004 to extend the SDF mission for another year. Not surprisingly, Japanese public opinion was divided. An opinion poll conducted by *Nihon Keizai Shimbun* showed that 54 per cent of the Japanese were against the extension of the dispatch and only 32 per cent in favour.[21] Similarly, there was an absence of consensus in the Japanese press.[22] Some newspapers offered strong support for the government's plan. *Sankei Shimbun* argued that the troop extension was a 'necessary course of action'. *Yomiuri Shimbun* believed that Japan needed to play its part in the international community. Withdrawing the SDF was therefore 'not an option'. Others, however, called for an exit strategy. *Asahi Shimbun* suggested that the troops should be withdrawn after Iraq's elections in March 2005 to coincide with the withdrawal of the Dutch military who had been responsible for the security in Samawah and protection of the Japanese mission. The paper questioned the argument that withdrawal of the troops would harm the US–Japan alliance and urged the government seriously to consider alternative ways of assisting Iraq.[23] Still others, such as *Ryukyu Shimpo*, raised their concern at Japan's 'lack of independence' in its decision to back America. *Tokyo Shimbun* urged the government to pay more attention to the safety of the troops in Iraq and to be prepared to withdraw the mission if the situation required.

Koizumi was fully aware of public divisions and debate and stressed that the troops were deployed in a 'non-combat' zone. He also highlighted the importance of the mission to US–Japan security relations. As he commented at a news conference in December 2004: 'Japan's support activities in Iraq are the implementation of policies for the Japan–US alliance and international cooperation . . . such implementation is a national interest of Japan.'[24] To Koizumi's delight, the Australian Prime Minister John Howard agreed in February 2005 to send 450 more troops to Samawah where the SDF were based. This would provide security for the Japanese troops to perform humanitarian and reconstruction work in the 'relatively benign' area.[25]

Bush's foreign policy and North-East Asian security

While there is much continuity in US perceptions of North-East Asia, one can identify certain distinctive characteristics in Bush's foreign policy towards the area, in particular the greater importance of Japan in America's security strategy in the Asia-Pacific region. The Bush administration has made it clear that it wishes Japan to play a more prominent part in regional security affairs. On many occasions, US leaders have emphasized the indispensable role of Tokyo in maintaining US security interests in Asia, making a genuine effort to strengthen and expand the US–Japan security alliance.

Japan has also been encouraged by US politicians such as Colin Powell and Richard Armitage to amend its constitution, which has restricted Japan's international peace-keeping activities.[26] The Bush administration is seeking the support of its loyal ally in order to face various global and regional challenges. This is why Japan's backing for the US invasion of Iraq was vital, even though Japanese contributions to the war were essentially symbolic. In North-East Asia, Washington needs the cooperation of Japan in its development and deployment of the Theatre Missile Defence System. Japan is undoubtedly considered as America's most valuable and trusted ally in the region (Marquand 2005).

In contrast to Japan, China is perceived by the Bush administration as a strategic rival despite its willingness to collaborate with America in the war on terrorism. Indeed, there is a growing concern in the US about the security implications of an ascendant China.[27] The Americans are worried that China's rapidly expanding military power, especially its nuclear capabilities, will present an immense challenge to US security interests. A recently published Central Intelligence Agency (CIA) report estimated that China's ballistic missiles will increase severalfold by 2015 and that they will be deployed primarily against the United States.[28]

Concerns about China's defence modernization and its growing military capabilities have also been expressed in several Pentagon reports.[29] Most worrying is Beijing's possession of over 500 short-range ballistic missiles,[30] known to be targeted at Taiwan, which is regarded by Chinese leaders as a 'renegade province'. To Washington, the PRC's continued military intimidation of Taiwan represents a serious threat to regional stability. As the former US Deputy Secretary of State Richard Armitage has acknowledged, Taiwan is the biggest landmine in US–China relations.[31]

Another significant element of Bush's foreign policy in the region is its tougher stance towards the North Korean regime. In 2002, Bush referred to North Korea as a member of the 'axis of evil'. Since then, relations between Washington and Pyongyang have deteriorated. North Korea's withdrawal from the Treaty on the Non-Proliferation of Nuclear Weapons and its admission of possessing nuclear weapons have heightened tensions on the Korean Peninsula. But US officials have found it extremely difficult to apply the Bush Doctrine of pre-emption to the resolution of the nuclear impasse. A military confrontation with the North Koreans could result in calamity not only for Japan and South Korea but American soldiers in the two countries.

Hitherto, the Bush administration has tried to handle the crisis through the six-party talks involving America, North Korea, South Korea, China, Japan and Russia. However, North Korean leaders decided in February 2005 to suspend the talks indefinitely, citing Secretary of State Condoleezza Rice's reference to the DPRK as an 'outpost of tyranny' as a reflection of Washington's continued hostility towards Pyongyang.[32] Following intense diplomacy, North Korea rejoined the six-nation talks in July 2005 and some progress has been made towards the goal of denuclearization of the Korean Peninsula (Kerr 2005).

Japan, America and North-East Asia security in the Bush era

Japanese leaders and politicians who are keen to upgrade Japan–US security relations welcome Bush's North-East Asian policy. Despite their different views on Japan's involvement in the Iraq war, most Japanese elites believe that it is in Tokyo's interest to maintain a robust alliance with the United States and to expand its security role in a changing international environment. Japanese response to US policy should be understood within the context of the changing domestic security debate under the Koizumi government.

Ever since the end of the Cold War, Japan has been struggling to find a new place in the world. However, Japan's global activities have been severely curtailed by its pacifist constitution. Many Japanese elites are frustrated by the constitutional constraints that have prevented Japan from assuming more international responsibilities. Some have advocated a revision of their constitution, whereas others have argued that Japan should regain its status of an 'ordinary nation' and serve as a permanent member on the UN Security Council.

In recent years, several high-level government advisory groups have called for greater flexibility in allowing overseas deployment of the SDF and its participation in collective security activities. Indeed, Japan has become more active in participating in UN missions and initiatives in East Timor, Afghanistan and elsewhere. In addition, there have been various legislative initiatives on expanding the SDF's peace-keeping role in relation to the war on terrorism. Other proposals that have been put forward include the transformation of Japan's Defence Agency into a government ministry and the establishment of a regional collective security organization. More controversially, some senior Japanese politicians have questioned the tradition of forbidding nuclear weapons development in Japan.[33]

In December 2004, Japan published its third National Defence Programme Outline,[34] which would enable Japan to play a broader role in international security. Specifically, it would allow the SDF to defend Japanese security interests and carry out anti-terrorist missions around the world. The outline also reiterated the need for closer Japan–US security cooperation, especially in the area of missile defence.[35] To facilitate joint development of missile defence systems with America, the Koizumi government decided to lift its long-standing ban on weapons exports, which had symbolized Japan's pacifist image for 40 years. This, together with the new defence outline, signified a major shift in Japanese defence policy.[36]

Japan's widening security role has certainly had the blessing of the Bush administration as both nations share a range of common security concerns, particularly their apprehensions about the rise of Chinese power. Although the PRC is Japan's biggest trade partner, the Japanese are acutely aware that a stronger China would present a huge challenge to Tokyo's position in the Asia-Pacific region. Especially worrying are Beijing's growing military capabilities (Drifte 2003: ch. 2). Indeed, this concern was conveyed in the recently published defence outline where, for the first time, China was named as a potential threat.[37]

The Koizumi government also shared the Bush administration's concern over the PRC's threat of using force against Taiwan. In a joint US–Japan security statement of 19 February 2005, both countries agreed that encouraging 'the peaceful resolution of issues concerning the Taiwan Strait through dialogue' should be one of their 'common strategic objectives'. They also agreed to 'encourage China to improve transparency of its military affairs'.[38] Yoshinori Ono, Director General of Japan's Defence Agency, is reported to have said: 'While we should maintain good relations with China, we must also pay attention to its military moves'.[39] The Japanese saw the intrusion of a Chinese nuclear submarine into Japanese territorial waters in November 2004 as evidence of a growing China threat.

Japan and China, moreover, are competing for Russian oil and gas. They also have unresolved disputes over the sovereignty of the Senkaku/Diaoyu islands where rich deposits of natural gases are believed to exist. Japan's suspicions of Beijing's intentions were reflected in a recent government-sponsored survey, which showed that Japanese people felt less friendly towards China than at any time since 1975. A poll conducted by the *Nihon Keizai Shimbun* indicated that most Japanese wanted their government to adopt a tougher stance towards Beijing.[40]

Another major concern bringing Japan and America together is the perceived threat from North Korea. Undoubtedly, North Korea's nuclear programmes and ballistic missile activities have posed a tremendous threat to Japanese security given the geographical proximity between the two countries. North Korea's missile launch in August 1998 is a vivid reminder of how vulnerable Japan is to a missile attack. Despite the difficulties in dealing with North Korea, Japanese leaders have been trying to develop a stable relationship with Pyongyang. They do not wish to see a military confrontation on the Korean Peninsula, nor face the consequences of a sudden collapse of the North Korean regime.

For many years, Japan has provided generous economic support for the North Koreans. Koizumi's visit to Pyongyang and his meeting with the North Korean leader Kim Jong-il in September 2002 demonstrated Japan's desire to engage with North Korea through diplomacy and dialogue. This is why Japan has serious reservations over pre-emptive strikes against North Korea. To Tokyo, a desperate North Korean communist regime could fire missiles at Japan and South Korea where US troops are stationed. Indeed, Japan, along with the United States and South Korea, has actively encouraged China to persuade the DPRK to return to the six-party talks. Both countries regard a peaceful resolution of the North Korean issue as a 'common strategic objective', as outlined in their recent joint security statement.[41] In the meantime, the Koizumi government is collaborating with the Bush administration to maintain 'preparedness for any situation'.[42]

China, America and US–Japan security relations

Chinese leaders and elites have long been suspicious of the sincerity of US policy towards China, which is characterized as 'engagement plus containment'. They are of the view that the Bush administration, like its predecessors, does not wish to see a strong and prosperous China, which can potentially contest its regional and global interests. To Beijing, the 'war on terror' has enabled the US to consolidate its defence ties with traditional allies and develop new security relations across Asia. The Chinese are worried that their country would be encircled by the US through its military presence in Asia and enhanced alliance relationships with a range of countries surrounding China (Gao 2004).

The Chinese expect that the Bush administration will continue to use Taiwan to constrain the growth of China's power and possibly intervene in a China–Taiwan conflict (Wu 2004). Thus, Beijing has closely observed America's recent military operations, especially 'Operation Iraqi Freedom', in order to gain a better understanding of the strengths and weaknesses of the US military.

The PRC government has always considered Taiwan to be a matter of 'national sovereignty and territorial integrity'. To Beijing, Taiwan has drifted further away from the mainland under the pro-independence leadership of President Chen Shui-bian. They are convinced that Bush's closer links with and arms sales to Taipei have given a greater impetus to the independence forces on the island (Liu 2003). Chinese leaders have therefore stepped up their military pressure on Taiwan recently. Their resolve to use force to thwart Taiwanese independence is stated unambiguously in China's National Defence White Paper published in December 2004.[43] China has also passed an anti-succession law in March 2005, which threatened to achieve 'reunification' with Taiwan through military means should peaceful negotiations fail.[44]

To PRC leaders, Japan has been working closely with America to frustrate China's great power aspirations since the early 1990s (Li 1999b). They have therefore reacted strongly to the February 2005 US–Japan security statement, which listed Taiwan as one of their common security concerns.[45] It was the first time that the Taiwan issue had been mentioned publicly by both Japan and America in their bilateral security statement. Chinese leaders considered this as an indication of US–Japan collaboration to interfere with China's 'internal affairs'. Tokyo's decision to issue a visa to former Taiwanese president Lee Teng-hui to visit Japan in December 2004 was interpreted as another attempt to challenge China on the Taiwan issue.

Chinese leaders are particularly troubled by Japan's expanding security role and its plan to revise the pacifist constitution and to gain a permanent UN Security Council seat. Koizumi's regular visits to the Yasukuni Shrine, where executed war criminals are venerated along with other war dead, are seen as a sign of Japanese reluctance to accept the past. A remilitarized Japan allied with the United States, the Chinese fear, will present a tremendous threat to China's security. Chinese distrust of Japan seems to be prevalent among PRC citizens. A recent survey conducted by the Chinese Academy of Social Sciences showed that 53.6 per cent of the Chinese 'do not feel close' to Japanese people.[46] Indeed, anti-Japanese sentiment is growing in China following widespread public protests in April 2005 over the Japanese government's approval of eight history textbooks that allegedly downplay the magnitude of Japan's wartime crimes.[47]

Another important security issue in North-East Asia is the North Korean nuclear crisis, which directly affects China's interests. For over 50 years, the PRC and DPRK have had a close relationship of 'lips and teeth'. Today, China remains North Korea's major source of energy and food supplies. To Chinese leaders, Bush's reference to North Korea as part of the 'axis of evil' does not help to reduce regional tensions. According to some Chinese analysts, it was America's menace to the DPRK's regime survival and its refusal to engage in a direct dialogue with Pyongyang that led North Korea to play the 'nuclear card'. Thus, America is thought to be the primary source of instability on the Korean Peninsula, although Chinese leaders are unhappy with Pyongyang's provocative behaviour. A nuclearized Korean Peninsula would only encourage other countries in Asia to acquire a nuclear capability, thus threatening China's security environment (for detailed analysis, see Li 2003b).

While Chinese leaders do not particularly want to see a united Korea, the demise of the North Korean regime does not serve Chinese interests either. This explains Beijing's strong opposition to any pre-emptive attacks on North Korea. If the DPRK regime were to collapse, China would find it very difficult to cope with a massive refugee crisis. Another consequence would be the loss of a buffer area between China and American forces in North-East Asia. Should the United States maintain its military presence in a united Korea, PRC leaders would face rising American influence in an area that is strategically vital to China. For all these reasons, Beijing has played an instrumental role in persuading North Korea to accept the six-party talks on dismantling its nuclear programme (Li 2003b).

Conclusion: the 'strategic triangle' and the future of North-East Asian security

It is clear that the Bush Doctrine has had a significant impact on the strategic thinking and security policy of Japan and China. In particular, Bush's foreign policy has played a major part in shaping the interactions among the key players within the 'strategic triangle' in North-East Asia.

China is apprehensive of the strengthening of US–Japan defence cooperation in the light of 9/11 and the Iraq war, while Japan and America are uncertain of the security implications of a rising China. Despite their different perceptions on various issues, the three major powers share a common interest in maintaining regional security and economic prosperity. They all have a vested interest in promoting trade relations and preserving regional economic stability. The Chinese market is important to both Japan and America, while China needs the two economic powers for its economic modernization. America also needs the PRC's cooperation in dealing with a variety of global security issues such as combating terrorism and non-proliferation of WMD.

The three countries are in agreement that a nuclear confrontation on the Korean Peninsula would seriously destabilize the region with wider security and economic repercussions. Although Japan stood by the US in its war in Iraq, it prefers a non-military solution to the North Korean issue. Even the US, which has adopted a hardline stance towards Pyongyang, has so far accepted the six-party talks as the most viable channel of defusing the crisis. Indeed, both the US and Japan have relied heavily on Beijing to persuade North Korea to return to the negotiation table. South Korea, another ally of America, is also against pre-emptive strikes on the DPRK, although it supported the US-led invasion of Iraq.

It is the case that there are serious perceptual gaps among the US, Japan and China over Taiwan, but they all hope that the issue can be resolved peacefully. America does not wish to have a military engagement with China, given its preoccupation with fighting the global war on terrorism. In any case, the costs of fighting a war with China are incalculable. While opposing the use of force against Taiwan, US officials have been exerting more pressure on Taiwanese leaders not to alter the status quo that might provoke China.

Japan is also not keen to be involved in a cross-strait confrontation, even though it would be obliged to provide support for America in such a conflict. The Japanese government has recently reassured PRC leaders that Japan does not support Taiwan's independence.[48] For its part, China is loath to confront US forces despite its commitment to the reunification with Taiwan. The priority of Chinese leaders remains economic development, which requires a stable and peaceful international environment. China has emphasized the 'peaceful' aspects of its anti-succession law but also demonstrated its willingness to use force to achieve the national goal of reunification. Meanwhile, Washington and Tokyo are sending a clear signal to the PRC through their joint security statement and other official pronouncements that any non-peaceful resolution to the status of Taiwan is unacceptable.

It can be argued that the future of North-East Asian security will be shaped primarily by the dynamics of the strategic interactions of the three great powers – the United States, China and Japan. This is not to say that Russia is irrelevant to the security of the region. However, its role is less significant compared with that of the three players within the 'strategic triangle'. Russia's contributions to North-East Asian security will be made mainly through multilateral security forums.

Nevertheless, one must not underestimate the potential implications of Russia's 'strategic partnership' with China. After all, Moscow is the PRC's biggest arms supplier, and Russian weapons are important to future Chinese military development. But it is unlikely that the two countries will form a military alliance against America and Japan. Whether peace and stability in North-East Asia can be maintained will be determined largely by the foreign and security policies of the US, Japan and China and how they manage their triangular relationships in the coming years.

Notes

1 The countries in North-East Asia include China, Japan, Mongolia, North Korea, Russia, South Korea and Taiwan.

2 'China cautious on Iraq action', 14 September 2002, http://edition.cnn.com/2002/WORLD/asiapcf/east/09/14/china.iraq/index.html.

3 *The National Security Strategy of the United States of America*, September 2002, http://www.whitehouse.gov/nsc/nss.pdf.

4 'China adds voice to Iraq War doubts', 23 January 2003, http://edition.cnn.com/2003/WORLD/asiapc/east/01/23/sprj.irq.china/index.html.

5 'China calls for diplomatic solution on Iraq', 27 January 2003, http://edition.cnn.com/2003/WORLD/asiapc/east/01/26/china.iraq/index.html.

6 'More inspections enjoyed broad UN support', 14 February 2003, http://edition.cnn.com/2003/WORLD/meast/02/14/sprj.irq.un.world.reax/index.html.

7 Led by Hu Jintao, the Chairman of the Chinese Communist Party and Chinese President, this secretive group is responsible for coordinating China's foreign and defence policies.

8 Willy Wo-Lap Lam, 'China readies for future US fight', 25 March 2003, http://edition.cnn.com/2003/WORLD/asiapc/east/03/24/willy.column/index.html.

9 'China says peace still possible', 18 March 2003, http://edition.cnn.com/2003/WORLD/asiapc/east/03/17/china.iraq/index.html.

10 Lam, 'China calls for end to war', 24 March 2003, http://edition.cnn.com/2003/WORLD/asiapc/east/03/24/sprj.irq china/index.html.

11 Willy Wo-Lap Lam, 'China readies for future US fight', 25 March 2003, http://edition.cnn.com/2003/WORLD/asiapc/east/03/24/willy.column/index.html.

12 Lam, 'Beijing curbs antiwar protests', 30 March 2003, http://edition.cnn.com/2003/WORLD/asiapc/east/03/30/sprj.irq china.protests/index.html.

13 Lam, 'Beijing bans antiwar protests', 11 March 2003, http://edition.cnn.com/2003/WORLD/asiapc/east/03/11/china.demos/index.html.

14 *Strategic Survey 2001/2002*. Oxford: Oxford University Press for IISS, p. 279; *Strategic Survey 2002/2003*. Oxford: Oxford University Press for IISS, p. 255.

15 Axel Berkofsky, 'Koizumi: US ties beat out public opinion', *Asia Times*, 20 March 2003, http://www.atimes.com/atimes/Japan/EC20Dh01.html.

16 'China says peace still possible', 18 March 2003, http://edition.cnn.com/2003/WORLD/asiapc/east/03/17/china.iraq/index.html.

17 'No war, please', http://kanzaki.com/jpoll/2003/.

18 '84 per cent of Japanese oppose Iraq attack', *Mainichi Shimbun*, 3 March 2003.

19 'Japan to send troops to Iraq', 9 December 2003, http://edition.cnn.com/2003/WORLD/asiapc/east/12/09/japan, troops/index.html.

20 *Mainichi Daily News*, http://mdn.mainichi.co.jp/news/20041229p2a00m0fp006000c.html.

21 *Nihon Keizai Shimbun*, 29 December 2004.

22 'Japan's press split over Iraq mission extension', 10 December 2004, http://news.bbc.co.uk/1/hi/world/asia-pacific/4084993.stm.

23 'Koizumi must think beyond US ties', *Asahi Shimbun*, 10 December 2004.

24 'SDF mission in Iraq extended', *Asahi Shimbun*, 10 December 2004.

25 'Aussie troops to protect Japan contingent in Iraq', *Japan Times*, 23 February 2005.

26 'US questions Japan's pacifism', 13 August 2004, http://news.bbc.co.uk/1/hi/world/asia-pacific/3561378.stm.

27 See, for example, *2004 Report to Congress of the US–China Economic and Security Review Commission*, June 2004, http://www.uscc.gov.

28 *Foreign Missile Developments and the Ballistic Missile Threat Through*

2015,   January   2002,   http://www.cia.gov/nic/pubs/other_products/
Unclassifiedballisticmissilefinal.htm.

29 The latest one is *Annual Report on the Military Power of the People's Republic of China*,
    Department of Defence, July 2005, http://www.defense.mil/news/Jul2005/
    d20050719china.pdf.

30 Ibid.

31 See Richard Armitage's interview with Charlie Rose on PBS, 20 December 2004,
    http://www.state.gov/s/d/rm/39973.htm.

32 Sarah Buckley, 'Why North Korea won't talk', 10 February 2005, http://news.bbc.
    co.uk/go/pr/fr/-/1/hi/world/asia-pacific/4253563.stm.

33 *Strategic Survey 2002/2003*. Oxford: Oxford University Press for IISS, pp. 254–7.

34 The first defence outline was published in 1976 and the second one in 1995.

35 *National Defence Programme Guidelines for FY 2005 and After*, 10 December 2004,
    http://www.jda.go.jp/e/index_.htm.

36 'Good ally of US: 40-year arms ban eased for missile defence', *Asahi Shimbun*, 11
    December 2004.

37 See *National Defence Programme Guidelines for FY 2005 and After*, 10 December 2004,
    http://www.jda.go.jp/e/index_.htm.

38 *Joint Statement: US–Japan Security Consultative Committee*, http://www.mofa.go.jp/
    region/n-america/us/security/scc/joint0502.html.

39 'Japan, US set security goals, eye Taiwan, N. Korea', *Kyodo News*, 20 February
    2005.

40 *Kyodo News*, 20 December 2004; AFP, 28 December 2004.

41 See *Joint Statement: US–Japan Security Consultative Committee*, http://www.mofa.
    go.jp/region/n-america/us/security/scc/joint0502.html.

42 *Joint Statement on North Korea*, http://www.mofa.go.jp/region/n-america/us/
    fmv0502/n_korea.html.

43 *China's National Defence in 2004*, Xinhua, 27 December 2004.

44 'Anti-Succession law', *Renmin ribao*, 14 March 2005.

45 *Renmin ribao*, 20 February 2005.

46 Frank Ching, 'Strained Japan–China ties bode ill for region's future', *Japan Times*,
    25 December 2004.

47 'Thousands join anti-Japan protest', 16 April 2005, http://news.bbc.co.uk/1/hi/
    world/asia-pacific/4450975.stm.

48 *Kyodo News*, 15 March 2005.

7 India and Pakistan

Samina Yasmeen[1]

The US National Security Strategy (NSS) assigned a special place to South Asia. After the Israeli–Palestinian dispute, South Asia was mentioned as the region where the Bush administration had invested time and resources building strong bilateral relations with India and Pakistan. The expected outcome of this involvement was for the two states to resolve their disputes. Given such an emphasis on two states that had been embroiled in a near conflict for most of 2002, how did India and Pakistan react? Did the two states differ in their responses or do common threads exist in their understanding and engagement with the essential components of the new doctrine? How did these understandings have an impact upon their responses to regional and extraregional developments? What is the likely course that these two countries would adopt in future in dealing with the US primacy and presence in and around South Asia?

This chapter attempts to answer these questions in terms of global, regional and state levels. It argues that, when viewed as an expression of strategic ideas underpinning policies of the dominant international actor, the Bush Doctrine has been criticized by groups in both India and Pakistan. At the regional and state levels, however, perceptions differ on the utility and relevance of the doctrine. Not only do differences exist between the two states on the applicability of notions of pre-emption and relevance of deterrence, but groups within these states also have varying understandings of the meaning and impact of the Bush Doctrine. These differences have played a role in shaping the policies adopted by India and Pakistan to events unfolding in close proximity to South Asia, including the US invasion and occupation of Iraq in March 2003.

US policy towards South Asia: the context

Indian and Pakistani understandings of and responses to the Bush Doctrine cannot be divorced from the nature of the strategic community dealing with issues of power and politics in these two states. Strategic issues, views on global and regional balances of power and the implications of these views for state security have largely remained the preserve of a select few who are generally based in the capital cities of the two countries. Not that the strategic assessments from other select cities do not emanate. In fact, the last decade has witnessed the emergence of new centres of strategic thinking in both India and Pakistan. But the process continues to be largely dominated by a few who belong to the 'strategic community' located in New Delhi and Islamabad. These individuals and think tanks regularly provide opinions on how regional and international developments have an impact upon their respective states and suggest appropriate courses of action.

This exclusivist approach to strategic issues exists in tandem with the prevalence of 'popular images' of world events among ordinary citizens. A combination of the continued relevance of oral tradition, the proliferation of electronic media, satellite television networks and Internet technologies enables these citizens to develop their opinions on the nature of global and regional balances. These views are not necessarily presented by using 'language of strategy' but, nonetheless, remain significant as they reflect the popular understandings of the relationship between domestic and international actors and events.

Interestingly, these two sets of views have created images of the US in both India and Pakistan that broadly coalesce round two different ends of the spectrum. At one end, America is viewed through the prism of social and cultural understandings of relationships and identified as a 'reliable' partner and/or ally.[2] At the other end lie images of the US as a state motivated by national interest that is not necessarily reliable. It is seen as a dominant actor that is prepared to ignore the interests of others if and when needed. The US is accorded Machiavellian attributes with little or no guarantee of reliability. However, the realist approach enables some to entertain the notions of interest-based engagement and cooperation with Washington.

Essentially, the views have grown out of the history of America's South Asian policy and its perceptions in India and Pakistan since 1947 (Burke and Ziring 1990: 147–240; Kux 1993, 2001). Washington has vacillated between being excessively engaged in South Asia and ignoring the region during the last five decades. When engaged, it has shifted between a Pakistan-centric and an Indo-centric policy, which has been interpreted by the 'other' as evidence of Washington not fully appreciating South Asian realities. During the 1950s, for instance, the US interest in containing communism resulted in a predominantly Pakistan-centric policy: Washington secured Pakistan's membership of its alliance system in return for military and economic assistance. Given the animosity between India and Pakistan since independence, this assistance was viewed critically by New Delhi, thus causing the US to be perceived as an unfriendly state. At the turn of the 1960s, Washington shifted to a relatively equidistance policy in the region. As India's relations with China worsened, Washington moved to support New Delhi and sided with it in the Sino-Indian border war of 1962. While originating from Washington's global concerns, the move was interpreted by Islamabad as evidence of American unreliability, which prompted it to establish close links with China. Meanwhile, as India moved closer to the Soviet Union, the US shifted its attention away from South Asia. By the end of the 1960s, America's need to use Pakistan as a link with China caused it to adopt a relatively Pakistan-centred policy. Indian leaders viewed the US support for Pakistan during the 1971 war, or absence of outright condemnation of Islamabad's handling of the crisis in east Pakistan, as evidence of American Pakistan-centric policy. By extension of this logic, America was cast in the role of pursuing anti-Indian policies. Interestingly, Pakistan soon assigned similar attributes to Washington as the latter attempted to prevent Islamabad from building nuclear capability to match that acquired by India in May 1974. By the late 1970s, America was perceived as being unfriendly and unreliable by both India and Pakistan.

The Soviet invasion of Afghanistan in December 1979 once again changed the nature of US South Asia policy. It identified Pakistan as a 'front-line state' in the struggle to roll Soviet forces back, and offered billions of dollars in military and economic assistance to Islamabad. Those across the border once again perceived the change as essentially being anti-Indian because of the quality of weapons (such as F-16s) Washington transferred to Islamabad. This was despite the fact that the US remained interested in building a relationship with India as well. The US overtures were reciprocated by New Delhi only in the 1990s when Washington ceased its support for Pakistan and India embarked upon a process of economic liberalization. The ensuing economic and security relationship was viewed by some groups in Pakistan as evidence of US unreliability as well as its preference for an Indo-centric policy. Others in Pakistan questioned these views on the grounds that a unipolar system necessitated a cooperative relationship between the US and Pakistan. The US government did little to dispel the negative images or to support the pro-engagement groups until May 1998 when India and Pakistan tested their nuclear weapons. Interested in capping their nuclear capabilities, Washington adopted dual policies of imposing sanctions while urging leaders in the two states to rethink their nuclear policies. In less than a year, faced with Pakistani incursions into Kargil, Washington was cast as an undeclared mediator between India and Pakistan. The mediation, however, did not usher America into an era of equidistance policies *vis-à-vis* the South Asian neighbours. President Clinton's visit to South Asia in March 2000 clearly demonstrated that the US had adopted an Indo-centric policy while casting Pakistan into the role of a pariah and failed state.

The 9/11 terrorist attacks forced both Washington and Islamabad to reassess their relationship. Pakistan's willingness to side with the Bush administration in its war on terrorism and America's need for allies in the region resulted in Washington once again identifying Pakistan as a front-line state. American sanctions against Pakistan were lifted, and it emerged as a major recipient of US assistance in the new millennium. The shift, it is essential to note, did not occur at the expense of the US–Indian relationship. Washington continued to emphasize its commitment to a close economic and strategic relationship with New Delhi. Nevertheless, for some groups in India, the revival of US assistance to Pakistan equalled a Pakistan-centric policy and evidence of US unreliability. Interestingly, meanwhile, sections from both moderates and Islamic orthodox groups in Pakistan also perceived Washington as being selfish and 'using' Pakistan after a decade of ignoring and actively undermining Pakistan.[3] Such perceptions were reinforced after the terrorist attacks on the Indian parliament in December 2001. As India and Pakistan came close to a major conflict in 2002, US interest in managing the crisis by engaging and putting pressure on both sides was seen by groups in both India and Pakistan as favouring 'the other side'. These voices were present both within and outside the decision-making circles. At the same time, other groups in the two South Asian states viewed the US involvement as evidence of its strategic interest in the region with a possibility of further engaging Washington in a cooperative relationship.[4]

Given the presence of multiple images and views in India and Pakistan on American policy towards South Asia, it was inevitable that the articulation of the Bush Doctrine would also attract multiple responses.

India and the Bush Doctrine

The Bush Doctrine attaches significance to democracy as the preferred state of existence for countries. At the same time, it expresses US determination to promote a liberal agenda on a global scale and to combat any threats to this agenda. Instead of awaiting the emergence of the threats and then responding to them, Washington favours pre-emption, based on the notion that deterrence as the basis for state relations has lost its validity. Terrorism and the acquisition of weapons of mass destruction (WMD) are classified in this category of threats that need to be combated as they emerge or even before they become a reality. To this end, the Bush Doctrine emphasizes US willingness to take unilateral action if multilateralism does not work. It also includes the preference to form issue-based coalitions of the willing to achieve its goals. A realist outlook that accords significance to power and the US primacy in the post-Cold War era underpins the promotion of a liberal agenda at state and global level.

Indian responses to the doctrine have been shaped by a combination of the idealist and realist streams in its foreign policy, as well as the adversarial relationship with Pakistan that is perceived as having supported terrorist activities against India. As a prescription of the shape of the international order, the Bush Doctrine has come into conflict with the idealist trends prevalent in Indian society. 'The Doctrine', one critic has maintained, 'seems to be to free [the US] of alliances of any kind in order to retain all options in picking allies for specific operations.' While it is seen as a possible model for India to emulate, its weaknesses are recognized and criticized as 'a sure recipe for disaster'.[5]

The perceptions and responses at the regional level, however, are varied.

They are closely linked to the assessment of how elements of the doctrine impact upon India, especially in the South Asian context. One school of thought among analysts identifies India as a natural contender for a close relationship with the US due to the declared preference for democracy as the preferred form of state organization. Given that India is the second largest democracy, the argument goes, Washington has made an implied choice in favour of New Delhi and, therefore, the Indian government and society can expect a closer relationship between the two countries for a number of years.[6] This view is contested by other analysts who approach the issue in terms of American need to find allies in its war on terrorism and its geostrategic implications. They argue that the requirements of a policy of countering terrorism in south and west Asia have prompted Washington into establishing a close relationship with Pakistan and identifying it as a front-line state. That Pakistan was identified as the major non-NATO ally in early 2004 is presented as an additional proof of this US need to retain close links with Pakistan.[7] This view of the US–Pakistani relationship does not deny that US–Indian relations have improved since the early 1990s. Nor does it question that the relationship has been strengthened in the new millennium. But the dictates of a policy of countering terrorism, in their view, limit the extent to which the Bush Doctrine singles out India as the natural and preferred ally in South Asia.[8]

These differences shape the nature of debate in India on the relevance of the Bush Doctrine for South Asia as a region. The debate is conducted in terms of the applicability of pre-emption as a policy option in the region and the relevance of deterrence as a concept underpinning Indian defence posture. Pakistan remains the main reference point in these debates: views are presented in terms of how the Bush Doctrine may or may not be used as a policy prescription in India's relationship with Pakistan. For some analysts, the concept of pre-emption in conjunction with the ideas of waging a war on terrorism enshrined in the Bush Doctrine could be applicable to South Asia. They argue that India has been a victim of terrorism promoted and supported by Pakistan since the late 1980s. Not only has Islamabad created groups such as Lashkar-e-Toiba and Jaish Mohammad to infiltrate into the Indian part of Kashmir, but Pakistan has also provided sanctuary to known terrorists who have posed threats to India. Such support for them reflects the process of Islamization of Pakistani society and the military, which is seen as the main decision-maker in the country.[9] Instead of deterrence, they argue, pre-emption provides the best policy option for India to respond to the threat posed by Pakistan. It is important to mention that the precise meaning of pre-emption has varied. In one form, it refers to the idea of pre-emptive strikes across the line of control (LOC) in Kashmir to target the training camps supported by the Pakistan government. In another form, it also encapsulates the notion of a limited war with Pakistan including the possibility of crossing the Indo-Pakistan border 'to teach' Pakistan a lesson.

Others remain sceptical of the applicability of the doctrine of pre-emption in South Asia.[10] This scepticism is linked to their acceptance that the US interest in retaining Islamabad's support in the war on terrorism prevents Washington from branding Pakistan as a terrorist state. It also excludes the possibility of the Bush administration endorsing a pre-emptive strike in Pakistan even on selected targets. Such views direct some defence analysts into arguing for the need to 'take a serious look at other policy options', including an end to being obsessed with Pakistan.[11] Others in the community of Indian defence analysts, however, have emphasized the continued relevance of deterrence in Indo-Pakistan relations. The argument is based on the assumptions that the currently existing deterrence relationship with Pakistan could fail. Pakistan, in their view, would use nuclear weapons against India not only when its existence is threatened but also when its image or military capability is challenged. The prevalence of Islamic fundamentalism in the state and societal structures are seen as contributing to this possibility. However, instead of adopting pre-emption as the preferred option, they argue for strengthening Indian ability to deter Pakistan by adopting a multi-pronged policy. Two different suggestions emerge: some favour consolidating and augmenting Indian nuclear weapons and missile capabilities by 'purposefully following through negotiations on missiles and related technologies' with the US, Russia and Israel.[12] Others, including some retired defence officials, favour a policy of minimum nuclear deterrence while accepting the possibility of deterrence failing at some stage.[13] Interestingly, some, such as J.N. Dixit, who accept the continued relevance as a way of shaping Indo-Pakistan relations have not excluded the possibility of a demonstrative and selective pre-emptive strike against Pakistan. Such a strike, it is argued, would convince the US and others that India should not be seen as remaining restrained 'in the face of structured and continuous provocations by [the Pakistan Government]'. Instead, India could also opt to 'replace reason ... by use of structured force as the final arbiter for resolving issues'.[14]

The diversity of views in India on the meaning and relevance of the Bush Doctrine appears to have influenced New Delhi's approach to a number of strategic and foreign-policy issues. While it is not possible to establish a direct causal link between the multiplicity of views and the policies adopted by New Delhi, the nature of Indian foreign policy vindicates such an assumption. On the one hand, India appears to countenance the idea of deterrence losing its relevance in global politics: New Delhi's initial endorsement of National Missile Defence (NMD) is a case in point.[15] At the same time, New Delhi has occasionally indicated that pre-emption may be an acceptable response to counter terrorist threats to Indian security. During the Indo-Pakistan tensions in 2002, for instance, the Indian government did not exclude the possibility of launching pre-emptive strikes against selected targets in Pakistan. Such attacks, it was suggested, would be an appropriate response to Pakistani support for anti-Indian terrorist activities. On the other hand, however, Indian nuclear policy continues to be guided by an acceptance of the logic of deterrence.

The emerging strategic relationship between India and the US has also played a role in determining Indian responses to the Bush Doctrine. A combination of the Indian policy of economic liberalization and American interest in forging a strategic partnership with India has created a momentum for continuing expansion of Indo-US ties. In the economic arena, Indian trade with America has increased: Indian exports to the US reached $19 billion in 2002 with the balance of trade in India's favour.[16] In the strategic arena, the two countries have established close relations. Coupled with the supportive role played by the Indian diaspora in America, these factors have brought the two states closer to each other. The process has created a constituency for American interests in India that identifies with Washington's views on global politics. At the same time, those subscribing to a realist perspective (such as the former head of the Institute for Defence Studies and Analyses, Jasjit Singh) have argued for and accepted the need to build closer interest-based ties between the dominant actor at the global level (the US) and the emerging global power (India). Not that groups opposing a close alliance with the US have ceased to exist, including some in the socialist/Marxist organizations, but an interest in sustaining the emerging entente appears to direct New Delhi towards a cautious and mixed response to the manifestations of Bush Doctrine. This has been most apparent in the manner in which New Delhi reacted to the US invasion and occupation of Iraq in 2003.

From the very beginning, the US intentions of toppling the Saddam regime on the basis of alleged Iraqi possession of WMD had received little support from Indian analysts and the public. This was apparent in the manner in which strategic analysts shied away from explaining the American government's policy in terms of WMD. As it became apparent that, despite the international criticism, Washington was determined to invade Iraq, concerns emerged in India about the repercussions of the imminent moves for Indian security. Some argued that the US had embarked upon an agenda of restructuring the Middle East that included both costs and benefits for India. The invasion was seen as causing problems for the large Indian diaspora employed in the Gulf states. The potential rise in oil prices was seen as another cost for India at a stage when its energy requirements were increasing at a fast pace.[17] At the same time, a restructured Middle East was viewed as opening avenues for a greater Indian role in the region including its participation in the reconstruction of Iraq.[18] These views were opposed by Muslims in India, the leftist faction in the Indian National Congress, as well as Hindu fundamentalist groups from the Rashtriya Swayamsevak Sangh (RSS), who objected to the US invading an independent country without ample proof of its WMD capability or culpability in promoting terrorism. Their criticism also centred around the unilateralism adopted by Washington in its pursuit of its Middle East interests. These groups held rallies against the impending invasion of Iraq and demanded that the Indian government should take a categorical stand against the impending invasion.[19]

The Indian government's response was tailored to mollify the critics at home without compromising the progress in its relations with the US. To this end, it adopted an ambiguous policy that could indicate its opposition to the US moves against Iraq without costing it a role in the post-invasion Middle East. Such a pragmatic approach was reflected in a number of statements given by Indian leaders prior to the US invasion of Iraq. In January 2003, for instance, the Indian Minister for External Affairs, Yashwant Sinha, stressed the significance of multilateralism in dealing with the Iraqi situation. He said that 'military action was not a solution and that India did not favour external interventions in the internal affairs of any country . . . It is not the responsibility of any country, however high or mighty, to interfere in another country's affairs.' But he stopped short of criticizing the US military build-up on the pretext that the US fleet was either in international waters or being allowed in by the respective Gulf states.[20] A few weeks later, the Indian Prime Minister Atal Bihari Vajpayee adopted a similar stand on the US policies towards Iraq: speaking at the Non-Aligned Movement (NAM) summit in Kuala Lumpur in February 2003, he identified both the US and the UN as being engaged in Iraq. While acknowledging the limits to a role played by NAM in averting the war, India became party to a resolution that asked Iraq to destroy its WMD. By implication, it clearly extended the blame for the invasion to Iraq.[21]

The policy of not openly criticizing the Bush Doctrine continued as the US launched its attack on Iraq on 20 March 2003. The statement issued by the Indian government did not blame or 'even name the US and the UK which had bypassed the UN and gone ahead'. Instead, it acknowledged 'the full force and validity of the objective of the international community to disarm Iraq of its weapons of mass destruction'. The statement also expressed an interest in India playing its part in providing humanitarian assistance to the Iraqi people.[22] This reluctance to criticize the US was echoed in the resolution passed by the Indian parliament 20 days after the invasion. The resolution had used the Hindi word 'ninda' while referring to the US invasion. The Indian government was keen to emphasize that it translated as 'deplore' and not 'condemn'![23]

The cautious response to the invasion stemmed from New Delhi's interest in not impeding the process of improving relations with US. It was also interested in using a less than critical stand for securing contracts in the reconstruction of Iraq. Such motivations were evident in the refusal by the Indian Defence Minister George Fernandes to let the invasion affect India's military relationship with Washington. A number of senior Indian officials and leaders also visited the US during and after the Iraq invasion. The list included the Indian Secretary of External Affairs Sibal, the National Security Adviser Mishra (May 2003) and the Indian Deputy Prime Minister Advani (June 2003). New Delhi also tried to ensure that Indian companies would be given a share in the reconstruction of Iraq. However, the willingness to operate in Iraq was not extended to sending Indian troops as part of an international stabilization force. Despite requests by the US government, New Delhi was careful not to accede to such a request. After discussion in the

Cabinet Committee on Security, the Indian Prime Minister announced on 14 July 2003 the decision not to send Indian troops to Iraq except under UN supervision.[24] Two months later, the Indian Permanent Representative to the UN repeated his government's commitment to send troops to Iraq only within the framework of multilateralism. The invitation to send troops, he specified, could only come from the Iraqi leadership, and New Delhi would respond favourably only if the command and control of the troops occurred under a UN mandate.[25]

The Indian government's response to the Iraq situation in 2003 indicated the limits of Indian ability to question the Bush Doctrine. The logic of its strategic partnership with Washington limited New Delhi's ability to voice criticism of the invasion. At the same time, however, the Indian approach in 2003 indicated the government's reluctance completely to identify with the US position on unilateralism and pre-emption. This mixed approach, one could argue, has provided the framework in which New Delhi has shaped its relationship with Washington despite the concerns among some Indian sections about the assumption underpinning the Bush Doctrine.

Pakistan and the Bush Doctrine

The Bush Doctrine was enunciated within a year of Pakistan undertaking a major foreign policy shift. Instead of supporting the Taleban regime, it had joined the US war on terrorism and provided needed support for American operations against al-Qaeda and the Taleban in Afghanistan. Coupled with the resentment against American unreliability, as evidenced in the 1990s, the shift in Pakistan's foreign policy provided the backdrop against which various groups interpreted the significance of the Bush Doctrine. Two distinct strands of opinion could be discerned in this respect. Those critical of the doctrine have highlighted its negative implications for global, regional and national security.

At the global level, these critics argue that the doctrine had been evolving since the end of the Gulf War in 1991 and was an expression of the imperialist tendencies in the US.[26] At the same time, 'the doctrine of pre-emptive self-defence justifying unilateral military action based on a subjective assessment of any potential future threat from international terrorism or from possession of weapons of mass destruction' is identified as being 'pregnant with alarming implications for the security of the smaller states and the stability of the world order'. Such ideas are seen as contradicting international law, particularly 'Article 51 of the Charter of the United Nations which recognizes the right of individual and collective defence in the specific case of an armed attack by an aggressor state' (Shahi 2002: 3). The 'vague notion of "failing states" and the more precise definition of "rogue states"', in their opinion, are to enable the US to make pre-emptive strike against 'any government or state that [is] seen as hostile to the US' (Mazari 2004: 20). Significantly, the critics view the doctrine as being directed primarily against Muslim states.

The war on terrorism, they maintain, has been religion specific; it ignores certain kinds of terrorism while focusing on Muslim countries. That four of the seven states identified in terms of WMD in the Nuclear Posture Review (NPR 2002) were Muslim is also presented as anti-Muslim bias in the doctrine (Shahi 2002: 3).

At the regional level, the doctrine is seen as providing India with a blueprint for action in South Asia. The logic of equating freedom fighting with terrorism, in their opinion, enables the Indian government to employ a similar language in its relations with Pakistan. Coupled with the idea of pre-emption, it is seen as opening the possibilities for the Indian government to thwart the genuine struggle for freedom by Kashmiris. Statements by Indian leaders and their reluctance to negotiate on issues are frequently presented to support such an assessment of the meaning of pre-emption for Pakistan's foreign policy. At the same time, instead of questioning the assumption that deterrence had become irrelevant, these critics focus on the meaning of the assumptions for Pakistan's nuclear policy. The downgrading of deterrence in the doctrine is analysed as 'directly impact[ing] . . . upon countries like Pakistan' that have opted for 'minimum nuclear deterrence' and have 'exercised nuclear restraint' (Mazari 2004: 21).

Most of the criticism of the Bush Doctrine, however, has been linked to its perceived implications for Pakistan as a Muslim state. Critics argue that the US presence in Afghanistan and the Middle East forms part of a grand strategy that aims to neutralize 'strong' Muslim states. Pakistan, with its nuclear capability and the large Muslim population, it is argued, is a natural target. The process of targeting Pakistan is seen as being 'gradual' in nature. According to this perspective, Washington has secured Pakistan's participation in the war on terrorism. But the logic of confusing the freedom struggle with terrorism, which lies at the heart of the Bush Doctrine, enables the US also to side with New Delhi against Pakistan. By building a strategic partnership with India, it is slowly reducing the options for Pakistan to find a fair resolution of the Kashmir issue. This process is viewed as occurring in tandem with American moves against other major Muslim states: the US invasion of Iraq and its declared opposition to Iran acquiring a nuclear weapons capability are presented as the evidence of this anti-Muslim bias in the Bush Doctrine.

Eventually, it is important to note, these critics expect the Bush Doctrine also to provide a basis for the US to put pressure upon Pakistan to relinquish its nuclear capability. They argue that Washington has already started pushing Pakistan into signing the Nuclear Non-Proliferation Treaty as a non-nuclear state in the NPT Review Conference of 2005. Without naming them, these analysts also argue that top US officials have been asking Islamabad 'not to conduct nuclear tests, to end the production of fissile material for nuclear weapons, and to tighten the export controls'. There is also a suspicion that the Pakistan government might already have allowed the US to 'acquire partial control [of its nuclear weapons] and mark them down' (Irshad 2004). The process has been paralleled by the allegation that the architect of Pakistan's nuclear programme, Dr A.Q. Khan, had shared nuclear technology with Iran, Libya and North Korea. These allegations are seen as part of the process of putting extra pressure on Pakistan to roll back its nuclear programme. Interestingly, the critical discourse surrounding the revelations of Khan's role in nuclear proliferation portrays him as a hero who has willingly shouldered the blame to avert negative US reaction within the framework of the Bush Doctrine. The Pakistan government, in contrast, is presented as an accomplice unwilling to take a stand against US pressure on the nuclear issue. This weakness, they argue, has also been apparent in Islamabad's policy of appeasing the US and acting as a pawn in the latter's moves in the regions bordering Pakistan. The campaign by the Pakistan military against al-Qaeda remnants in South Waziristan is presented as a case in point. The policy of cooperating with the Bush administration, however, it is argued, would not avert the danger of US retribution in future: Islamabad would come under additional pressure from Washington to give up its nuclear capability and drastically alter its stand on Kashmir. Failure to comply with this demand would attract US retribution along lines similar to the ones experienced by Iraq. Effectively, therefore, critics expect the Bush Doctrine to pave the way for America targeting Pakistan as well.[27]

The critical voices also include some liberal analysts and political leaders who focus on the inherent contradictions between different elements of the Bush Doctrine. The need to counter terrorism, they argue, has prompted Washington into aligning itself with a military dictator, General Pervez Musharraf. In the process, the US has strengthened his position *vis-à-vis* those demanding the reintroduction of democracy in Pakistan. Interestingly, such a view presents the Pakistan government as the manipulator that provides lip service to ideas of introducing democracy. The US is seen as the misguided hegemon that cannot fully appreciate the ability of some at the periphery to exploit the inherent contradictions of the Bush Doctrine.[28]

Other voices in the academic and strategic community in Pakistan contest such negative analysis and present a more positive assessment of the Bush Doctrine. While not denying the threats to international stability inherent in the notions of unilateralism and pre-emption, they focus on the American agenda of democracy. They distinguish between assumptions of 'instant' and 'gradual' democratization of Muslim states (Rais 2002). Instead of accepting the notion that the US–Pakistan alliance militates against democratic movement in the country, they suggest that Washington has embarked upon a process of gradual democratization of Pakistan. The economic assistance extended to Pakistan as a result of its participation in the war on terrorism is part of creating conditions that would make this transition possible. Hence, Musharraf is seen as a benevolent dictator who is guided in his alliance with Washington by the need to introduce enlightened moderation in the country and introduce 'real' democracy in which liberal voices could also be heard. US cooperation with the military regime, in other words, is seen as part of the historical evolution of democracy in Pakistan, and not as a reflection of an inherent contradiction in the ideals of democracy and the war on terrorism.

A small minority of supporters of the Bush Doctrine also identify the indirect benefits to Pakistan: the doctrine's opposition to WMD is seen as introducing an element of realism in Pakistan's defence and foreign policy. Having invested in the nuclear capability at the expense of improving economic conditions, they argue, Pakistan is forced to reassess its relationship with India and the relevance of nuclear capability in 'countering' the Indian threat. The long-term implications of such a reassessment are considered to be beneficial for Pakistan as well as the whole of South Asia.[29]

Against the background of these differing strands of opinion, the Pakistan government has adopted a mixed attitude towards the manifestations of the Bush Doctrine. At one level, guided by the need to retain US support in the economic and military arena (including the supply of additional F-16s), Islamabad has been reticent in equivocally condemning the doctrine. On the contrary, it has highlighted its credentials as a state that is playing a major role in the war on terrorism. Active cooperation between the Federal Bureau of Investigation (FBI) and Pakistani authorities as well as the patrolling of the Pakistan–Afghan border to prevent infiltration by al-Qaeda members are often presented as evidence of Pakistan's acceptance of one element of the Bush Doctrine. That the Pakistani authorities have also managed to catch a number of al-Qaeda operatives within Pakistan is presented as part of this activism and acceptance.

At another level, the need to balance opposing views within Pakistan has prompted the government to take decisions to assuage the concerns of the critics of the doctrine at home. This dual approach has been apparent in the pronouncements by the Musharraf government on the relevance of pre-emption and deterrence in South Asia, particularly with reference to Pakistan. In September 2002, for instance, Musharraf categorically declared at an international conference:

> This doctrine of pre-emption ... can apply between unequal opponents or equal adversaries. In the case of unequal adversaries, the world reaction could only be diplomatic condemnation. In the case of equal opponents, the application of pre-emption will lead to war. It will be extremely dangerous. It will be more dangerous in case the opponents, being equal, also have nuclear potential. Let there be no doubt that this doctrine does not apply in the India–Pakistan context at all, at least in the foreseeable future.
>
> (Musharraf 2002)

Such pronouncements have been combined with references indicating that deterrence as a concept remains relevant in the South Asian context. That Islamabad is unwilling to deny itself the ability to maintain a deterrent relationship with India has been expressed in the government's assertion of sovereignty over its nuclear programme. Musharraf has made numerous statements insisting that the Pakistan government would not compromise its nuclear capability. This assertion of sovereignty extends to the way in which the Pakistan government has dealt with the allegations against A.Q. Khan. While being critical of his actions, Islamabad has refused to let the scientist be interrogated by the US and/or the International Atomic Energy Agency.

The Pakistan government's assertion of sovereignty also finds expression in its operations along the Pakistan–Afghan borders. It has opposed incursions by US forces into Pakistani territory in hot pursuit of terrorists. At the same time, careful to retain its credentials as an active state, it has launched an independent operation in south Waziristan against members of al-Qaeda. Despite accusations of Pakistan playing the American game in the tribal regions, the policy is used to highlight the government's resolve to draw clear lines between sovereignty and cooperation with Washington.

The dual approach to the Bush Doctrine has also been apparent in Islamabad's response to the US invasion of Iraq. Even prior to the invasion, it was keen to emphasize the helplessness of weaker states in conflicts involving unequal adversaries. However, as the invasion became imminent, mindful of the negative reaction among the general public, the Pakistan government stressed its preference for multilateralism over unilateralism. As a member of the Security Council, it came under pressure from Washington to support the second resolution. Senior US officials also visited Pakistan to secure its support. Instead of caving in, Islamabad adopted a mixed approach: it stated that war was not a good option but did not categorically condemn the impending invasion. It suggested that inspectors be given more time to establish the presence of WMD in Iraq. At the same time, it insisted that all UN resolutions be respected, thus diluting the criticism.

The Pakistan government's response to the US request for troops in Iraq also demonstrated its dual approach. In June 2003, Musharraf stated after a meeting with Bush at Camp David that 'in principle' Pakistan could send troops to Iraq if some 'conditions' could be met.[30] This was followed by a formal request from the US Chairman Joint Chief of Staff, General Myers, in July 2003. Initially, some sections of the Pakistan government responded favourably as a means of securing US goodwill. However, the concerns of domestic backlash changed the preference. Prime Minister Jamali refused to commit troops without taking parliament into his confidence. At the same time, however, Islamabad left the option open for such a commitment in future. During his trip to the US, for instance, Prime Minister Jamali said that Pakistan might send troops if the Organization of Islamic Conference (OIC) or the Gulf Cooperation Council (GCC) became active in Iraq. That Pakistan did not wish totally to alienate the US became apparent as it agreed to its ambassador in Washington, Jehangir Qazi, taking up the position of UN envoy in Iraq.[31]

Effectively, Pakistan has been keen to show that, while declaring its opposition to unilateralism, it is prepared to accept American presence and policies around South Asia. It is also prepared to accept the limits of multi-lateralism provided the US continues to support Pakistan within the context of the Bush Doctrine.

Conclusion: different concerns, similar responses

The mixed Indo-Pakistani responses to the Bush Doctrine stand out for their marked similarity. Elites in both countries are interested in improving relations with Washington as part of their own global agenda. Realizing the limits to the ability of regional states to manipulate the US, as was the case in the Cold War, they have adopted a mixed approach. They use the elements of the Bush Doctrine that suit them best to elicit US support. At the same time, aware of the reactions against the doctrine's underlying assumptions, they avoid overly committing themselves in its favour. This is evident in their views on unilateralism, multilateralism, pre-emption and deterrence. Their mixed approach to the US invasion of Iraq provides a similar example of making the most of what is available without excessive commitment.

The similarities and the interest in building links with Washington can and have worked to create a situation in which the US has emerged as the main facilitator between India and Pakistan. However, if it appears that Washington is focusing on a single element of the doctrine at the expense of others, the situation may change in South Asia as well. Relative calm may give way to another round of animosity between the two neighbours.

Notes

1 The author wishes to thank Daniel Vujcich, Wendy Chew and Chengaiz Khan for their help with researching this chapter.
2 This assessment draws upon a number of personal interviews and discussions with opinion makers and analysts in Pakistan and India during the 1990s.
3 Such portrayals of the US were more common in statements given by Islamic groups including Jamaat-i-Islami. But some officials of the Pakistan Government expressed similar sentiments and viewed American policy as being motivated by US national interest.
4 Based on personal interviews with officials and policy analysts in Pakistan and India in 2002.
5 See, for example, S. Nihal Singh, 'Response to war clouds in Gulf', *Tribune*, Chandigarh, 19 February 2003, in *Selections from Regional Press*, Islamabad, 16 February–1 March 2003, pp. 9–10.
6 Amar Chandel, 'Time to woo India: major think tank tells Bush', *Tribune*, Chandigarh, 3 January 2003, in *Selections from Regional Press*, Islamabad, 1–15 January 2003, p. 6.
7 See, for example, Raja Mohan, 'Beyond India's Monroe Doctrine', *Hindu*, 2 January 2003, in *Selections from Regional Press*, 1–15 January 2003, pp. 11–12.
8 See, for example, 'Major non-NATO ally: Indian concern', *Behind the News*, 5 July 2004, India News on Line, http://news.indiamart.com/news-analysis/major-non-nato-ally-5135.html, accessed 10 April 2005; see also Sridhar Krishnaswami, 'Doublespeak on terror', *Frontline*, 23 April 2004, p. 37.

9 Based on personal interviews with Indian analysts in New Delhi in January 2003.

10 Prem Shankar Jha, 'After Iraq, Kashmir?', *Outlook*, New Delhi, 14 April 2003, in *Selections from Regional Press*, 1–15 April 2003, p. 3.

11 Raja Mohan, 'Beyond India's Monroe Doctrine', *Hindu*, 2 January 2003, in *Selections from Regional Press*, 1–15 January 2003, pp. 11–12.

12 J.N. Dixit, 'Reality check', *Hindustan Times*, New Delhi, 8 January 2003, in *Selections from Regional Press*, 1–15 January 2003, p. 4.

13 Brijesh D. Jayal, 'Look beyond the madness', *Telegraph*, 18 February 2003, http://www.telegraphindia.com/1030218/asp/opinion/story_1664570.asp.

14 See, for example, J.N. Dixit, 'Reality check', 8 January 2003, in *Selections from Regional Press*, 1–15 January 2003, p. 4.

15 John Cherian, 'Courting Uncle Sam', *Frontline*, vol. 18, 26 May–8 June 2001, http://www.frontlineonnet.com/fl1811/18111050.htm.

16 R. Krishnan, 'Westward ho!', *Hindustan Times*, 12 March 2003.

17 Personal interviews with a senior Indian journalist, New Delhi, January 2003.

18 See, for example, Raja Mohan, 'India and the Iraq War', *Hindu*, 27 March 2003.

19 'Protest march against war on Iraq', Press Statement issued by Communist Party of India (Marxist), 10 February 2003, http://www.cpim.org/, accessed 10 April 2005.

20 'India against removal of Saddam: Yashwant Sinha', *Hindu*, 20 January 2003.

21 'India walks tightrope between US, Iraq', *Indian Express*, 26 February 2003, in *Selections from Regional Press*, 16 February–1 March 2003, p. 9.

22 'Attack lacks justification, says India', *Times of India*, 22 March 2003.

23 Interestingly, the opposition chose to translate the word as 'deplore'. 'Deplore or condemn; what is the difference?', *Statesman*, 12 April 2003.

24 'India rejects US plea, says troops to Iraq only under UN', *Sentinel*, 15 July 2003.

25 Jyoti Malhotra, 'PM lunch with Bush has joint statement and Iraq on the menu', *Indian Express*, 23 September 2003.

26 A former diplomat and well-known Pakistani analyst, Maqbool Bhatty, presented this argument. See, for example, 'The US and Islamic world', *Dawn*, 15 December 2003.

27 Based on personal interviews with analysts in Pakistan, January 2004 and January 2005.

28 Aitzaz Ahsan has been one of the most vocal political leaders in Pakistan who link the absence of democracy in Pakistan with Musharraf's usefulness in the war on terrorism.

29 Based on views expressed by some analysts to the author in Islamabad, January 2004.

30 'Editorial: Is there a connection between Qazi's appointment and sending troops to Iraq?', *Daily Times*, 13 July 2004; http://www.dailytimes.com.pk/default.asp?page=story_13-7-2004_pg3_1.

31 'Pakistan's Qazi is UN's new Iraq envoy', *Acorn*, 13 July 2004, http://www.paifamily.com/opinion/archives/000967.html.

8 The Middle East

Between ideology and geo-politics

Anoushiravan Ehteshami

The Bush family has a particularly long legacy of engagement with the Middle East, whether in corporate terms or in political and diplomatic ones. So, when one speaks of the Bush Doctrine in this region, one has to draw a distinction between the policies and policy environment of the 41st president of the US and the 43rd. While the analysis of the latter's policies will form the core of this chapter, it is of some importance that we do so with the benefit of a much wider backdrop that can place President George W. Bush's doctrine, policies and policy implications in the more appropriate broader regional context. The Middle East has been at the heart of the Bush Doctrine, which has, not surprisingly, generated a series of regional responses.[1] On the whole, the actual responses have been less than positive, but in practice it is possible to argue that the Bush agenda of reform, as a democratization–security nexus, has been yielding impressive results. It is of course impossible to identify cause and effect in the relationship between the Bush strategy for Middle East reform and regional responses to it. But what it is possible to do is to argue that the Bush administration's emphasis on democratization and wholesale reform has helped in pushing the agenda forward within the region, shifting the mindset of all the players, leaders and activists alike. While the responses to the war on terror have been rather defensive, at the policy level, several Arab states – Algeria, Egypt, Jordan, Morocco, Saudi Arabia and its Gulf Co-operation Council neighbours, Tunisia, Yemen – have chosen to bandwagon with the US and curry favour with it by joining in the battle to contain and then defeat Islamic-inspired violence at home. The war on terror offered them a golden opportunity to tackle their own Islamist radicals with US support. The Iraq war and the democratization drive of the Bush administration, on the other hand, have been seen as nothing more than American-style neo-imperialism.

Of course, no party in the region has accepted any links between Islam and 'Islamic terrorism', with the latter phrase being rejected outright by commentators in the Muslim world. In Saudi Arabia, the cradle of Islam, any suggestion that the hijackers of 9/11 were somehow representative of the life and norms of the Kingdom has been dismissed as anti-Islam nonsense. But the fact that so many of the 9/11 hijackers (15 out of the 19) were citizens of the Kingdom has profoundly affected the close US–Saudi partnership, which had stood the test of time for over 50 years.

For the non-Arab Middle East states, the Bush Doctrine has brought fortune and fear, at times in equal measure. Iran, for example, has stood to make great strategic gains from the fall of the Taleban in Afghanistan and the Ba'ath regime in Iraq, but Tehran has at the same time found itself at the top of the US target countries. Turkey has not seen its influence weaken, but regime change in Iraq has raised concerns in Ankara over Kurdish resurgence there spilling over into Turkey. And Israel, finally, has found the Bush Doctrine to be bountiful in so many ways, but it has also brought with it, for the first time, the explicit recognition by a US president of the need to establish the state of Palestine on land occupied since 1967.

The New World Order

The Middle East, defined in this chapter as the sum of the Persian Gulf and the Levant states, is perhaps unique in the international system for not only being the birthplace of the first 'Bush Doctrine',[2] but also to have been the first region in the world to have seen the doctrine implemented and subjected to its 'laws'. The 'New World Order' (NWO) of Bush Senior was designed to rebuild on the ashes of the Cold War structures an inclusive world in which the principles of justice and fair play would replace power bloc politics. Multilateralism, as enshrined in the UN Charter, would guide US policy and set global standards. The principle of collective security and collective action would replace that of unilateralism and isolationism. Bush provided regional actors with a new 'code of conduct', to use Emma Murphy's (1997: 110) words, which anticipated 'the moral will and military might of the United States ... ensuring the protection of weak and vulnerable states from the roguish elements of the international community'. As Robert Tucker (1993: 164) has noted, Bush Senior appeared to have 'virtually reversed the outlook that informed the Reagan Doctrine'. The new vision

> not only placed emphasis on the maintenance of the law and order; in assigning to the USA the role of insuring order, it did so by pledging that this role would be undertaken within the institutional constraints of the UN. The change this represented from the position of the preceding administration was striking.
>
> (Tucker 1993: 164)

Contextually, prior to 9/11, the Middle East had spent the previous decade not only coming to terms with the end of the Cold War but also finding the means for adjusting to the deep security and political upheavals that had followed the decade-long implementation of the NWO doctrine. Bush Senior's policies had led to the region's biggest military campaign since World War

II, the almost complete isolation of Iraq internationally and the stationing of US forces in and around the Arabian Peninsula. His NWO also paved the way for the introduction of Bill Clinton's 'dual containment' strategy for both Iraq and Iran and an acceleration of the peace talks between Israel and several of its Arab neighbours. Despite their many shortcomings, the 1993 Oslo accords (and the 1994 Jordan–Israel peace treaty) were a direct result of the so-called Madrid process initiated by Bush Senior in the autumn of 1991. Bush Senior's NWO doctrine, therefore, had already left a strong impression on the Middle East, uprooting many of the existing norms in interstate relations.

Furthermore, the campaign for the liberation of Kuwait also fundamentally altered the Arab regional order, fracturing, polarizing and, ultimately, atomizing it. After the Kuwait war of 1991, there was not an Arab order to speak of any longer. The drive for collective pursuit of 'Arab national interests' gave way to the pursuit of territorial interest as defined in nation-state terms. Local Arab actors found partnership in some regional, but largely external, players. It was thus that the US emerged as the chief military and political ally of all the Arabian Peninsula states bar Yemen, in addition to Egypt (the largest and most influential Arab state). With Saudi Arabia, Washington consolidated its partnership in 1990, for the first time openly providing the US with military access and basing rights. Virtually every Gulf Co-operation Council state signed a defence cooperation agreement with the US, and they all increased their military reliance on the US as a consequence.

By the turn of the century, the US had become the predominant actor in the Middle East, regulating the regional agendas as much as setting them. The Clinton presidency's active involvement in the Middle East's two main arenas – the Arab–Israeli theatre and the Persian Gulf subregion – testifies to this reality. His administration had built on Bush Senior's NWO world view to present its own 'national security strategy of engagement and enlargement' in 1994. This strategy gave priority to three key goals: sustaining American security with military force; bolstering America's economic revitalization; and promoting democracy abroad (Hansen 2000: 83–6). Through 'engagement' (globalization), the US was tied to the world, which required 'enlargement' of free market democracies as a precondition of its post-Cold War global dominance. This Clinton national security strategy also specifically identified regional conflicts and theatres as challenges, particularly where weapons of mass destruction (WMD) proliferation was involved. These and related themes were of course touched upon during George Bush's presidency as well, but Clinton seized the moment of pre-eminent American power to create a set of linked policy priorities for the US.

The makings of the Bush Doctrine

President George W. Bush came to power in 2001 with essentially two foreign policy priorities: China and the Persian Gulf sub-region. In China, the concern was how to contain the influence of this rapidly emerging Asian power. In Condoleezza Rice's (2000: 56) words, China 'is still a potential threat to stability in the Asia-Pacific region . . . China is not a "status quo" power but one that would like to alter Asia's balance of power in its own favour. That alone makes it a strategic competitor, not the "strategic partner" the Clinton administration once called it.'

It was Robert Zoellick (2000: 68) who argued, even before Bush's victory, that the first principle of Bush's foreign policy 'is premised on power, being neither ashamed to pursue America's national interests nor too quick to use the country's might'. In the Middle East, the US did follow the broad outlines of policies in place since 1990: to contain Iran and Iraq and maintain Israel's strategic lead. These two agendas had been linked at least since the 1979 Iranian revolution and the rise of Iran's anti-Israel regime but, in the aftermath of the 1991 Kuwait war, the link became more structural. That this was so was demonstrated by Zoellick. In formulating his version of a Bush foreign policy before the November 2000 presidential race, he argued that the US 'must counter those dangerous states that threaten its closest friends, such as Israel, or its vital interests, such as maintaining access to oil in the Persian Gulf' (Zoellick 2000: 76). The strategic link drawn between the two is clear, even though it may have been made unintentionally.

In the Persian Gulf, the agenda was very much Iraq driven, with an eye also on neighbouring Iran. Iraq was ripe for 'regime change': 'Saddam Hussein's regime is isolated, his conventional military power has been severely weakened, his people live in poverty and terror, and he has no useful place in international politics . . . Nothing will change until Saddam is gone, so the United States must mobilize whatever resources it can . . . to remove him' (Rice 2000: 60). Iran too was set for renewed American pressure. As, Rice (2000: 61) noted, Iran supported terrorism, had tried to destabilize America's regional Arab allies and was making advances in the military field, it presented 'special difficulties in the Middle East, a region of core interest to the United States and to our key ally Israel'. This assessment was not new of course and, with regard to Iraq, the Clinton administration too had been 'planning for post-Saddam Iraq and our efforts to speed its arrival' (Berger 2000: 36).

Post-9/11 order

In its first year, the administration had shown little interest in the broader Middle East problems such as the stalled Arab–Israeli peace process or the threat of political Islam. Where 'Islamic terrorism' was noted as a problem, it was largely in the context of Israel's security dilemmas. After the horrific events of 9/11, however, the 'greater' Middle East (including North Africa, Central Asia, Afghanistan and Pakistan) emerged as Bush's main foreign policy preoccupation, and pursued, some have suggested, for very narrowly defined ends (see, for example, Ahmed 2003). While interest in 'regime change' in Iraq had already been demonstrated from 2000, 9/11 helped in creating a security calculus for the Middle East that not only produced the 'axis of evil' doctrine in January 2002 but also brought into sharp focus in this region the application of the pre-emptive strike doctrine, and the war on terrorism.[3]

In relation to pre-emption, the talk in the immediate aftermath of 9/11 was of US preparations for a strike on Iraq for its alleged role in the September attacks and the development of WMD. Although no links were established, after Afghanistan, Iraq was to find itself at the top of the US hit list, with its leader branded as 'evil' by the American president.[4] Fears of a pre-emptive strike on Iraq were so rife that one of the US's closest regional allies, King Abdullah of Jordan, went on record in October warning of the disastrous consequences of such an act for the region and for the US's finely balanced anti-terror coalition. He told the *Financial Times* that 'there is no proof of Iraqi responsibility *vis-à-vis* the September 11 attacks' and that 'it would be a serious blow if Iraq was targeted and it would be detrimental to the international effort against terrorism'.[5] Leaders of several other Arab states, including those unfriendly to Iraq (Syria, Saudi Arabia and Egypt), expressed similar reservations. The Arab League, the 'mouthpiece' of the Arab world, did likewise on more than one occasion.

Taking no heed, Bush reinforced his administration's growing anti-Iraq position by hinting twice in two days in November 2001 that action could be taken against Iraq. The State Department's Richard Haass mused that 'we'd be able to make the case that this [attack on Iraq] isn't a discretionary action but one done in self-defence'.[6] In the late Hugo Young's perceptive words, uttered before even 2001 was out: 'Americans want a war on Iraq and we can't stop them.'[7]

The spread of democracy to the Muslim Middle East, particularly the Arab world, as a US political and security imperative emerged at the same time. By late 2002, the need for political reform (democratization) in the greater Middle East had became an added condition of US concerns over guaranteeing global security, creating with one stroke a security–democratization nexus in the Middle East region.

But it was the post-9/11 war on terror, conducted against al-Qaeda and its related militant Islamist groups, that became the single most important dimension of Bush's interaction with the Middle East. The multifaceted and multidimensional war on terror threatened the stability of many of America's regional partnerships, at the same time as affording the regional actors the chance to jump on the bandwagon of the US-led anti-terror campaign (for a discussion, see Rabasa *et al.* 2005).

At the same time, the US position fuelled suspicion in virtually every Muslim state capital, friend and foe alike. But, as will be shown, Middle East responses to the 'Bush challenge' were by no means uniform. In broad terms, the differences were over emphasis when it came down to the war on terror and the hunt for al-Qaeda, and over substance when it came to the spread of democracy to the Arab world and the 'greater Middle East'. Ironically, as most of America's Arab allies were autocracies of the first order anyway, already engaged in their own bloody campaigns against radical Islamist groups, the strengthening of security relations with the US in the global war on terror not only helped them to consolidate these security ties with the US but at the same time afforded them the opportunity to tighten their grip on power without much fear of retribution from the West. But not all Middle East states warmed to America's war on terror. Saudi Arabia, for example, whose nationals were among the 9/11 conspirators, and bin Laden himself was from that country, felt the heat of US reactions; as indeed did Iran, although for very different reasons. But other Middle East and North African countries, from Morocco to Oman and Yemen, found common cause with the US in this campaign. Ruling regimes in Egypt, Jordan and several Gulf Arab states formed the Middle East frontline in the anti-al-Qaeda drive, sweeping up in the process many of their own Islamist opponents. Even Sudan, Syria and Libya, which were not known for their affections for the US, joined the bandwagon.

But the democratization drive did get virtually every state's back up. From Iran westwards, Washington's agenda was seen as blatant interference in domestic affairs of sovereign international actors. Saudi Arabia and Egypt, in particular, both close US allies, objected most strongly to the tenor and content of the administration's reform agenda.

The Bush Doctrine and the Middle East

To be able to gauge fully the impact of the Bush Doctrine on the Middle East, it is proposed here that, as much as possible, we look at its three constituent parts as the key variables in the complex relationship between the US and the Middle East.

If the attack on Afghanistan was to be classed as an example of military action in the course of the war on terror, then the Iraq war of March 2003 demonstrated the full force of the pre-emption element of the Bush Doctrine. In his State of the Union address, the president laid out the essential components of his administration's post-9/11 stance in these terms:

> Our nation will continue to be steadfast and patient and persistent in the pursuit of two great objectives. First, we will shut down terrorist camps, disrupt terrorist plans, and bring terrorists to justice. And, second, we must prevent the terrorists and regimes who seek chemical, biological, or nuclear weapons from threatening the United States and the world.[8]

Thus, the 'linkage' in policy terms between the war on terror and counter-proliferation was made. The war on terrorism – fighting terrorist groups – had become subsumed in the much broader war on terror, which placed counter-terrorism operations alongside pre-emption as a counter-proliferation strategy. In this campaign, the Middle East was to emerge as a central theatre. Stoking up the administration's rhetoric against Iraq, deputy US Defence Secretary Paul Wolfowitz had explained at an international gathering in Munich as early as February 2002, held soon after President Bush's 'axis of evil' speech, that the US 'has to aim at prevention and not merely punishment. We are at war [and] those countries that choose to tolerate terrorism and refuse to take action – or worse, those that continue to support it – will face consequences.'[9]

The Iraq war unsettled the region to a much greater extent than the war in Afghanistan, but the Afghan campaign did prompt much criticism of the US action in the Middle East. From Iran westwards, regional actors openly expressed their reservations about US policies. Even in a country such as Iran, which stood to make strategic gains from the fall of the Taleban and the decimation of the anti-Shia al-Qaeda network, support for the military campaign could only be given indirectly and behind closed doors. Most telling were the public criticisms of the US-led action made by President Bashar al-Asad of Syria in his Damascus press conference with the visiting British Prime Minister: 'we cannot accept what we see every day on television screens, the killing of innocent civilians [in Afghanistan]. There are hundreds now dying every day. I do not think anybody in the west agrees with that.'[10] He was publicly articulating the Arab position on the bloody process of the war on terror. But while, in Afghanistan, its immediate neighbours formed the zone of conflict, with Muslim action against it emanating from South-East Asia and some parts of the Middle East, in Iraq, the fallout from the war proved to be all-encompassing, reaching the furthest corners of the Arab and Muslim worlds. In the Arab world, however, hostility to any military attack on Iraq was expressed in Damascus and Riyadh (which stood to make some gains in security terms from the Iraqi dictator's fall) as much as in Cairo and elsewhere. Indeed, the only Arab country that did not oppose military operations was the tiny Gulf Arab state of Kuwait, which had suffered hugely from Iraqi aggression in 1990.

The attack on Iraq, therefore, for many opened what Richard Perle (a leading Republican figure and former assistant secretary of defense) had referred to in early November 2001 as 'phase two' of the war on terror. Apart from Iraq, he named Syria, Lebanon, Iran, Libya, Sudan, Somalia and North Korea as being on the target list.[11] Of this list of eight states, all bar one fell in the Arab or Muslim worlds. The impression being reinforced in the Middle East, therefore, was that the war on terror was, at its core, an anti-Muslim and anti-Islam exercise, fought to strengthen the west's position in the strategically important Persian Gulf region, and also to ensure Israel's long-term security by eradicating any remaining sources of opposition to its presence and policies in the region (see, in particular, Laurent 2000: 77–92). The Iraq and the Afghan wars, then, had quickly acquired significant geopolitical dimensions to them, in terms that saw in every American-led move the strategy for domination of the heart of the Muslim world.[12]

More broadly, it is not too implausible to argue that the Iraq war changed the geo-political dimensions of Middle East politics as well. A new regional order may well be fast emerging from the ashes of the war in Iraq. On the one hand, we see the perceptible shift in the balance of power between the region's Arab states and the three prominent non-Arab states of Iran, Israel and Turkey. In different ways, the latter trio have stood to gain from the fall of Baghdad. Iran's access through its western gateway to the Arab world, in the shape of Iraq, has been swung wide open, as has its reach to the Shia heartlands in Iraq. Israel can, for the first time in its existence, freely boast that it no longer faces a serious threat from the Arab order, but that the strategic depth – provided by Iraq – that its one remaining Arab adversary, Syria, had always counted on has now been filled. For Turkey, the fall of Saddam brought political bounties of a different kind in terms of improved relations with the EU and a freer hand in its dealings with the west and the region as a whole. It also has a much more direct role in assessing the impact of the Iraqi Kurdish factor on its own territory.

On the other hand, there is a less tangible, but equally significant, intra-Islamic shift taking place in the region, characterized by the tensions between the Shias and the majority Sunnis. Baghdad's fall has, for the first time since the Iranian revolution of 1979, added real impetus to the Arab Shias' cries for a stronger political voice in the Arab world. The fall of the Sunni-dominated Ba'ath regime has enabled the Shias to emerge as a powerful political force in the Arab world and, by virtue of their numbers in such a strategically important country as Iraq, has given them a greater hand than ever before in the shaping of the political map of the fractured and highly polarized Arab system.

The fall of Baghdad at the hands of the US in April 2003 lifted, possibly for good, the centuries-old Sunni domination of Mesopotamia and the pivotal Shia sites of central and southern Iraq. The end of the Ba'ath regime instantaneously and effectively invigorated the Shia communities of Iraq, mobilizing them into mass action. Within months of the fall of Baghdad, several hundred *ulama* and their families decamped from their refuges in Iran (and elsewhere) and returned to the cities of Najaf, Karbala and Kazemiah to rediscover their holy pasts and to engage in the task of rebuilding their country. Some came with their new Iranian families, but most came to build new homes and help in the rebuilding of the Shia holy sites and cities. They all brought with them massive extra power, however. Although low key at first, the marking of the two key Shia festivals of Ashura and Tasua in Najaf and Karbala in late spring 2003 demonstrated to the world the cultural depth and vigour of Shiism in Iraq; it also gave a fright to those Sunni neighbours who had for years feared the emergence of a 'Shia international' that would openly challenge their interpretation of Islam, on the one hand, and also ultimately threaten their regimes by demanding more rights for the Shia minorities in those states, on the other.

Baghdad's fall has also helped in reducing the one-dimensional Arab–

Persian divide that had so successfully been exploited by Saddam Hussein alongside the older Sunni–Shia one. With the Shia factor now acquiring an open and strong Gulf Arab dimension in its own right, Tehran at long last had a chance to try and separate the Iran–Shia 'double whammy' so masterfully exploited by Saddam in the 1980s to win favours from the fearful Gulf Arab states. Through the 'liberation' of Iraq, the Arab Shias not only gained an independent and a more formal presence in pan-Arab circles, but also acquired a Shia Arab voice in the sea of Sunni Arabs dominating the Arab world. Thanks to US action, Shiism could no longer be packaged as an Iranian curse imposed by Iran's Islamic republic on the Arab world. Despite the active presence in, and engagement with, the Arab world of the vibrant and powerful Shia communities of Lebanon, the independent voice of the Shia hailing from Najaf and Karbala has had an altogether more qualitative, but perhaps still unquantifiable, impact on the region. The Shia awakening can shake, if allowed to grow and consolidate, the very foundations of the political orders that were resurrected atop the old Ottoman territories early last century. In the Persian Gulf, they can shake them from within, and elsewhere they can challenge Sunni orthodoxy by presenting alternative Islamic discourses on a broad range of issues.

To the chagrin of radical Sunnis, the reach of the Shia extends in other directions and ways as well. In South Asia, for instance, a population greater than the size of Iraq are Shias and, in Turkic Azerbaijan, the vast majority are from the Shia sect of Islam. Thus, the Shia network has a broad Arab and non-Arab dimension to it, with Iran and Iraq providing the geo-political anchors for this active community of Muslims. One can talk about a new Shia 'crescent' having been born, stretching from South Asia to the heart of the Levant in Lebanon, tied together by the virtue of their unique belief system, which is underlined by the vast Marja'a (emulation) superstructure that brings Shias together from all nationalities and territories. Thus, such a key Najaf-based figure as Grand Ayatollah Sistani, in whose hands seems to lie the destiny of the state of Iraq, will have millions of Shia 'followers' in Iraq itself, as well as in his native Iran, Lebanon, the Gulf Arab states and even Azerbaijan. One also finds that other Shia activists are in place, such as Hojjatoleslam Muqtada al-Sadr in Iraq, to ably exploit their immediate political environment for the accumulation of influence and, ultimately, power. The fact that such relatively junior Shia personalities as Muqtada al-Sadr can use their family heritage to such good effect is testimony to the broad reach of the Shia clerical establishment, and the ease with which personal can become political in Shia Islam, and vice versa. By the same token, the senior ayatollahs in Qom will have a large following in other parts of the Muslim world. Such networks not only strengthen the internal pillars of the Shia Muslims, providing moral and practical support to the Shia communities, but also act as powerful supporting bulwarks in defence of the faith as a whole. Shias, therefore, are often found to be much better organized than their Sunni counterparts, and are more fully engaged as communities.

This same network, however, can also generate a dangerous counterflow. The religious requirement for emulation among Shias has been known to lead to deep rivalries between Marja'as, at times feeding into political debates and differences as well.

It can be suggested, therefore, that there was another important dimension to 'Muslim politics' that had been overlooked by the Bush policy-makers in Washington as they prepared to wage war on Iraq: that of an intra-Islamic dispute being violently contested in places such as Afghanistan and Iraq. Salafi Islam took on the US as well as the Shias as its common enemy, unleashing violence against both in equal measure. Ironically, 9/11 brought an unexpected, but badly needed, sense of purpose to the Muslims, whose own civilization was already tearing itself apart over ideology, purpose, governance, distribution of political and economic power and control of the Muslim agenda in a post-bipolar world. We had failed to notice that, before 9/11, an intensive 'clash of civilizations' was already going on in Afghanistan between various Muslim states supporting or fighting the Taleban. Today, this same kind of turf war is going on in Iraq. Where it will strike tomorrow, nobody can tell, but the rise of the Shia will grow to impinge on many domains hitherto assumed to be the prerogative of the Sunni majority in the Middle East and North Africa (MENA) region. The movement we can surely detect; its direction, however, is much harder to predict at this stage.

On another front, the impression of intervention as part of a grand strategy was further reinforced by the democratization component of the Bush Doctrine. Bush brought this issue to the forefront of his national security strategy in November 2003, in the course of two major speeches delivered in Washington (6 November) and London (19 November).[13] In speaking of a 'forward strategy of freedom in the Middle East', he spoke of the need to change America's relations with the region. In Washington, the president put the emphasis on the need for reform: 'the freedom deficit', he said, 'has terrible consequences for the people of the Middle East and for the world. In many Middle Eastern countries poverty is deep and it is spreading, women lack rights and are denied schooling, whole societies remain stagnant while the world moves ahead.'[14] In London, however, he was more critical of the interstate bargain between the west and its authoritarian elites. He said that 'we must shake off decades of failed policy in the Middle East ... in the past [we] have been willing to make a bargain, to tolerate oppression for the sake of stability. Longstanding ties often led us to overlook the faults of local elites. Yet this bargain did not bring stability or make us safe. It merely bought time, while problems festered and ideologies of violence took hold.'[15] Together, these speeches demonstrated his administration's Wilsonian appetite for democracy promotion in the Middle East and the Arab world in particular. The forward strategy of freedom was to become as controversial in regional terms as the war on terror and its associated pre-emptive military campaign in Iraq.

The elements of the democratization campaign as a security imperative of the US found even more concrete expression in the 2004 'Greater Middle East Initiative' (GMEI). Vice-President Cheney first brought the initiative, in its original form, to light at the World Economic Forum meeting in Davos in January 2004, where it was called 'the most ambitious US democracy effort since the end of the Cold War'.[16] Its existence was made public a year after the Arab world's own 'Arab Charter', which Saudi Arabia tabled in January 2003. The charter, which was seen as a revolution of sorts in its own right, had called for 'internal reform and enhanced political participation in the Arab states'.[17] The later US plan, in contrast, had encompassed a wide range of diplomatic, cultural and economic measures. The GMEI had deliberately moved the agenda on by calling for the US and its European allies and partners (in the G8, NATO and the EU) to press for and assist free elections in the Middle East, foster the growth of new independent media there, press for judicial reforms, help create a 'literate generation' by helping to cut regional illiteracy rates in half by 2010, train 'literacy corps' of around 100,000 female teachers by 2008, finance the translation of Western classical texts into Arabic to foster better understanding of the West among Muslims, establish a European-style Greater Middle East Development Bank, an IFC-style Greater Middle East Finance Corporation to assist the development of larger enterprises and give $500 million in microloans to small entrepreneurs, especially women, in order to spur 1.2 million small entrepreneurs out of poverty.

The concern from the region, however, was that the 2004 US initiative, like its predecessors in 2003, had tried to explain its arrival in purely Western security terms: 'So long as the region's pool of politically and economically disenfranchised individuals grows, we will witness an increase in extremism, terrorism, international crime and illegal migration', its early 2004 draft stated.[18] Furthermore, there was a concern that the initiative perceived the region in largely Cold War terms. For example, it spoke of creating MENA security structures based on the 1975-launched Helsinki process and NATO's Partnership for Peace programme. It anticipated that a complex set of security structures could bring six Middle East countries, including Egypt, Morocco, Tunisia, Qatar and Israel, into partnership with NATO. But leaving such prominent regional players as Iran, Syria and Saudi Arabia out of such regional security arrangements would only fuel discontent, creating new divisions and breeding further instability across national boundaries.

It was precisely because of the ambiguities attached to the initial proposal that President Mubarak of Egypt 'denounced with force the ready-for-use prescriptions proposed abroad under cover of what are called reforms'.[19] As he headed home from a meeting with King Fahd and Crown Prince Abdullah of Saudi Arabia, Mubarak told Egyptian journalists, 'we hear about these initiatives as if the region and its states do not exist, as if they had no sovereignty over their land ... these kinds of initiatives do not deserve a comment, [but] need to be confronted by scientific and convincing answers from thinkers, so as not to leave people to fall prey to misleading impressions and misconceptions disseminated by such initiatives'.

The voices of some other Arab leaders, including those from Jordan, Morocco and Syria, were added to this objection, all rejecting the plan as an external imposition as the news of it began to filter out in February 2004. 'No matter how well-intended the Americans and Europeans say their initiatives are, it will take more than words to comfort sceptical Arab rulers and a worried Arab public. The regimes see many signs suggesting that the United States is determined to enforce change or "reforms", while the public – initially desperate for real reforms – suspect that the foreign calls for democracy are only an excuse to interfere in the region and redraw it in accordance with the West's own interests. The occupation of Iraq and the disinterest in Palestinian suffering have reinforced those fears', noted the *Cairo Times*.[20] Former National Security Advisor, Zbigniew Brzezinski, added that 'There is no question that the administration has its work cut out for it. For starters, the president unveiled the democracy initiative in a patronising way: before an enthusiastic audience at the American Enterprise Institute, a Washington policy institution enamoured of the war in Iraq and not particularly sympathetic toward the Arab world. The notion that America, with Europe's support and Israel's endorsement, will teach the Arab world how to become modern and democratic elicits, at the very least, ambivalent reactions. (This, after all, is a region where memory of French and British control is still fresh.)'[21]

Large sections of Middle Eastern elites are not yet ready to consciously open their national borders to external political, socio-economic and cultural influences. Judging by the bemoaning that goes on, they recognize that such influences have already jumped the barriers and are active on the inside, but the elites have put their hope in their ability to reverse the westernizing trends embedded in Bush's doctrine. It is in this context that, in the Middle East, the religious elites want to protect the cultural realm from globalization, while the political elites want to ensure that their grip on the levers of power are not loosened by the broader democratization and reform agenda or the war on terror campaign being foisted on them. As Michael Scott Doran (2004: 35–51) has shown with reference to Saudi Arabia, for example, the dichotomy of the various factions of that country's power elite has, in recent years, fed directly into perceptions of, and relations with, the West, most notably the US. He has shown that, as the Wahhabi establishment openly views the US as a hostile power – seen as the 'Idol of the Age' and one of Islam's greatest enemies since its birth – the domestic power struggle is largely couched in polemics about the Middle East policies of the US and the relationship of the al-Saud political elite with the sole superpower. With the considerable influence of the anti-US camp in the Kingdom – which today may consist of the heart of the Wahhabi religious establishment and a powerful group of the al-Saud princes gathered around Prince Nayef – the religious elite's role becomes critical in the process of reform, as well as its content and direction, in this most important of Arab and Muslim countries.

These competing forces can play out their competing world views and attitudes towards the US on their home turf, in one of the region's most important economic and political players.[22] The rejectionists can show their displeasure of the US and play out their opposition to it through attacking the power base of the reformers in the political establishment, such as that of Crown Prince Abdullah. The reformers can in turn attack the power base of the conservatives, religious endowments and cultural organizations. This rather futile rivalry will in the end actually weaken the Kingdom's power elite as a whole, ultimately pitting faction against faction, prince against prince, alem against alem. With mounting internal and external pressures, one could find the principal groups of the elite locked into a perpetual confrontation over the control of the country's national agenda. Internal pressures will undoubtedly have played an influential part in the coming crisis of the Saudi state, but the real harbinger will have been the targeting of the Kingdom by the American neo-conservatives for the role that several of its citizens played in 9/11.

Although not unique, the Saudi case well illustrates the socio-political contradictions in policy terms that the divergent views of members of the power elites in the Muslim Middle East constantly generate. The political elite has declared total war against al-Qaeda and participated in the West's war on terrorism, while the religious elite continuously criticizes the US for its regional policies. The contradictions in policy terms that the Saudi case highlights are of course daily played out elsewhere in the region as well, affecting the daily lives of millions of ordinary citizens across the region, permanently shaking the ground under their feet. The same also tests the nerve of those who seek to introduce substantive reforms into the region: can they take risks in introducing reforms without destroying the fabric of society and its delicate social balance?

The tensions between the US role perception in the Middle East, on the one hand, and the existing political process in the region, on the other, have been identified here as major causes of instability in the post-9/11 regional environment. This tension is a key feature of the post-9/11 regional order in which the war on terror has come to play a major part. As noted with relation to Saudi Arabia, the nature of US regional engagements today plays a significant part in the domestic politics of most MENA states – from the Mashreq to the Maghreb. The role of the US factor has been in evidence in the political processes of an ally such as Saudi Arabia, as well as in those of an adversary such as Iran. In Iran's February 2004 parliamentary elections, in which Iran's conservative forces manipulated the electoral roll in order to ensure the defeat of the reformist camp in the poll for the Seventh Majlis, one could feel the ghost of US power present in every debate. In the end, a real fear of the US policy agenda in the Persian Gulf subregion encouraged the success of the conservative factions in the parliamentary elections. The irony of the impact of the US factor in these elections has been deliciously captured by an editorial in the *Guardian* newspaper:

Tension between the secular and religious in Iran is nothing new. What has changed is the external context. Iran feels tremendous pressure, principally from the US, over nuclear arms, terrorism, human rights and the occupation of neighbouring Iraq and Afghanistan . . . . Alive to these threats and exploiting them, anti-western mullahs seem to be circling the wagons. Thus has George Bush's grandiose bid to democratise the Middle East helped produce in Iran the exact opposite; a democratic derailment.[23]

Is the US democratization drive for a pluralist future in the Middle East in fact further de-democratizing the region? Are its double standards and contradictory policies in fact emboldening the conservative and radical forces in the Muslim Middle East, while undermining the position of the very progressive reformists that it desperately needs to see in power in order to push through the 'root and branch' reforms it wants to see introduced? With the region now regarding the US as part of the problem, it is hard to predict how Washington intends to nurture the rise of democratic forces in the region and see democracy introduced when one of the first acts of such democrats (as much in response to the demands of their constituents as their own conscience) will be to condemn the US superpower for its occupation of Iraq, for the behaviour of its troops and political agents there, for its unconditional support for Israel and blatant disregard for international law and norms in the Palestinian–Israeli conflict and for its continuing support for many of the region's authoritarian regimes. Is a direct but unintentional outcome of the Bush Doctrine the birth of an illiberal democracy as the norm that the peoples of the region will have to endure in the twenty-first century? It is still too early to tell, but much of the outcome will depend on what kind of an Iraq emerges from the ashes of war and decades of destruction.

Conclusion

By late 2002, the need for political reform (democratization) in the greater Middle East had became an added condition of US concerns over guaranteeing global security, creating with one stroke a security–democratization nexus in the Middle East region (Khalidi 2004). This was an unprecedented development. Regime change (in the context of countering terrorism and preventing the spread of WMD in the wrong hands), imposed democratization and far-reaching reform emerged as the key drivers of the Bush administration's agenda, causing considerable anxiety across the region. If the Clinton legacy was to be summed up as one of 'profound politicization of foreign affairs' (Haass 2000: 139), then surely Bush's must be seen in terms of the profound ideologization of the same. By the end of 2002, the roots of the Bush Doctrine were to be found in the exercise of hard power at the expense of the use of soft power.[24] Three cardinal principles acted as the drivers of his doctrine: pre-emption as a central feature of US foreign policy;

ensuring American supremacy; and predominance in military and economic terms through the utilization of whatever means necessary.[25]

In 2001, before the events of 9/11, Fred Halliday (2001: 107) had noted that, for all the subtle differences that may exist between different US administrations, under any American president, 'Washington is going to pursue its own interests, with its allies if it can, against them or independent of them if it cannot'. What we have seen in the evolution and implementation of Bush's doctrine is the reality of this observation.

Bush has begun his second term with his policy of transforming the greater Middle East taking centre stage, judging by the State of the Union address in January 2005. America is committed to nurturing new democracies in Afghanistan, Iraq and Palestine, an astonishing about-face since 9/11 for an administration originally hostile to nation-building altogether, notes Harvey Sicherman: 'thus, it may be said that whatever the prospects in the Middle East, US foreign policy itself has surely been transformed. Will it work? A thousand obstacles obstruct the way, yet some things have begun to move. Insofar as elections signal a potentially democratic direction, 2005 begins with important auguries for the development of local partners capable of working with the United States. Sharon's new government gives proof of his readiness to withdraw from Gaza. The vote for Abu Mazen ratified a potential Palestinian partner for peace. Renewed Israeli–Palestinian cooperation, taken in tandem with local legislative and party elections scheduled for late this year, could give a big boost to a nascent Palestinian democracy.' In the same vein, the success of the Iraqi elections held in January 2005 provided more than a glimmer of hope that national revival after the war was possible. 'For the advocates of democracy in the Middle East, the Palestinian and Iraqi elections focus on a quintessential virtue: citizen choice. Yet this beginning, potentially the birth throes of popular government, should also remind us of the distance yet to go. These polls will matter little if in the end those who oppose democracy can abort the results through violence. US policy will still be poised on the brink of failure so long as that battle remains in doubt' (Sicherman 2005).

Sicherman's perceptive analysis reminds one of an earlier set of equally insightful comments made by the President of the Council on Foreign Relations in New York in November 2002. Then, as American military planners were putting the final touches to their war plan, Leslie Gelb said:

> I think we're about to cross a Rubicon, and in modern times it's every bit as fateful as Caesar's crossing. I believe we should cross it, for [Saddam Hussein] really is a serious threat, and a danger. And it's important for us to go after him, to get rid of him. But I shudder at my beliefs and my conviction that we should do this, because I think this act of war will set off momentous events. This is a war maybe beyond anything we've done since the end of the Second World War, in its potential overflow into our lives here and abroad. I think it has the potential to do more to the world

and to us than Korea, than the first Gulf War, and maybe even Vietnam. I think the war as a military battle will probably be over quite quickly. US military might, at this point, to fight a straight-up conventional war, is awesome. And Saddam is weaker. Whatever his tactics will be, the shock of American military power in a straight-up military battle will be fearsome. I think it's what happens after the victory that engages us and worries me. Good things can come of it, and I hope they will . . . . At the same time, it is a terrible roll of the dice. And it could unleash a terrible anti-Americanism, and a fanaticism, an active fanaticism, even beyond what we've seen.[26]

His emphasis on the war's importance proved well-founded, but it is also clear to all that all that Gelb feared has come to pass in Iraq and, without a clear exit strategy in sight,[27] it is hard to see how the administration's other noble goal of democratizing the Middle East can be squared with the underlying currents that drive the Bush Doctrine today. Shortly before the Iraq war, a Bush insider and Pentagon staffer confided to the *New Yorker* that

you have the phenomenon that this greater freedom that came to Latin America, that came to various parts of Asia, largely missed the Middle East. And there are all kinds of writing on the subject, on whether there is anything inherently incompatible between either Muslim culture, or Arab culture, and this kind of freer government. This administration does not believe there is an inherent incompatibility. And if Iraq had a government like that, and if that government could create some of those institutions of democracy that might be inspirational for people throughout the Middle East to try to increase the amount of freedom that they have, and they would benefit both politically and economically by doing so.[28]

The difficulty that the administration continues to face is how to square its militaristic instincts with the implementation of long-lasting reforms in the Middle East. Being a prisoner of the Bush Doctrine, the way forward seems to be one in which the war on terror itself is refined by the administration (Andreani 2004–5) before it can safely take forward the strategy of freedom so loudly announced back in 2002 and confirmed in 2005.

Notes

1 For an excellent summary of some of the issues, see 'The impact of 9/11 on the Middle East', *Middle East Policy*, vol. IX, no. 4, December 2004.
2 Bush Senior crafted the famous New World Order in 1990 in his international effort to build a coalition to reverse Iraq's invasion and annexation of neighbouring Kuwait.
3 With regard to the latter, President Bush's 20 September 20001 address to the nation had made the US position clear: 'Our war on terror begins with al-Qaeda,

but it does not end there. It will not end until every terrorist group of global reach has been found, stopped, and defeated.' As the war on terror was unleashing American military power against the al-Qaeda and Taleban strongholds in Afghanistan, the president further elaborated on 7 October that while 'today we focus on Afghanistan . . . the battle is broader. Every nation has a choice to make. In this conflict, there is no neutral ground. If any government sponsors outlaws and killers of innocents, they have become outlaws and murderers themselves.'

4   'Afghanistan is just the beginning of a war on terrorism', he said in November 2001. *Guardian*, 27 November 2001.
5   *Financial Times*, 31 October 2001.
6   Nicholas Lemann, 'The next world order: the Bush administration may have a brand-new doctrine of power', *New Yorker*, 1 April 2002.
7   This was the title of an article he wrote in the *Guardian*, 27 November 2001.
8   See the White House website, http://www.whitehouse.gov.
9   *Guardian*, 4 February 2002.
10 *Financial Times*, 1 November 2001.
11 *The Times*, 10 November 2001.
12 The US was being seen by some Sunni Arabs (who form the majority sect of Islam) as a co-conspirator in a plot to empower the Shia in Iraq as a barrier against the influence of Sunni-inspired Salafi and Wahhabi Islam in the Muslim world. Radical Sunni Islamists in particular saw in the rise of the Arab Shia in post-Saddam Iraq (a country of great strategic importance for its history, geopolitical location and vast hydrocarbon resources) the means for the suppression of mainstream Islam in the Arab world.
13 The former was to celebrate the 20th anniversary of the National Endowment of Democracy, and the latter was at Whitehall Palace to mark his official visit to the UK.
14 'Bush on democracy in the Middle East', *Washington Post*, 6 November 2003.
15 'President Bush discusses Iraq policy at Whitehall Palace in London', Office of the Press Secretary, The White House, 19 November 2003.
16 Robin Wright, 'US readies push for Mideast democracy plan', *Washington Post*, 28 February 2004.
17 *Arab News*, 17 January 2003.
18 Ibid.
19 Wright, op. cit.
20 Khaled Ezzelarab, 'Everyone else wants reform', *Cairo Times*, 26 February–3 March 2004.
21 'The wrong way to sell democracy to the Arab World', *New York Times*, 8 March 2004.
22 Nawaf Obaid, 'The clerics cannot be allowed to block reform', *International Herald Tribune*, 23 April 2003.
23 'Iran: supremely subversive', *Guardian*, 19 February 2004.
24 As much was clear from the Bush administration's National Security Strategy document unveiled in September 2002. The strategy of preventive strike formed the very heart of this document.
25 The phrase used is 'to dissuade potential adversaries from . . . surpassing, or equaling, the power of the United States'. See the White House website for details.
26 'The Next War: Richard Holbrooke, Jeffrey Goldberg, Lawrence Wright, Isabel Hilton, and Leslie Gelb discuss America's next war', *New Yorker*, 18 November 2002.
27 See *Foreign Affairs* 84 (1) February/January 2005.
28 Nicholas Lemann, 'After Iraq: the plan to remake the Middle East', *New Yorker*, 17 February 2003.

9 Africa

Robert D. Grey

Since the Cold War's end, the African continent has been seen by successive US administrations neither as a significant source of threats nor as an arena of great opportunities (Hentz 2004). The 9/11 attacks, the Bush Doctrine and the invasions of Afghanistan and Iraq have altered these calculations to some degree. American security, to a greater degree, is now tied to Africa (Mills 2004). Nevertheless, despite some increased attention, the continent remains peripheral to America's war on terrorism.

The increased attention was symbolized by Bush's brief visit to Africa in July 2003.[1] In discussing the trip, he and his advisers enunciated a number of elements of American policy.[2] While they expressed a new concern with terrorism, emphasis remained on long-standing priorities in Africa: promoting economic development, ending regional and internal conflicts, dealing with the AIDS crisis and providing humanitarian assistance. These priorities reflect the primary concerns of the State Department, which are somewhat different from those of the Defence Department and the US military. Although pressure for change from the latter is beginning to have an impact, so far there has been little policy change.

Terrorism has long been an issue of low-level concern to the State Department. Every year, it issues a list of countries that support terrorism, including a small number of African states. In the past two years, the US has moved to neutralize these threats. State and Defense Department officials have expressed fears that terrorists may attack other governments or US interests in those states. A major effort has been made to cooperate with these governments to reduce these threats. These efforts are also directed at preventing potential terrorists from using African countries as places in which to hide or bases from which to strike elsewhere. America has responded to such threats – real or merely perceived – with both diplomatic efforts and military cooperation. Diplomats have also sought African support for US policies elsewhere in the world.

Africa also offers opportunities for America. With recent discoveries of substantial oil reserves in a number of African countries, American officials feel that it is now possible for the US to reduce its dependence on vulnerable

Middle Eastern oil and replace it, to a significant extent, with African oil. Increasingly, the US is defining protection of oil as a national security interest.

Despite these new aspects of America's policies, emphasis remains on the traditional goals mentioned above. In fact, in terms of US expenditures, programmes to enhance peace-keeping,[3] promote economic development, support democratization, deal with humanitarian emergencies and confront the AIDS crisis far outpace anti-terrorism allocations. On his Africa trip, Bush discussed a billion dollars allocated for famine relief, 200 million for emergency famine relief, 10 billion in new money for combating AIDS, 600 million for an education initiative, as well as large amounts for a new Millennium Challenge to promote good governance, peace-keeping and economic development. This contrasts with 100 million in spending for anti-terrorism programmes. Such figures suggest that Bush regards Africa as largely irrelevant to his war on terrorism.

But, in various ways, America did bring the war on terrorism to Africa, and leaders there have differed in their reactions to evolving US initiatives. During the Cold War, Soviet support had enabled some African countries to challenge American policies. However, in the post-Cold War era, with America left as the sole superpower and no significant international actor willing to support such challenges, Africans tended to fall into line with American policies. Nevertheless, there was substantial variation. Thus, the leaders of Libya and Sudan, countries identified as supporters of international terrorism, knew that they were likely targets of American attacks, that they could expect no assistance from other powers and that there was some likelihood – however low – of their country being invaded. This awareness provided strong incentives greatly to improve their relationship with America.

A small number of African countries embraced the Bush Doctrine with eagerness. Both Ethiopia and Eritrea joined the 'coalition of the willing', supporting, albeit in very limited ways, the US invasion of Iraq. Rwanda later indicated its strong support for American policies. While most leaders on the continent were horrified by 9/11, shared the American sense of heightened danger from terrorism and passively supported the invasion of Afghanistan, they found the American turning of attention to Iraq both a diversion and a wrong-headed strategy. Both in the UN and elsewhere, some members of this group tried to prevent the attack on Iraq and distanced themselves from any participation once it had occurred.

US decision-makers saw many African states as potentially threatened by terrorism and/or as possible arenas for terrorist activity. This view led America to seek increased cooperation among these states in the war on terrorism, and led members of this group into at least limited forms of working with the US. In addition, a new theme became important to the relationship, an emerging emphasis on the strategic importance to America of African oil. Military cooperation complemented the other, older forms of US–African cooperation, far more significant to both the US and Africa.

This chapter explores the US–Africa relationship, concentrating on the military elements. Such a focus seems justified by the Bush administration's emphasis on the use of military force to realize its central foreign policy goals. It argues that, despite the Bush Doctrine and a somewhat increased sense of the strategic importance of Africa, American policy towards Africa under Bush has not really changed very much, and that African states, despite broad cooperation with the US in military matters, remain marginal to America's war on terror.

The US and Africa in the post-Cold War era

During the Cold War, the conflict with the Soviet Union in Africa had provided US foreign policy with a focus and a justification for involvement on a continent that seemed to offer the US few opportunities and fewer threats. With the loss of that focus, the US, to a great degree, disengaged from the continent. At the same time, its continuing involvement reflected a number of rather low-priority concerns: conflict resolution; democratization or improved governance; humanitarian assistance in crisis situations such as drought or civil war; promotion of economic development and of neo-liberal economic policies as a means to that goal; and AIDS prevention and relief.

Early in the post-Cold War era, the Somali state's collapse led to a peace-keeping and humanitarian initiative there, with American troops as the largest single national presence in a UN force. Caught up in an internecine conflict among contending warlords, US troops took a number of casualties, and the corpses of American troops were dragged behind vehicles in the streets of Mogadishu. The resulting media furore in the US led to the withdrawal of troops and a decision by Pentagon officials that exposure of troops to the possibility of such humiliation where no obvious American interests were at stake was politically unacceptable. That decision was a powerful factor in America's reluctance to respond in any significant way to the genocide in 1994 in Rwanda or to commit soldiers to the numerous UN peace-keeping efforts on the continent during the 1990s or 2000s (Herbst 2000). On the other hand, US presidents recognized that the political instability reflected in the numerous conflicts within and between states represented both a significant humanitarian problem and a potential source of long-range threats to US security. This led to the provision of humanitarian assistance as well as funding and transportation of UN peace-keepers.

The Cold War's end was accompanied by an opportunity to raise to first priority the goal of world democratization. The fall of the Berlin Wall seemed to trigger moves towards democracy in Africa. Most analysts assign much weight in the process to external actors and forces, arguing that the International Monetary Fund (IMF) and World Bank have especially pushed African democratization. While these institutions are reasonably seen as agents of American policies and priorities, the US has not seemed to make a major bilateral commitment to promoting African democratization. Moreover,

America's limited commitment to African democratization began to clash with what were increasingly seen as intense and growing American strategic concerns, the war on terrorism and access to African oil.

The third of America's foci in post-Cold War Africa has been humanitarian assistance. Both natural causes, such as rainfall shortage, and person-made problems, such as civil wars limiting the planting and harvesting of crops, have contributed to famine in multiple areas of the continent. The US has made significant contributions of food, blankets, medicine and the transportation facilities to bring these to Africa and to distribute them within Africa.

Fourth on the list was the promoting of neo-liberal economic policies. The World Bank and IMF were active throughout the continent. While they partly promoted democracy, they – more basically and for a longer time – pushed a model of neo-liberal economic development. Finally, the US viewed with distress the rapid spread of AIDS, as both intrinsically horrible and as a threat to the realization of other American goals.

The Bush Doctrine and Africa

None of these priorities, however, loomed large in US foreign policy. As America searched for an appropriate post-Cold War role for the world's only superpower, Africa seemed to offer neither threats nor opportunities. 9/11 changed this. Rather quickly, administration officials identified Africa as of some concern.

The State Department had long included both Libya and Sudan on its list of countries supporting terrorist activity. In the 1980s, Qadhafi, the Libyan president, had been a target of a US bombing (an attack that killed his daughter), while a cruise missile attack had been made on a Sudanese chemical plant, falsely identified as a manufacturing site for chemical weapons in 1998. The Bush Doctrine made it clear that both these African states were potential targets, once Iraq had been successfully invaded, occupied, pacified and democratized.

Other African states, while not seen as promoting terrorism, were viewed as likely to be either targets of terrorist attacks or arenas where terrorists could operate with impunity. Many of the states of North Africa, the Sahel and the East African coast had overwhelmingly Muslim populations. Their governments tended to either be secular or have a very moderate Islamic cast. Some, such as the governments of Algeria and Egypt, had been under attack by domestic fundamentalist insurgents, and others were viewed as possible targets. Both the US and African governments felt that there was a potential security threat. Even where governments were unlikely to be targets, groups such as al-Qaeda, deprived of its base in Afghanistan, were likely to seek other countries in which to operate. From that perspective, the notoriously weak governments in much of Africa might be unable either to detect or to do anything about terrorist activity. The collapsed state of Somalia (Dange 2002; Menkhaus 2002)[4] was seen as particularly vulnerable.

Moreover, the Bush administration – and particularly Pentagon officials and energy analysts – had begun to realize that US dependence on imported oil from the Middle East left America vulnerable both to attacks on the region's oilfields and supply lines and to long-term political instability. The presence of substantial reserves of oil in Nigeria and Angola, and the discovery of additional oilfields from Equatorial Guinea in the Gulf of Guinea through Chad and into the Sudan, offered an alternative to Middle East oil supplies.

The conjunction of these two security priorities raised relationships with Africa to a higher priority than they had been since the Cold War. Africa, however, was not central to US foreign policy. Afghanistan and Iraq absorbed most US military capabilities, and the possible acquisition of nuclear weapons by North Korea and Iran captured diplomatic attention. Economic links with Europe, Japan, China and elsewhere were far more important than those with Africa. But a continent that had been largely marginalized since 1989 became somewhat less so after 9/11.

America and Africa: the diplomatic web

In its conflict with terrorism, the US sought diplomatic support from African states, both within the UN – in the lead-up to the Iraq invasion – and in the wider battle against terrorism. During the early months of 2003, the US, backed by the UK and Spain, worked desperately to produce a UN resolution that would authorize its planned invasion of Iraq. Immense pressure was put on six undecided members of the Security Council, including the three African states, Guinea (temporarily chairing the Council), Angola and Cameroon. France, closely linked to its former colonies, Guinea and Cameroon, applied counterpressure on these states. The US ultimately decided not to push for a formal vote, fearing not only France's veto but also that it might not even get the majority it sought.

Despite an African Union resolution opposing a unilateral decision of the 'coalition of the willing' to go to war without UN authorization, Ethiopia and Eritrea became part of the State Department's initial list of members of the coalition. Each seemed to think that its declaration of support might make America more sympathetic to its claim in their mutual border conflict. Eritrea, especially, tried to add a significant military component to its expression of support, offering America use of its Red Sea naval facilities. A second State Department list later added Rwanda and Uganda as coalition members.

Diplomatic support in the UN was important to the US, but only part of a larger web of diplomatic commitments it sought from other states, including those in Africa. In its Resolution 1373, adopted on 28 September 2001, the UN Security Council called on all member states to become parties to a group of 12 universal conventions against terrorism. These conventions,

adopted between 1963 and 1999, defined various acts as terrorist and specified penalties for those who committed them. As part of its war on terrorism,
the US encouraged African states to sign and ratify all 12 conventions and
then monitored the extent of commitment in each African state.

The military component of the war on terrorism in Africa

The State and Defence Departments considered Africa an important
secondary arena in the conflict with terrorism. Qadhafi in Libya (Alterman
and Morrison 2003) and Bashir in Sudan (Morrison 2002) espoused a more
fundamentalist role for Islam in their states, and both had previously been
identified by the State Department as state sponsors of terrorism. Each,
moreover, had been a previous target of limited US pre-emptive strikes.
Thus, they became possible targets of future US preventive invasions.
At this point, little is known about the dynamics of US–Sudanese or US–
Libyan relations. However, relations between each of these dyads improved
dramatically at the end of 2003 and the beginning of 2004. First, Libya
assumed responsibility for, and paid compensation for, an earlier plane
bombing.[5] More importantly, it announced that it had had a weapons of mass
destruction (WMD) development programme, renounced that programme
and opened its facilities to international inspection. In return, both the US
and various European countries signalled their acceptance of a Libyan return
to international respectability.

In addition to promoting a fundamentalist state and sponsoring terrorism, Sudanese President Bashir had long been waging a war against Christian and animist insurgents in the south. In 2004, Khartoum also seemed
to be responsible for militias waging war against the populations of Darfur Province, in western Sudan. Despite this horrendous record, relations
between Washington and Khartoum improved radically during 2004.[6] On
Washington's side, this may well have been the result of Bashir seriously
negotiating to end the conflict in the south and implementing anti-terrorist
activities and, perhaps, of growing American interest in Sudanese oil. The
increased willingness of the Sudanese and Libyan governments to cooperate
with Washington may have reflected their awareness that, as identified sponsors of terrorism, they fell just below Iran and North Korea as possible US
targets and that they were essentially helpless to avoid such a fate, with no
powerful international friends.

The US has thus dealt with its most serious threats in Africa. The Pentagon, and particularly the European Command, however, has argued that
there remains a large number of countries potentially vulnerable to terrorist
attack or sites of terrorist operation as well as several states that are actual
or potential sources of oil. These arguments might be seen as an effort by
a European Command with relatively little to do since the collapse of the
Soviet threat to redefine its central purposes and to justify maintenance of
or increase in its funding. To a limited extent, the Bush administration has

accepted this argument. Thus, the administration adopted a number of different programmes to deal with such threats. First, it established a small group of reasonably powerful African states with which it proposed to work closely in its anti-terrorist campaign. South Africa and Nigeria were the most significant regional powers in sub-Saharan Africa with military and intelligence capabilities surpassing others. Both were willing to work closely with the US in combating terrorism, yet each had certain domestic constraints in doing so. Islam is the dominant religion in northern Nigeria and, at least in parts of the north, becoming more fundamentalist. The national government in Abuja is confronted with significant domestic battles with such forces. An alliance with the US complicates an already complex situation. The South African government has confronted a number of terrorist incidents within its own borders, although not from fundamentalist Muslims. That strengthens its willingness to be part of an international anti-terrorist effort. But human rights groups within the country are sensitive to possible trade-offs between aggressive anti-terrorist activities and restrictions on civil and political liberties (Goredem 2003).[7] For these very different reasons, neither state has cooperated as fully as Bush wished.

The other two 'core states' in Washington's planning are Ethiopia and Kenya. Although lacking the resources of Nigeria and South Africa, these are more conveniently located, adjacent to the Red Sea and Indian Ocean, and thus across from the Arabian peninsula, a focus of terrorist activity. As indicated above, Ethiopia's Prime Minister, Meles Zenawi, enthusiastically joined the coalition of the willing. In 1998, Kenya had suffered a large death toll when the US embassy there was car bombed and then, in 2002, endured a second attack on a resort largely patronized by Israelis, as well as an attempted shooting down of an Israeli chartered flight. As a victim itself of terrorism, and as a country heavily dependent on tourism, the Kenyans have been close allies of the US in the counter-terrorism effort. Nevertheless, given the limited resources of these two states, their efforts could hardly contribute significantly to the American-led campaign.

The US military is stretched very thin. Despite its concentrations elsewhere, it has sought ways in which it could, with minimum personnel and minimum expense, provide a military response to the perceived threats in Africa.[8] As part of the Combined Joint Task Force – Horn of Africa (CJTF-HOA) programme,[9] the US has created a military base in Djibouti, which it has embedded in a diplomatic/military initiative to work with the militaries of the Horn of Africa and East Africa. It has initiated comparable arrangements with the militaries of West Africa, North Africa and the Sahel. Finally, it has continued a long-standing programme to bring to the US for additional training military personnel from across the continent.

The area of operation of the CJTF-HOA[10] includes the airspace, land areas and costal waters of Djibouti, Eritrea, Ethiopia, Kenya, Somalia, Sudan and Yemen. In 2004, Tanzania and Uganda were also put under the CJTF-HOA umbrella. The base at Djibouti is the only true US base on the continent.[11]

Initially, the headquarters for this operation was a flagship, the *USS Mount Whitney*, which arrived in the area in December 2002 and patrolled the Red Sea, the Gulf of Aden and the Indian Ocean for six months, presumably to intercept possible terrorist vessels. Soon after that, the CJTF-HOA conducted a 12-day Joint Readiness Exercise involving air, sea and land resources. The exercises focused on detecting, identifying and tracking terrorist activities in the region, ending with actions against those playing the terrorists. In May 2004, the headquarters was shifted from the *USS Mount Whitney* to a site on land, Camp Lemonier in Djibouti, with headquarters personnel joining other military personnel stationed there.[12] With the move ashore and the movement of additional units to Djibouti, US military and civilian personnel, as well as some personnel from coalition forces at Camp Lemonier, numbered some 1,800 individuals in the spring of 2004. The establishment of this base has been welcomed by a number of countries in the region. Isaias Afworki, the President of Eritrea, was an early visitor to the *USS Mount Whitney*,[13] and the President of Djibouti was hosted there in May 2004.[14] In addition, high-ranking officials of the CJTF-HOA paid official visits to top political officials in other countries in the region.

Using Djibouti as its headquarters, the CJTF-HOA has begun to operate in other countries. In July 2003, units from the US Army's 10th Mountain Division, attached to CJTF-HOA, began a three-month training programme for Ethiopian troops at an Ethiopian army training camp in south-east Ethiopia, fairly close to the Somali border.[15] By January 2004, what had been a training camp for the Ethiopian military was being described by US military sources as a 'forward base' for CJTF-HOA, the so-called 'Camp United'.[16] Then Commander of CJTF-HOA, Brigadier General Samuel Helland, was quoted in an AP interview: 'We've got forces now in almost every country and we've got representation in every country' except Somalia.[17] He went on to say that US training of regional militaries was increasing, and that the US task force was averaging one civilian–military operation every three days to promote anti-terrorist cooperation.

This activity must be put in context. On the one hand, the US government, and especially the US military, have been increasingly identifying the countries of Africa in general, and those of the Horn of Africa in particular, as potential terrorist targets and bases. For a host of reasons, African governments have agreed to accept that characterization and to cooperate with the US in combating terrorism. On the other hand, the US military effort in the Horn is an exceedingly limited one. While one commander of CJTF-HOA claimed that the small contingent in Djibouti could quickly be supplemented by additional forces from the US Central Command, as needed, the resources of that command are stretched thin by wars in Afghanistan and Iraq. It would take a very dramatic emergency to free up additional troops for CJTF-HOA. It appears that Bush continues to view the threat in the Horn of Africa as quite limited and is content to deal with this limited threat by a minimalist programme. What is true of the Horn is even truer of the rest of the continent.

While, elsewhere on the continent, there appear to be no bases equivalent to that run by CJTF-HOA in Djibouti – although there is talk of setting one up in Nigeria or elsewhere in West Africa – there are other operations parallel to those run by CJTF-HOA. The US military has assumed the role of training and, to a very limited degree, equipping anti-terrorist units in militaries across the continent. In 1997, an African Crisis Response Initiative (ACRI) was created, a programme through which small American units would train special units from a number of African states. During its three-year existence, it trained more than 6,000 troops from seven African countries, including Senegal, Uganda, Malawi, Mali, Ghana, Benin and Côte d'Ivoire. ACRI also paid for providing these troops with boots, generators, mine detectors, night vision goggles, vehicles and water purification devices.

ACRI was replaced in the spring of 2002 by the African Contingency Operations Training and Assistance (ACOTA) programme, which also supplements its training functions by providing limited amounts of arms and equipment to the forces it trains.[18] The US sends in 60-man special forces units from bases in Europe to work with targeted African units. Although funding is limited, $15 million in 2004, it can achieve much. In 2004 alone, the ACOTA programme trained 9,000 soldiers. Theresa Whelan, Africa Director of the US Department of Defense's Office of International Security Affairs, argued in November 2003 that ACOTA had to be more 'robust' than ACRI because of its 'expanded range' of security responsibilities.[19] The implication was that the troops trained, and perhaps their American advisors, were expected to be actively involved in violent confrontations with terrorist groups. Neither ACRI, whose creation far antedated 9/11, nor its successor, ACOTA, is typically characterized by American officials as a counterterrorist organization. Rather, unlike CJTF-HOA, which is so described, they are normally described as organizations doing military training for peace-keeping operations.

A comparable operation is the Pan Sahel Initiative (PSI), in which the US military works with military units from Chad, Niger, Mali and Mauritania. These are countries vast in area but very limited in population, with governments whose capacity to act against terrorists effectively is slight. The PSI seems to have been the one such group that has actually seen action. In 2003, an Algerian terrorist group, the Salafist Group for Call and Combat (GSPC), kidnapped a group of European tourists. After receiving ransom money, releasing the tourists and buying weapons and equipment, the group tried to flee across the desert.[20] The PSI-trained troops, presumably with US intelligence if not direct participation, captured one part of the group and defeated another part in battle.[21]

Yet another such military training programme is the East Africa Counterterrorism Initiative (EACTI), announced in June 2003. In addition to the military training component common to all these initiatives, it funds a number of other anti-terrorism measures, including programmes to strengthen border controls, improve aviation security and control financial systems to reduce the likelihood of terrorist money laundering.

These are small programmes, requiring only a limited number of US military personnel. Given competing demands, the military finds it difficult to carry out even these. Various remedial steps have been proposed, including a programme bringing into these activities National Guard units from the various American states. The National Guard State Partnership Program (SPP) is designed to work with 'lower priority nations'.[22] Another step is the contracting out of some of the training to private security firms. Such outsourcing is consistent with Bush administration emphasis on the positive role of the market. These initiatives are all part of what Major Neil Glad called 'cobbling together resources, funding and initiatives for Africa'.[23]

All these training programmes are designed inexpensively to enhance the capacity of African states, in coordination with the US, to detect and disrupt terrorist activities as well as to capture or kill the terrorists. Such programmes continue, but expand, initiatives begun during the Clinton years, but they remain poorly funded. While they have been expanded, they are not really a massive response to 9/11 nor a significant device for implementing the Bush Doctrine. Moreover, they are multipurpose programmes, designed to enhance peace-keeping capabilities as well as counter-terrorism programmes.

Another programme is IMET, the International Military Education and Training Program, which brings officers from African armies to the US; personnel from 44 countries have participated in this programme. Funded in recent years at around $10 million a year, the programme hoped to train some 1,600 officers in 2002.

The US also provides arms to Africa. In 2001, the US Defense Security Cooperation Agency sold some $21 million worth to nine African countries, with Nigeria spending $7 million on arms. Another $18 million were loaned to nine countries to pay for American arms, with Nigeria buying $10 million. Finally, US companies sold $2 million worth, with the approval of the State Department. Such provisions of arms, like training programmes, have long been in existence, are not large and have not been increased much by the Bush administration.

While such involvement began with neither 9/11 nor the Bush Doctrine, it has become more widespread. In addition, it is now commonly characterized as counterterrorist in character, whereas earlier it was framed solely as an American contribution to peace-keeping. Despite its growth, and this new 'framing', what seems to be the case is that it remains, in comparison with American efforts elsewhere in the world, very limited.

It is striking that almost all the leaders on the continent find it useful to cooperate with the Americans. In addition to whatever innate benefits these military links provide – and presumably they are seen as at least marginally enhancing the security of African leaders and/or their countries – they merely constitute part of a whole complex of programmes linking the US to African countries. African leaders may perceive participation in these military programmes as the price they must pay for continued American support of the other, non-military programmes. A substantial literature in African politics suggests that African leaders are adept at both diverting such funds to their personal use and using them to co-opt potential opponents into supporting their rule (Reno 1998; Leonard and Straus 2003: 21–56).

Africa, the USA and oil

A second national security front has quietly opened in Africa (Volman 2003). The US is heavily dependent on imported oil. African oil, particularly from Nigeria and Angola, constitutes a small but growing part of America's imports, some 15–16 per cent, with most of its imports coming from the Middle East (over 60 per cent). Given the Middle East's political volatility and the finite character of its oil reserves, during the past few years, the US has increasingly focused on the opportunities that African oil represent to diversify as much as possible. Thus, in 2002, Assistant Secretary of Defense for African Affairs, Walter Kansteiner, while in Africa, declared that 'African oil is of strategic national interest to us'.[24] General Charles Wald, Deputy Commander of the US military's European Command for Europe and Africa, echoed that theme in a number of speeches. The attraction of African oil has been enhanced by the discovery in recent years of rich reserves in a number of additional African countries. Daniel Volman lists five states with substantial reserves: Angola, Sudan, Republic of Congo, Nigeria and Chad.[25] Other oil-producing states in the region include Cameroon, Equatorial Guinea, Gabon and São Tomé and Principe. In a report for the oil industry, Douglas Stinemetz[26] argued that:

> Accessing oil from West Africa is clearly advantageous for the US. First it is prolific and relatively untapped. Many new discoveries in West Africa are coming into production just now, and new ones can reasonably be expected for the remainder of the decade. Nigeria alone expects its production of oil to increase almost 50% by 2004 as a result. Second, the oil itself is uniquely suited for the US market. The West African oil is good quality, low sulfur and perfect for refining in US Gulf port refineries which operate under tight environmental restrictions . . . Political risk in West Africa, while present, is not nearly as great as in the Middle East and many other oil producing provinces of the world.

Pierre Abromovici, writing for *Le Monde Diplomatique*, argues that the US is moving to protect both the supplies and the possible pipelines.[27] He treats the military measures discussed above neither as efforts to promote peace-keeping – for the most part Bush administration rhetoric – nor as part of the war on terror, the framework utilized in this chapter, but as part of a 'new scramble for Africa'. He argues that, in July 2003, there was an attempted

coup in São Tomé and Principe and that the attempt 'triggered US intervention in the archipelago'.[28] This view was clearly a French over-reaction to
any US presence, as the Americans kept a low profile, while African leaders
discussed a possible military response to the coup and put on enough pressure to force the military to withdraw.

While the US played a behind-the-scenes-role in ending the coup, it has
begun to explore the military implications of defining West African oil as
a national security interest. A feasibility study has been done in São Tomé,
exploring the island's possible use as both a naval and an air base.[29] There
have been hints that the European Command would like to establish two
types of forward bases in various West African states, one similar to the base
in Djibouti, able to hold several thousand US troops, and the other similar
to the Ethiopian base, rather bare bones.[30] Finally, there have been discussions of a naval task force cruising the Gulf of Guinea, protecting oil tankers
among other tasks. Military personnel have called for a substantial increase
in funding for these activities. Given these developments, concern about
oil converges with concern about terrorism. It may be that, in the future,
the economic importance of African oil becomes so great, and the perceived
threat to that oil represented by terrorism so salient, that my emphasis on
the relatively low level of US involvement in Africa will seem shortsighted.
But, at the moment, what now exists is a group of officials calling for, but
not yet getting, a significant increase in the military presence in Africa. For
the moment, that presence remains trivial in the context of overall US programmes in Africa.

America's other links with the continent[31]

An intrinsically desirable US goal for Africa is a reduction in the number and
severity of conflicts. Ambassador Aubrey Hooks, speaking to the New York
Council on Foreign Relations in 2000, said:

> Our on-the-ground engagement on behalf of African security is a multi-
> tiered effort. US diplomats are working day in and day out to promote
> the peaceful resolutions of conflicts in DROC (the Democratic Republic
> of the Congo), Sierra Leone, Angola, Burundi, the Horn of Africa and
> elsewhere. The US contributed over $100 million to support ECOWAS/
> ECOMAG efforts to build peace in Sierra Leone and Liberia in recent
> years and $8 million to the OAU and its Crisis Management Center . . .
> Over the past five years, we have contributed around $380 million to
> UN-assessed peace-keeping missions across Africa.[32]

These financial contributions to peace-keeping and conflict resolution
supplemented the on-site training of military units, the education in the US
of officers and the sale/provision of equipment. They exceeded spending on
anti-terrorist military funding, but were not particularly large. In fact, they

paled before the amounts spent on other American programmes in Africa. Thus, in fiscal year 1999, under the Clinton administration, the US spent $460.1 million on its Development Fund for Africa, $251.2m on its Child Survival and Disease Programs, $98.2m on its Economic Support Fund, $128m on its African Development Fund and $132m on various other non-food programmes. In addition, it provided $224.4m for food aid. The total aid package then amounted to $1293.9m, dwarfing the amount spent on the later anti-terrorist efforts.[33]

Despite the rhetorical emphasis of the Bush administration on the war on terrorism, its relationships with Africa continued to be dominated by these other goals.[34] Thus, for instance, in 2003 the US spent $1.1 billion on development assistance and child survival aid and requested just slightly less than that for fiscal year 2004. The total projected expenditure for economic and humanitarian aid for 2003 was $1.7 billion, with another $469 million projected for peace-keeping operations and only $90 million to be expended on the various military programmes described above. Requests for 2004 were similar. Starting in 2001, such sums made the US the largest single contributor of bilateral official development assistance (ODA) to the continent, although the US contributed a relatively small percentage of its total ODA to Africa.[35] Such sums spent on America's political, economic and humanitarian efforts in Africa also demonstrate the extremely limited character of its military activities on the continent.

Conclusion

Despite US disengagement from Africa since the end of the Cold War, America has undertaken a series of programmes designed to promote low-priority goals. With a heightened focus on Africa, the administration – under military prodding – has initiated or expanded programmes of military cooperation and is now looking for bases beyond Djibouti. The view that Africa's oil will be increasingly important to the US economy adds urgency to these activities. Hitherto, comparatively few dollars have been spent on military programmes and very few military personnel have been involved. The US remains essentially disengaged from Africa and its purposes remain overwhelmingly economic and humanitarian.

Notes

1 He was only the fourth US president to visit the continent while in office, and the first Republican president to do so.
2 See a White House statement at http://www.whitehouse.gov/infocus/africa. Also, then National Security Advisor Condoleezza Rice, http://www.whitehouse.gov/news/releases/2003/07/20030703-14.html#6. A presidential press conference prior to the trip expressed Bush's then priorities. http://www.whitehouse.gov/news/releases/2003/07/20030703-5.html.

3 It is proving increasingly difficult, however, to distinguish activities designed to promote peace-keeping from those designed as anti-terrorist.

4 Walter H. Kansteiner, 'Weak state and terrorism in Africa: US policy option in Somalia', Testimony before the Senate Committee on Foreign Relations Sub-committee on African Affairs, Washington, DC, 6 February 2002, http://www.state.gov/p/af/rls/rm/7872.htm.

5 http://www.terrorismfiles.org/countries/libya.html. See also Sharon A. Squassoni and Andrew Feickert, 'Disarming Libya: weapons of mass destruction', CRS Report for Congress, Congressional Research Service, Library of Congress, 22 April 2004. This can be found at www.fas.org/spp/starwars/crs/#libya.

6 For an analysis of this evolving relationship, see Ted Dagne, 'Sudan: humanitarian crisis, peace talks, terrorism, and US policy', CRS Issue Brief for Congress, Congressional Research Service, Library of Congress, 27 September 2004, pp. CRS 10–11, http://www.fas.org/man/crs/IB98043.pdf.

7 See 'South African Anti-Terror Bill draconian', http://www.globalissues.org/Geopolitics/WarOnTerror/SABill.asp?p=1.

8 Much of the material on US military involvement in Africa comes from Daniel Volman, 'US military programmes in sub-Saharan Africa, 2001–2003', Association of Concerned African Scholars, http://www.prairienet.org/acas/military/miloverview.html.

9 http://www.globalsecurity.org/military/agency/dod/cjtf-hoa.htm.

10 'Terrorism in the Horn of Africa', United States Institute of Peace, Special Report 113, January 2003, http://www.usip.org/pubs/specialreports/sr113.html.

11 Although this is currently the only base, see below for Camp United in Ethiopia and for efforts to explore the possibility of West African bases.

12 http://www.defendamerica.mil/articles/may/2003/a05080a.html.

13 http://asmara.usembassy.gov/eritrea/The_USS_Mount_whitney.html.

14 http://www.somalilandtimes.net/2003/68/6817.shtml.

15 http://www.dcmilitary.com/army/pentagram/9_03/national_news/27172-1.html.

16 http://www.globalsecurity.org/military/facility/camp-united.htm and http://www.Hartford.hwp.com/archives/27c/422.html.

17 www.geeskaafrika.com/djibouti_18aug04.htm.

18 Colonel Russell J. Handy, USAF, 'Africa Contingency Operations Training Assistance: developing training partnerships for the future of Africa', http://www.airpower.maxwell.af.mil/airchronicles/apj/apj03/fal03/handy.html.

19 http://usembassy.state.gov/nigeria/wwwhp070403d.html.

20 http://windsofchange.net/archives/004795.php.

21 Pierre Abramovici, 'United States: the new scramble for Africa: precious resources in need of protection', *Le Monde Diplomatique*, July 2004, http://www.mondediplo.com/2004/07/07usinafrica.

22 Major Neil C. Glad, 'Expanding security cooperation to North Africa through the State Partnership Program', Headquarters United States European Command, 25 August 2004, http://ngb-ia.org/public/library_file_proxy.cfm/lid/268.

23 Ibid, p. 6.

24 www.globalpolicy.org/security/natres/oil/2003/0114angola.htm.

25 Daniel Volman, 'Oil, arms and violence in Africa', Report prepared for the African Security Research Project, February 2003, http://www.prairienet.org/acas/military/oilandarms.pdf.

26 S. Douglas Stinemetz, 'Changing US policy toward West Africa', http://www.rigzone.com/insight/insight.asp?i_id=16.

27 Pierre Abramovici, 'United States: the new scramble for Africa: precious resources in need of protection', *Le Monde Diplomatique*, July 2004, http://www.mondediplo.com/2004/07/07usinafrica.

28 Ibid, p. 6.

29 http://www.derechos.org/nizkor/eguinea/doc/wa1.html.

30 www.flysouth.co.za/news/archive/2003-07-11/pentagon and www.globalpolicy. org/empire/analysis/2004/0902yeomans.htm.

31 While arguing that non-security goals should have the highest priority in America's dealings with Africa, Booker *et al.* (2003) assert that the war agenda has replaced those at the top of the list. I couldn't disagree more strongly.

32 Ambassador Aubrey Hooks, 'Promoting security in Africa – the US contribution', Presentation to the Council on Foreign Relations, New York, 10 February 2000, http://usinfo.state.gov/regional/af/acri/hookstx.htm.

33 Raymond W. Copson, 'Africa: US foreign assistance issues', CRS Issue Brief for Congress, Congressional Research Service, Library of Congress, 19 August 1999, available at http://www.crie.org/nie/econ-51.html.

34 Data for this section came from Raymond W. Copson, 'Africa: US foreign assistance issues', CRS Issue Brief for Congress, Congressional Research Service, Library of Congress, 5 September 2003, p. CRS 8, http://www.pennyhill.com/ africa/ib95052.html.

35 Ibid, p. 9.

10 Australasia

Brendon O'Connor

The Bush Doctrine has caused alarm among many of America's traditional allies, from its continental European NATO allies to its ANZUS partner New Zealand. One obvious exception, however, has been the Australian government, which has offered almost unreserved support for the US in recent years and seems remarkably comfortable with Bush's National Security Strategy and its much talked of notion of pre-emption. This chapter compares Australia's embracing of the Bush Doctrine with New Zealand's more ambivalent position and discusses how Australia's position has been received in the region. It argues that Australia's reasons for closer alignment with the US in recent years are twofold: to meet a broader goal of alliance fortification; and to meet the individual objectives of an extremely pro-US and pro-Bush Australian prime minister.

Australasia's differing views on the Bush Doctrine

The respective attitudes of the leaders of Australia and New Zealand towards the Bush Doctrine provide an interesting insight into how these two allies have so differently judged the costs and benefits of strengthening their ties with the US. At the grand strategic level, the Australian government is in agreement with America's plans to maintain its position as the pre-eminent global power. The US is not only seen as Australia's most important military ally but also as its best protection against possible outside threats, with many Australians believing that America saved Australia from Japanese occupation during World War II and that America would come to their country's aid again today. The notion that Australia exists in a hostile region has been an ongoing motif throughout Australian history (Burke 2001), although, apart from the Japanese during World War II, Australia has faced very few foreign threats. At present, the intelligence community is most concerned about China (White 2002), whereas the general public sees Indonesia as the greatest threat to Australian security (McAllister *et al.* 2004). In reality, it would seem reasonable to argue that neither nation poses anything close to an imminent threat.

New Zealand, in contrast, seems less concerned about threats, real or imagined, an attitude reflected in its comparatively low level of defence spending – only around 0.9 per cent of gross domestic product (GDP) compared with Australia's approximately 2 per cent.[1] Since New Zealand's decision to prohibit the entry of US nuclear-powered ships into its harbours – a policy driven by a strong anti-nuclear sentiment in the community that was taken up by the New Zealand Labour Party in its march to power in 1984 – the New Zealand–US relationship has cooled significantly. While the New Zealand government is not openly critical of a continuation of US hegemony, it is far less outwardly supportive than Australia. New Zealand's more limited emphasis on military, political and trading relations with the US is obvious when comparing annual reports and foreign policy speeches by the respective governments of New Zealand and Australia.[2] Australia stands out as far more US-centric in the foreign policy rhetoric of these documents. This is not to say that all New Zealanders are comfortable with their nation's position – the top New Zealand business organization, the Business Roundtable, has attacked the New Zealand government for generally distancing itself from the US (Kerr 2004). New Zealand also draws regular criticism from Australian politicians from both major political parties for its lack of defence spending, with these critics complaining that New Zealand is living in a fantasyland, with its security guaranteed by Australia.

Given such differences towards America's grand strategic objectives, it is not surprising that, when it comes to support for the more specific policies of the 'war on terror', New Zealand has played a much more limited role than Australia. Like many other nations, New Zealand is concerned about Bush's doctrine of pre-emption. This concern with pre-emption in general and opposition to America's pre-emptive attack on Iraq in particular dominated the response from many US allies. However, the Australian government not only sent troops to both Afghanistan and Iraq but also took its own steps towards pre-emption, asserting that Australia was also willing to use pre-emptive force against terrorists in its own region, a claim that has been widely condemned as provocative as such an action could clearly be seen as a declaration of war. The Australian Prime Minister John Howard has twice stated that Australia reserves this right: first in December 2003 (Broinowski 2003: 19; Garran 2004: 135–6) and then again during the election campaign in 2004. On both occasions, such unilateral statements disturbed leaders in the region, and one imagines that a fair degree of behind-the-scenes diplomacy was required to clarify exactly what the prime minister meant. Australia's countenancing of the use of pre-emptive force would seem to confirm one of the immediate criticisms of the Bush administration's pre-emptive doctrine; namely, that it would create a precedent or excuse for other nations who want to act outside the boundaries of international law.

The Australian prime minister and his people's own recent experiences of terrorism, discussed below, form a convincing argument as to why Australia has backed America's war on terror much more strongly than New

Zealand. On 11 September 2001, Prime Minister Howard was giving a press conference in a Washington, DC, hotel when American Airlines flight 77 hit the Pentagon. Being in the US meant that Howard was able to share in the disbelief and horror at the events, and he was the only foreign leader to attend the joint session of Congress held the next day. Howard then flew back to Australia on the vice-presidential plane, Air Force Two. While still in mid-air on this return to Australia on 12 September, Howard took the historic and highly symbolic mid-air decision to invoke the ANZUS treaty, placing Australia on alert to support the US in its response to the terrorist attacks (Garran 2004: 68–73). Howard's personal experience has also played into the very close relationship he has forged with President Bush. Howard spoke of his resolve when addressing a joint sitting of the US Congress on 12 July 2002:

> Through these times Australians have shared your shock and anger and have been partners in your resolve. We have taken our place beside you in the fight against terrorism, because what happened last year in the United States was as much an attack upon our nation and the values that we hold dear, as it was upon yours.

This shared experience was amplified after 12 October 2002, when 88 Australians were among over 200 people killed in a terrorist attack on the Sari Club in Kuta Beach, Bali, Indonesia. Like the attacks on 9/11, the Bali bombings were soon linked conclusively with Muslim extremists. Outside the Australian continent, few places hold as iconic a place in modern Australian identity as Kuta Beach, which keeps company with other destinations such as Earls Court, the Kokoda trail and Gallipoli. Like following a triumphant Australian sporting team at Lords or Twickenham, visiting these destinations is a rite of passage for many Australians. Kuta Beach is a much favoured holiday getaway for Australians in general and sporting clubs in particular, who visit in large numbers to celebrate the end of their competitive seasons (a significant number of those killed at the Sari Club were team members of Australian sporting clubs). There was much symbolism in the targeting of such a popular destination for Australians. As a result, the Bali bombing touched the psyche of the broad populace in a way an attack in a more unfamiliar place would not have. It created a reaction among many Australians somewhat similar to the American response to the 9/11 attack with references to the Bali bombing as 'Australia's September 11'.[3] Two weeks after the Bali bombings, a Hawker Britton–UMR poll in Australia reported that almost twice as many respondents said that the bombings made them more likely (24 per cent) rather than less likely (14 per cent) to 'approve of Australian military participation in an attack on Iraq' (Goot 2003).

The Australian government has also been fully supportive on both a personal and a policy level when faced with the discourse of the Bush administration. Howard is often found defending the latest announcement from Washington to the local press. On a policy level, too, the Howard government's mindset mirrors the less 'multilateralist' attitude of the Bush administration, sharing its concerns about the wisdom of the UN and also showing a similar reluctance to sign international agreements simply because they have been passed by most European nations. A notable example of this shared outlook is the negative position both governments have taken on the Kyoto Protocol. New Zealand, in contrast, recently ratified the Protocol, emblematic of a foreign policy outlook that has far more in common with the social democratic states of Europe than that of Australia or the US (Kerr 2004: 8). Even on the subject of America's controversial treatment of its Guantánamo Bay prisoners, the Australian government has remained silent despite the incarceration of two Australian citizens.

Australia as supporter of the Bush administration

The level of support the Australian government has given the US since 9/11 has been quite extraordinary. In addition to sending combat troops into war with the US in Iraq, Australia has signed up to the US missile defence shield and has generally strengthened its military, political and economic ties with the US whenever the opportunity has arisen. These decisions and actions make Australia part of a small group of nations that have continuously supported the Bush Doctrine and moved closer to the US since Bush's election. Reflecting on the Australia–US relationship, two leading experts on the alliance, Rod Lyon and Bill Tow (2003), recently described it as reaching a 'new zenith' under the Howard government.

The Howard government's embrace of the Bush administration has occurred in the face of considerable disagreement from Australia's main opposition party, the Labor Party, and at best lukewarm support from the public, who remain strongly supportive of the ANZUS alliance, but are considerably less taken with the Bush administration (McAllister *et al.* 2004). Thus, the Australian government's support of the Bush Doctrine is more ambivalent than the tag 'loyal Aussies' suggests. This is particularly reflected in opinion polls, which have shown little support for President Bush.[4] The various outbursts by Labor Party MP Mark Latham, such as his claim in the Australian parliament that Bush was the 'most incompetent and dangerous president in living memory',[5] reflect a viewpoint shared by 45 per cent of the population according to one poll.[6] Similarly, it would be incorrect to see New Zealand's leaders as completely anti-Bush. Although the current Labour government and Prime Minister Helen Clark have not been persuaded by Bush and his foreign policy, Don Brash, the leader of the biggest opposition party, the Nationals, sounds very much like a New Zealand version of John Howard, keen to see New Zealand offer stronger support to the Bush administration. Along with these differences between the major parties in New Zealand and Australia, another complicating factor is the often contradictory nature of public opinion. One example of public ambivalence towards the US can be found in a major survey of Australian public opinion on US foreign policy conducted on 16 May 2003 where 43 per cent of those questioned said 'American foreign policy has a negative effect on Australia' as opposed to 31 per cent who thought it had a positive effect. At the same time, 62 per cent thought the 'military action in Iraq by the US and it allies was justified'.[7] Such contradictions within the mindset of the general public remind us of how strong a role the government of the day can play in ultimately shaping a nation's position in the face of conflicting public opinion such as existed regarding the Iraq war in Australia. The pivotal role that governments play in this regard makes election victories and the visions and styles of individual political leaders particularly significant. John Howard presents as a case in point.

Howard has undoubtedly taken certain risks to strengthen the Australia–US alliance since 9/11. His decision to send Australian troops to Iraq in the face of general popular opposition throughout 2002 – one national poll showed support for an American attack as low as 33 per cent (Goot 2003) – and his personal support for a generally unpopular President Bush point to the importance he attaches to the US alliance. He has taken every opportunity to strengthen what he sees as Australia's special relationship with the US, a relationship that squares with his own sense of history and values; as he puts it 'it is a relationship steeped in history, but it's also a relationship that is built upon common values'.[8] The history that Howard is principally referring to is the shared service in the two world wars, a point he emphasized in his 2003 parliamentary welcome to President Bush.[9] Elsewhere, Howard has commented that Americans 'have a lot of the values and attitudes that we share' and that he is 'a great believer that you should have close relations with the countries whose way of life is closest to your own' (Harries 2004). The strengthened alliance with the US has afforded Howard closer contact with the president than is typical for an Australian prime minister. Reflecting this chumminess, Bush described Howard as 'a man of steel' during Howard's visit to Crawford, Texas, and, in Bush's address to the Australian parliament in October 2003, he proffered that 'Prime Minister John Howard is a leader of exceptional courage who exemplifies the finest qualities of one of the world's greatest democracies. I am proud to call him friend.'[10]

It is not inconceivable to imagine other Australian politicians, from both sides of politics, adopting a similar approach to that of Howard, such is the importance attached to the Australia–US alliance. It has been suggested that Australia–US bilateral relations are among the world's most intimate (Tow 2004). Although this would seem to overestimate the importance of Australia to the US, it is clear the Howard government would like to see the relationship as one of America's closest. In Australian government circles, the praise and attention of leaders such as George W. Bush[11] and other members of the US government is highly sought after (Tow 2004: 275). To doubt how crucial this alliance is regarded among a broad range of Australian politicians and in elite foreign policy circles would be to misread Australian politics. For example, when Mark Latham became leader of the Australian Labor Party in

December 2003, one of his first media events was a press conference in front of an Australian and an American flag reaffirming his commitment to the security alliance between the two nations,[12] an act that reflects the power the alliance ultimately holds in Australian elite politics. None of this, however, diminishes the significance of Howard's role in strengthening alliance relations. Howard has *achieved* the goal of a stronger Australia–US relationship, rather than simply favouring this outcome, and this makes an understanding of his leadership crucial for our purposes.

According to his critics, Howard has strengthened this relationship at a terrible cost to his nation. When comparing Howard's and Blair's reasons for supporting the US position on Iraq, the former Australian intelligence officer, Andrew Wilkie (2004: 74), wrote that they 'found themselves driven mostly by their obsession with fostering their countries' relationships with the US at any cost; in practice, what this amounted to was ingratiating themselves with Bush by supporting a war which they both had known for a long time was inevitable'. Both Howard and Blair reject the regular mocking of them as Bush's 'poodles', believing instead that they have actively engaged with the Bush administration to achieve short- and long-term benefits for their respective nations. These assumed benefits, however, have not been articulated to the public particularly well and, as a result, the fires of anti-Americanism have been stoked in both countries. The noted rise of anti-Americanism in Britain and Australia is certainly not just among the liberal intelligentsia – the 'café-latte set' as they are called in Australia – but is a broad-based phenomenon with the breadth of this dissent most apparent during the lead-up to the 2003 Iraq war. However, the absence of Australian military deaths in Iraq has probably reduced the issue's impact on Howard's political standing with the Australian public.

A Howard-led alliance

Howard has dominated Australian federal politics for the last decade. Since first being elected prime minister in 1996, he has gone on to win a further three terms in office. Howard did moot retiring after his 65th birthday but changed his mind in 2003, stating that the climate of international terror made it the wrong time to leave. He also seemed to be enjoying the job and his place in the Bush inner sanctum too much to retire.[13] John Winston Howard, like George W. Bush, is not particularly admired by academic commentators, with much of the commentary written on him decidedly negative (Manne 2001, 2004). Like Bush, his scruples and honesty are regularly questioned. However, Howard and Bush are decidedly different political characters. John Howard is a crafty lifetime politician, rather in the Bob Dole or, as one critic has suggested, Richard Nixon mould (Rundle 2001). Like Nixon, Howard is a fastidious worker and a formidable campaign strategist with an impressive command of the details of the political issues of the day. He also has something of Nixon's chip on his shoulder as the result of early and deep political scars. His 1987 loss as his party's leader and the bitter internal rivalries he has endured would have ended the career of a less tenacious politician. He also shares Nixon's discomfort in front of the camera, lacking the 'natural' political charm of a Clinton or even a George Bush.

To his critics, Howard also has Nixon's Machiavellian streak, with his election victories being delivered by means both fair or foul. Nixon is famously associated with the rise of wedge politics in US presidential politics with his 1968 'Southern strategy'. Howard is seen as the Australian master of wedge politics with his 2001 election campaign based significantly on attacking the arrival of illegal refugees on Australian shores (Weller 2002; Marr and Wilkinson 2004). This assessment of Howard has seen him regularly labelled as a poll-driven politician who calibrates his actions for public manipulation (Wesley 2001; Flitton 2002). The Nixonian view of Howard, however, coexists with a view of Howard as a conviction politician rather in the mould of Margaret Thatcher, whom Howard is known to much admire. Certainly, Howard can stubbornly hold a political position in a manner not unlike Mrs Thatcher. However, these two views of Howard create obvious contradictions and suggest that he is still something of an enigma despite being a member of the Australian federal parliament since 1974. Two seasoned commentators who have written recent books on Howard reflect this confusion. Alison Broinowski (2003: 23) wrote that Howard is 'the most poll-driven prime minister in years' with a 'reputation for following and appealing to popular opinion' (ibid.: 1), whereas Robert Garran (2004: 14) wrote, 'Like George W. Bush, Howard is a conviction politician who asserts his moral rectitude.'

More useful than seeing Howard as either the great manipulator or a man of conviction is to see him instead as a tenacious politician who is a traditionalist by nature, most comfortable forging an Australian nationalism that builds on existing traditions and alliances. For critics, this traditionalism has seem him turn his back on issues such as reconciliation with Australia's indigenous people and the fostering of a multicultural Australia. Rather than such progressive causes, Howard has returned to the conservative themes of strong families, a strong economy and strong alliances with powerful friends, reigniting the legacy of his Australian political forefather Robert Menzies.

According to his critics, Howard's traditionalism in the foreign affairs arena has seen him turn Australia away from Asia, with Australia becoming little more than an American proxy as a result (Garnaut 2002; Beeson 2003: Capling 2003). As one critic put it: 'Howard has resurrected an anachronistic and counterproductive image of Australia [in Asia] as an uncritical supporter of the United States' (Garran 2004: 203, discussing Verrier 2003). This critique overstates the reality. The obvious retort is that any talk of Australia's relations with 'Asia' is a misnomer as it homogenizes a diverse range of nations with which Australia has quite distinct and individual relations. Moreover, some Asian nations, like Australia, are closely aligned with the US, whereas others are much more sceptical of America. To comment on general Asian attitudes is probably only relevant on the broadest of issues such as

Bush's remark that the US sees Australia as a 'sheriff' of the Asia–Pacific. Obviously, loose talk by Bush or Howard of Australia as America's 'sheriff' or 'deputy sheriff' in the Asia–Pacific region is offensive and likely to provoke anti-Australian sentiment (Tow 2004) and reinforce the view of Australia as an American surrogate. It gave credence to the rhetoric of leaders such as Malaysia's Mahathir Mohamed who responded that Australia would not be accepted in the region while it continued to play 'deputy sheriff' to the US.[14] The Howard government's rhetoric – at times called megaphone diplomacy – is reminiscent of the Bush administration's brusque style, which has fanned the flames of anti-Americanism. In both countries, relationships with neighbours and allies could have been approached with far more subtlety and nuance. However, much of what is deemed offensive is principally calibrated for domestic audiences.

Although Howard has described the claim that Australia's closeness with the US hinders its capacity to develop close ties with Asia as 'one of the great myths of the foreign policy and trade debate in this country', it is not entirely surprising that this view is associated with Howard and his government. Howard has been the subject of long-standing suspicions regarding his attitude to the Asian region due to his own personal record on Asian immigration. As leader of the opposition in the 1980s, he questioned the volume of Asian immigration to Australia and speculated that it was changing Australian society for the worse. In his early years as Prime Minster, his at times tepid public responses to the rise of Pauline Hanson, who vocally attacked the 'Asianization of Australia', reinforced the belief that Howard was insensitive towards the Asian region. Howard's public rhetoric on Asia since becoming prime minister has often been a direct reaction to the engagement rhetoric of his predecessor Paul Keating, making the Howard government's change in direction similar to the current Bush administration's early 'anything but Clinton' approach to foreign affairs. Howard has described his position as seeking a better balance so that Australia does not feel forced to choose between 'its geography and its history'; however, there is undoubtedly a populist element to his rhetoric aimed at comforting a part of the electorate uneasy with the promotion of Australia's increased integration with Asia.

The Bush–Howard embrace

The election of the Howard-led Liberal Party/National Party coalition on 11 March 1996 could be seen as a turning point in Australia–US relations, with Australia refocusing its foreign policy towards the US from that date. This perception, however, has been strongly disputed by the former Labor Party leader Kim Beazley as under-representing Labor's strong relationship with the US (Beazley 1998). Independent commentators, such as the conservative columnist Gerard Henderson (2004), have similarly acknowledged that the Labor governments of Prime Ministers Hawke and Keating (1983–96) were firmly committed to the US alliance, with the Hawke government a strong supporter of the US during the 1991 Gulf War. The myth/perception that Australia moved away from the US is associated with the Keating government (1991–6). Paul Keating clearly made increasing Australia's engagement with Asia a priority of his foreign policy, with varying degrees of success achieved across the region. John Howard dubbed this policy Keating's 'Asia only' approach to foreign affairs. However, even Howard found 'astonishing' and 'absurd' (Garran 2004: 52) Samuel Huntington's (1996) assessment in *The Clash of Civilisations* that, during the mid-1990s, Australia was 'torn'[15] between the cultures and values of the West and Asia.

Howard did undoubtedly seize on negative perceptions about Keating's foreign policy approach, and his rhetoric towards the Asian region has generally been less cautious than Keating's. At the same time, from the outset, the Howard government emphasized its policy to 'reinvigorate' political, economic and strategy relations with the US (Tow 2004: 2). However, as Tow has argued, this 'somewhat puzzled American policy officials and independent observers' as the alliance already seemed in healthy shape. Nonetheless, the Howard government's rhetoric and offers to provide a site for the prepositioning of US military equipment (politely declined as it was considered too far from any potential conflict) did coincide with the US experiencing conflicts with Japan over Okinawa, with South Korea over US bilateral negotiations with North Korea, and with Thailand and the Philippines over the issue of US military access to their territories (Tow 2004: 3).

Despite the Howard government's friendly rhetoric towards the US and the upgrading of military training and intelligence exchanges, diplomatic relations certainly had their ups and downs during the Clinton administration's tenure. In a 1997 speech, the US Ambassador to Australia, Genta Hawkins Holmes, criticized 'Australia's support of "differentiated targets" based on national economic costs as a rationale for continuing to rely excessively on fossil fuel energy sources' (Tow 2004: 11). This disagreement over climate control seems a world away from recent Australia–US relations and reflects the significant differences between the Clinton and Bush administrations on the Kyoto Protocol and other issues related to global warming and the environment.

Another issue that highlighted less than perfect lines of communication between the Howard and Clinton governments was Australian military involvement in East Timor in 1999. The US was slow to confirm its support for this action, something that initially increased the risks of the operation for Australia. More generally, Howard's personal relationship with Clinton was far removed from his chummy friendship with Bush.[16] In a 1999 visit to Washington, Howard arrived to hear that the Clinton administration had announced the imposition of quotas on Australian lamb imports.[17] He was then accorded a rather short meeting with Clinton, at which the American president arrived late. In a recent interview, Howard's Foreign Minister Alexander Downer commented that Howard was not terribly excited by Clinton's victory in 1996; however, 'by the time the 2000 election came around, we [he and Howard] were absolutely keen to see Bush win'.[18] And 'when Bush was finally confirmed as the next president, Howard and Downer sat down in the prime minister's office and had a glass of champagne to celebrate'.[19] Downer had been cultivating a relationship with Bush Junior since visiting Austin in 1997 when the then Australian Ambassador in Washington, DC, Andrew Peacock – an old friend of Bush Senior's – had predicted that George W. Bush would be the next US president. Once Bush was elected, Howard and Downer obviously felt there was a new opportunity to become much closer to the US; the events of 11 September 2001 and the subsequent 'war on terror' brought Howard into the Bush administration's inner circle, making him one of Bush's most loyal and trusted international allies. However, the development of this bond faced a serious litmus test with the US declaration of war on Iraq.

The Iraq loyalty test

Public support for Australia to go to war with the US in Iraq was never strong. In the early months of 2003, a sizeable majority of Australians opposed Australian troops being sent to war without UN endorsement.[20] The government did enjoy a swing towards its position in opinion polls on the war's eve. However, at the same time, anti-war sentiment was considerable and vocal. On the weekend of 14–16 February 2003, over 500,000 people took part in rallies against the Iraq war across Australia, including Australia's largest ever demonstration of around 250,000 people in Sydney.[21] Despite the protests and calls for more time to be given to the UN weapons inspections process in Iraq, Australia went to war. Bob Woodward's (2004) revelation of Bush's eleventh hour offer to Blair for Britain to take a pass on sending troops to Iraq for the initial combat phase is fascinating to contemplate, given the very awkward position this would have left Howard in. The obvious question is 'would Australia also have been given this option or was its loyalty taken for granted?'

The official engagement of Australian troops covered a 21-day period in March/April 2003 in which Saddam's regime was comprehensively defeated without a single Australian soldier being killed. Howard's shrewd commitment of Australian troops for the duration of the war with a limited post-war role[22] has not totally alleviated public scepticism about the war, but this more limited role, coupled with a lack of casualties, has reduced the political fallout. At the same time, the role Australia has played has strengthened its alliance with the US. In some circles, this has been seen as a masterstroke. However, the general public seems decidedly ambivalent about these closer ties; this was reflected in Howard not making Australia's strengthened relations with the US a major election issue in the October 2004 federal election.

In the lead-up to the Iraq conflict, the Howard government's line on why war was necessary mirrored the American position. Although Iraq posed no direct threat to Australia (Wilkie 2004: 65–6), the government gave the public a list of reasons for grave concern. In his parliamentary case for the war, the Foreign Minister Alexander Downer stated that the 'issue about Iraq' was 'whether the world has any choice but other than to live in the constant fear of chemical, biological and nuclear weapons left in the hands of vicious dictators'.[23] Following the US lead, the prime minister argued that these weapons of mass destruction (WMD) could 'fall into the hands of terrorists', which he said would be the 'ultimate nightmare not only for us but other peoples in other nations. That, more than anything else, is the reason why we have taken the stance we have.'[24] However, a less circuitous and more honest reason why Australia went to war was because America did.

In Australia, Andrew Wilkie, on resigning on 11 March 2003 from his job at the Office of National Assessments (ONA), where he had been working on intelligence on Iraqi weapons, highlighted cracks in the case against Iraq:

> Iraq does not pose a security threat to the US, to the UK, to Australia or another country at this point in time . . . Their military is very small, their weapons of mass destruction program is fragmented and contained, and there is no hard evidence of active cooperation between Iraq and al Qaeda.
>
> (Barker 2003: 48)

Former ONA employees Carl Ungerer and David Wright-Neville also repeated this dissent from within the intelligence community.[25]

The likely fallout of the Iraq war on the Australia–US alliance is that future American military actions in the Middle East or elsewhere are likely to be met with even greater public scepticism than this conflict, potentially leaving future Australian governments less willing to join any US-led coalition (for a more detailed discussion of this issue, see O'Connor 2004). The image of the Howard government as a pliant deputy to the Bush administration definitely has traction in the community and is an image reinforced by Australia's overly accommodating approach in the recent Australia–US Free Trade Agreement (FTA) negotiations (Weiss *et al.* 2004). As Owen Harries (2004) suggested in his recent Boyer Lectures, powerful allies are often unreliable friends. An overenthusiastic pursuit of the alliance could lead to faulty decisions about Australia's national interests or an inability to heed independent judgements and opinions from within Australia. The debates over prewar intelligence on Iraq and the Australia–US FTA bring these concerns to the fore. It had been suggested that Australia's support of America in Iraq would speed up trade negotiations between the two countries[26] and help Australia secure important concessions from US negotiators on exports dear to Australia such as sugar and beef. However, reports in the *Australian* newspaper have it that a direct plea from Howard to Bush for greater concessions to Australia in the FTA were rebuffed by Bush as the negotiations reached the critical phases of putting final offers on the table.[27]

Conclusion

The Bush presidency has strained America's foreign relations with numerous nations, including many long-time friends. Australia, however, presents as an interesting contrast to this general trend, unquestionably strengthening its relationship with the US during Bush's term in office. On the other hand, Australia's neighbour New Zealand has shown little enthusiasm for the Bush administration and continues to craft an independent foreign policy on a shoestring budget. The differing paths of these two nations are not just a product of the policies and actions of the Bush administration; their foreign policy trajectories have been diverging ever since New Zealand's 1984 decision not to allow nuclear weapons or nuclear-powered ships into its harbours. Nonetheless, recent events have substantially widened the gap between the foreign policies of these two countries. Clearly, the Australian government has made significant decisions since 9/11 that have seen Australia forge a very close relationship with the US. As I have argued throughout this chapter, the role of Australia's Prime Minister John Howard has been crucial in cementing this new intimacy between the US and Australia. The President and other leading officials such as US Deputy Secretary of State Richard Armitage, who fought alongside Australians in the Vietnam War and formed strong bonds with a number of them, have shared Howard's push for a stronger relationship.[28] The benefits of a closer relationship with the US are at times so immediately assumed by Australian politicians that they often do not care to articulate them particularly well or to examine countervailing evidence, with a classic example being the manner in which most incumbent federal and state government politicians lined up automaton-like to support the Australia–US FTA (Weiss *et al.* 2004). Like increased trade with the US, a closer strategic and military relationship is always assumed to be in Australia's best interest. However, there are questions that require more vigorous debate. Does Australia's closer relationship with the US make it a target of America's enemies? Is Australia wise to be purchasing US military equipment that is of little use in defending the Australian mainland but allows easier integration into US defence systems and training manoeuvres?[29] Those who question the wisdom of such decisions look to New Zealand admiringly, believing it has struck upon a more sensible path.

Notes

1 These estimates use the Australian standards for defining defence spending. For Australian defence spending, see http://www.defence.gov.au/budget/04-05/pbs/2004-2005_Defence_PBS_03_Ch2.pdf and, for New Zealand, see http://www.defence.govt.nz/public_docs/elecbrief2002/.

2 Helen Clark, Address to the NZ Institute of International Affairs, 23 June, 2004; New Zealand Ministry of Foreign Affairs and Trade, Report of the Ministry of Foreign Affairs and Trade, 2003.

3 Colin Powell, 'Interview with Barrie Cassidy', http://abc.net.au/insiders/content/2002/s705789.htm.

4   Peter Hartcher, 'Anti-Bush not anti-American', *Guardian*, 15 October 2004.

5   Latham also claimed that 'President Bush's foreign policy looks more like American imperialism than a well thought through and resourced strategy to eliminate terrorists' and dismissed Howard as a 'yes-man to a flaky and dangerous American president' (Mark Latham, Address to the House of Representatives, Canberra, 5 February, 2004). These remarks and others by ALP politicians prompted US Ambassador J. Thomas Schieffer briefly to enter the political fray to express his disapproval of the ALP rhetoric (see Maxine McKew, 'Tom Schieffer United States Ambassador', *Bulletin*, 12 February, 2003). This entry into domestic Australian politics by a foreign diplomat was widely criticized. Latham's 2004 promise that he would bring the troops home by Christmas again saw Schieffer publicly criticize him (see Brendon O'Connor, 'Australia, an ally, not a servant', *Courier Mail*, 5 April 2004). This criticism of Latham was later strongly repeated by George W. Bush during Howard's June 2004 visit to the US, http://www.abc.net.au/am/content/2004/s1124330.htm.

6   In a 2004 AC Nielsen AgePoll, 45 per cent of Australians agreed with Latham that Bush was 'incompetent and dangerous', http://theage.com.au/articles/2003/12/09/1070732212139.html.

7   Morgan Poll 'Is the US too keen to use military force in other countries?', 16 May 2003, http://www.roymorgan.com/news/polls/2003/3627/index.cfm.

8   John Howard, Address to the Australian American Association, Melbourne, 2 September 2003.

9   John Howard, Address to the House of Representatives, Canberra, 23 October 2003.

10 George W. Bush, Address to the House of Representatives, Canberra, 23 October 2004.

11 John Wright, 'Dear John', *Bulletin*, 10 November 2004.

12 Ross Peake, 'Latham backs US alliance', *Canberra Times*, 5 December 2003.

13 Wilkie, writing on Howard's reasons for supporting the war against Iraq, states it was 'part ideological, part egotistical' (Wilkie 2004: 74).

14 Mark Baker, 'Mahatir signs off with swipe at Australia', *The Age*, 9 October 2003.

15 Huntington's description of Australia as a 'torn country' does make one question the quality of his research, as it is a serious misreading of Australian national identity (see Huntington 1996).

16 Wright, 'Dear John', *Bulletin*, 10 November 2004.

17 Ibid.

18 Downer quoted in Wright, ibid.

19 Wright, ibid.

20 Newspoll, 2003, http://www.newspoll.com.au/cgi-bin/display_poll_data.pl.

21 Valerie Lawson, 'With one voice, the world says no', *The Age*, 17 February 2003; Marcus Priest, 'PM not swayed by size of peace rallies', *Australian Financial Review*, 17 February 2003.

22 For the type of forces Australia provided, see Andrew O'Neil, 'Issues in Australian foreign policy: January to June 2003', *Australian Journal of Politics and History* 49 (4) 2003, p. 544. See also http://www.defence.gov.au/opfalconer/, which provides a list of initial and immediate post-war Australian military involvements in Iraq. Since 16 July, the defence personnel commitments in Iraq have been titled Operation Catalyst, with details of this commitment available at http://www.defence.gov.au/opcatalyst/.

23 Alexander Downer, Address to the House of Representatives, Canberra, 18 March 2003.

24 John Howard, Address to the National Press Club, Canberra, 14 March 2003.

25 Mark Forbes, 'Iraq claims hardened after Bush call', *The Age*, 3 March 2004;

Cameron Stewart, 'The blame game', *Australian*, 7 February, 2004; Carl Ungerer, 'Iraq intelligence driven by politics', *Australian*, 2 March 2004.

26 *The Australian*, 'Scrapbook', 12 February 2004.

27 Christine Wallace, 'Bush rebuff stunned negotiators', *Australian*, 25 February 2004.

28 Peter Hartcher, 'From dunny escape to a done deal', *Sydney Morning Herald*, 29 November 2004.

29 Gary Brown, 'Life with a superpower', *Australian Financial Review*, 1 October 2004.

11 International security

Alastair Finlan

In the words of *The 9/11 Commission Report* (2004: xv), 'September 11, 2001, was a day of unprecedented shock and suffering in the history of the United States. The nation was unprepared.' It has been estimated that just under 3,000 people died in the combined attacks (Woodward 2004: 24). What made this attack so different from a previous surprise attack on the US, that of Pearl Harbor in 1941, was its very nature, stemming not from a nation-state but rather from a small band of transnational terrorists, and consequently seeming 'in some ways more devastating' (*The 9/11 Commission Report* 2004: 339).

The use of American commercial aeroplanes as the means of inflicting this humiliating blow added to the sense of shock, as it was breathtakingly asymmetric. Above all other considerations, it easily overcame America's defences that were attuned to traditional methods of attack along symmetric lines in terms of either an assault by another state (ballistic missiles or conventional forces) or traditional-style terrorists using bombs. On an equally worrying scale, it demonstrated an ability to imagine warfare in a different way – one that was unorthodox and used aspects of globalization (international travel, technology transfer/training and modern communications) to the full. The upshot of this deadly combination was that, the day after 9/11, the US was filled with an almost unprecedented sense of danger and vulnerability. As David Campbell (1998: 2) reminds us, 'danger is an effect of interpretation' and, in this light, it is unsurprising that the sheer magnitude of 9/11 has been reflected in one of the most radical reinterpretations of international security in half a century.

The National Security Strategy 2002

It is easy to underestimate the reverberations of 9/11 on the American psyche. The enormous size and power of the US that is taken for granted on a global scale on so many different levels, from Coca Cola to Microsoft, belies a simple fact that the US is a rather sensitive giant. Unlike other developed nation-states, the US has enjoyed a peculiarly sheltered existence in which, apart from the torrid days of independence from colonial masters, warfare (excluding the Civil War) has been at a distance for the vast majority of Americans. Even in the twentieth century, unlike the continental European powers, wars were fought in other people's lands while the American homeland remained safe, to the point that Americans could virtually detach themselves in a social sense from their returning warriors who had fought in an unpopular military adventure in South-East Asia. Had 9/11 occurred on mainland Europe, then for people still steeped in the social memory of the Blitz, the firestorms of Hamburg and Dresden, with living relatives of such tragedies, the impact – although great – would have been mapped in the mass consciousness within the context of much greater catastrophes. For America, the airliners crashed not only into buildings but also into its social awareness of the outside world without the consoling memory of worse experiences with similar characteristics that could help to temper the trauma. For a nation without a national newspaper, 9/11 reminded the entire continent that another world existed beyond state county lines and outside US federal jurisdiction. Consequently, in the light of this horror and the gradual transition from shock to anger, it was not unexpected that radical expressions of how to look at the outside world (beyond the now less protective Atlantic and Pacific Oceans) should emerge from government.

Arguably, the most important policy document to arise from the aftermath of al-Qaeda's attack was *The National Security Strategy of the United States of America* (NSS; White House 2002). The foreword, signed by George W. Bush, is revealing:

> Today, the United States enjoys a position of unparalleled military strength and great economic and political influence. In keeping with our heritage and principles, we do not use our strength to press for unilateral advantage. We seek instead to create a balance of power that favors human freedom.

It is significant that this statement should give primacy to the *unparalleled military strength* of the US over economic and political considerations. This prominence, in combination with concepts such as 'balance of power' and 'great powers' (White House 2002), mirrors the ideas of the remarkable number of neo-conservatives[1] in his administration and their interpretation of world affairs.[2] The foreword also reveals a broadening of the remit of future military operations to include 'tyrants' as well as terrorists. Taken at face value, this overtly muscular approach to international security promises a conflict-rich future, as the US will antagonize every non-free and closed society by encouraging their citizens to embrace the American vision. Extending 'the peace' will really mean engaging – with aggressive intent – nations who do not meet the critical criteria for non-interference: great power status. This will, of course, encourage weaker powers to acquire great power status (which in the modern age necessitates the development of nuclear weapons) in order to avoid a future conflict with the US.

The NSS is an intriguing *tour d'horizon* of the Bush administration's view of international security that has parallels in thinking with his father's government but, given the number of policy-makers who have served both presidents (such as Cheney, Rice and Wolfowitz), it is, to a degree, unsurprising. First and foremost, the document has echoes with his father's idea of a 'new world order' set out in 1990 (Bobbitt 2003: 243). It argues that 'The US national security strategy will be based on a distinctly American internationalism that reflects the union of our values and our national interests. The aim of this strategy is to help make the world not just safer but better' (White House 2002: 1). It is a truly global vision of security and one that clearly identifies the threat from 'failing' (ibid.) states and 'catastrophic technologies in the hands of the embittered few' (ibid.). That said, it is important to note that the context is very different from that of 1990, particularly as the structure of the international system was not changed by 9/11 (see Litwak 2002–03: 58, who stresses that 'the 11 September attacks did not alter the structure of international relations'), unlike the collapse of the Soviet Union that ended the Cold War. Consequently, there is a clear danger that the NSS's grand design may be asymmetric in terms of scale to the nature of the threat (a relatively small band of transnational terrorists[3]) and will, inadvertently as well as unnecessarily, widen the scope of conflict. After all, tackling terrorists requires considerably less resources than openly declaring war on a state (failing or not). The declaration of a 'war on terror' after 9/11 certainly runs the risk of an almost infinite conflict because it raises the question of whether an abstract noun can be defeated. The NSS, however, displays no such concerns by confidently asserting that 'The struggle against global terrorism is different from any other war in our history. It will be fought on many fronts against a particularly elusive enemy over an extended period of time' (White House 2002: 5). Once more, it has an eerie resonance with the 'war on drugs' promoted by George Bush Senior (Mutimer 1999: 90), which continues in its own immeasurable fashion to the present day. From a costs/gains analysis, the lack of care that the Bush dynasty has consistently demonstrated in the use of powerful terms such as 'war', the significance of which, as Sun Tzu warns, 'is a matter of vital importance to the State' (Griffith 1971: 63), means the US faces the prospect of two open-ended conflicts with no foreseeable conclusion. Finally, the strategic vista of the NSS is simply breathtaking, in particular the manner in which the world is divided up on a regional basis into theatres of operations to generate a 'coordinated effort that isolates the terrorists' (White House 2002: 6). Each region is tackled in order of importance from the Middle East to South Asia, Latin America and lastly Africa (White House 2002: 9–10). It makes the focus on blocs during the Cold War, between East and West with a notable emphasis on the Western European theatre, seem limited and constrained at best; however, it is important to note that US military forces, despite increased spending in recent years,[4] are significantly smaller than during the bipolar division of the world.[5]

New security environment

The most radical aspect of the NSS concerns its conception of the new security environment and how old ideas such as deterrence are inappropriate for the 'new deadly challenges' posed by 'rogue states and terrorists' (White House 2002: 13). Its underlying assumptions encapsulate an extremely dark vision of the future.[6] Through this harsh lens, it is assumed that there is a connection between rogue states and terrorists that has yet to be proved,[7] but it does provide a bridge (that spans a massive chasm of credibility for linkage arguments) between weapons of mass destruction (WMD) and terrorists. Additionally, the employment of the term 'weapons of mass destruction' conveniently blends a variety of different weapons that range from the mildly difficult to the extremely difficult to produce. In essence, it lowers the acquisition threshold for terrorists, which can be dropped to an even lower level if a linkage with rogue states is established. However, this opaque and threatening fog of strategic worst-case scenarios is quickly dispelled by a specific analysis of the difficulties in producing such weapons on a category-by-category basis.

The development of nuclear weapons, for instance, took all the resources of the US, virtually the entire course of World War II and $2 billion (Alperovitz 1995: 654) to drop two quite small fission bombs on Japan in 1945. No terrorist organization has (or is likely to have in the near future) the necessary level of finance or infrastructure to produce a bomb from scratch even with the benefits of contemporary knowledge. Only states have the resources to manufacture such weapons. Biological weapons are likewise very difficult to produce *in a weaponized form*, and the recent use of anthrax in the US suggests that it can be effectively contained.[8] Chemical weapons are the easiest to produce; however, they need to be used in relatively large quantities and are heavily dependent on environmental conditions (surface temperature and wind) to work effectively. In addition, they can be countered by gas masks and NBC (nuclear, biological and chemical suits) relatively easily. Analysed from this perspective, the link between terrorists and WMD is tenuous at best (although such organizations may openly articulate desires to acquire them), and the worst-case scenario (of the smoking gun being transformed into 'a mushroom cloud')[9] becomes credible only if the resources of a state are somehow brought to bear to aid them. In other words, it demands a suspension of disbelief that, having spent vast resources on developing these weapons on a covert basis, a rogue state will just 'give' (or perhaps sell) one of these great power status bombs to a ragtag terrorist group. Notwithstanding this unlikely scenario – that appears to draw more from Hollywood movies than hard evidence – the number of states with WMD to dish out is still quite small ('Over two dozen states possess WMD'; see Clarke 2004: 267). These worst-case assumptions without the vital balancing caveats offer a frightening portrait of the future that bears little relation to the actual strategic situation.

Deterrence is not enough

The assault on the strategy of deterrence in the post-9/11 world is the critical foundation stone of the argument that 'times have changed' in terms of international security. For decades, deterrence has been at the heart of US international policies to prevent the outbreak of World War III and the subsequent chaos that it would bring to the international system of states. In the last 50 years, nuclear weapons have moved a long way from the devices (atomic bombs) dropped on Hiroshima and Nagasaki in 1945 to the infinitely more powerful thermonuclear weapons (hydrogen bombs) developed from the 1950s onwards. In crude terms, whereas the former are measured in kilotons (thousands of tons of TNT), the latter fall into the megaton category (millions of tons of TNT) and represent a much greater threat. In the light of the superpower rivalry between America and the Soviet Union, it was clear that, with the evolution of these extremely destructive weapons, a new strategy was needed: deterrence.

Deterrence has always been much more than just a strategy related to nuclear weapons. Its perpetuation and popularity across the millennia rests almost totally on its permanence in human affairs. According to Krause (1999: 121), deterrence can be defined as 'the use of threats to induce an opponent to act in desirable ways. In this respect, deterrence can be considered an enduring part of the calculus of war and peace, with *nuclear* deterrence merely being a special case in which the threat of punishment is overwhelming.' The absence of a nuclear exchange during the Cold War provides a degree of validation to the idea that the strategy of deterrence did play a significant part in preventing the use of these weapons. This, however, cut little ice with the NSS. In contrast, it argued that 'Traditional concepts of deterrence will not work against a terrorist enemy whose avowed tactics are wanton destruction and the targeting of innocents; whose so-called soldiers seek martyrdom in death and whose most potent protection is statelessness' (White House 2002: 15). The underlying assumption in the document is that terrorists without a state cannot be deterred by nuclear weapons.

Thus, the human element has been carefully drained out of the strategic equation based on the assumption that all terrorists are seeking 'martyrdom in death' and they cannot be deterred. In other words, these are irrational death-seeking automatons intent on killing innocents who do not adhere to accepted boundaries within the global political discourse. This vision of the new security environment is, however, debatable and ignores the idea of existential deterrence (see Freedman's (1988) discussion of McGeorge Bundy's concept of existential deterrence). In other words, the mere existence of America's arsenal of nuclear weapons, regardless of any strategy to use them, maintains the credibility of deterrence. It plays down the conclusion, which transcends global events such as 9/11 or even structural shifts (such as the Cold War's end), that anyone – whether state leader or terrorist – who breaks the nuclear taboo (Herring 1995: 42) and uses such weapons on the

American mainland will face nuclear retaliation. Furthermore, it is inconceivable that an American president will not respond to a nuclear strike in kind and with devastating effect on the point of origin of the threat. After all, the US quickly ascertained after 9/11 that the attacks had been directed from Afghanistan. In addition, the US remains one of the few countries that possesses the disposable power to destroy any country, region or, if necessary, continent if it so wishes. From this perspective, deterrence still operates at all levels of politics, from presidents to pariahs, beyond the state level down to the very personal human level. Times may have changed in the light of 9/11, but the cold logic of nuclear deterrence and its focus on values, cherished by people (regardless of belief or designation) around the world, has not. As Ken Booth (1991: 50) once remarked about the famous American strategist, Bernard Brodie, the founding father of the concept of nuclear deterrence, 'By insisting upon the centrality of politics in strategy, he tried to ensure that the study of war and the threat of war had a human face.' In contrast, the authors of the NSS have conveniently removed the human factor in order to strengthen their case against deterrence.

These concerns about the strategy of deterrence reflected a new appraisal of America's nuclear weapons arsenal that was published earlier in 2002, called the Nuclear Posture Review (NPR). According to one authoritative source, 'the NPR calls for a transformation of US strategic deterrence' (*Strategic Survey 2003/4* 2004), and the ideas contained in this document have significant ramifications for international security if they are fully implemented. In terms of defensive systems, the Bush administration, in the same vein as Reagan's proposed Strategic Defence Initiative (SDI) in the 1980s, is keen to develop 'an effective missile defence system' (White House 2002: 14) or, as it is more commonly called, national missile defence (NMD). Developing a successful anti-ballistic missile system has been the 'holy grail' of American strategic thinking since the early days of the Cold War, and policy-makers have set out on the quest on a regular basis every decade or so from the 1950s onwards. The reason is quite apparent, as Steve Andreasen (2004: 118) notes, 'Ballistic missiles armed with nuclear warheads remain the most fearsome weapon system ever devised. One missile fired in anger or by accident or miscalculation could produce tens of millions of casualties within minutes.' The quests have generally failed because of the technological difficulties of trying to defend against a mass ballistic missile attack and the sheer cost of trying to install missiles systems with their associated radars across the whole of the US. More importantly, and equally relevant to the current debate, is the impact of successfully deploying such systems for international security as a whole, in particular the consequences for deterrence. After all, deterrence was underpinned by 'the idea that *defensive* preparations such as civil defence or antiballistic missile systems were negative, and could upset deterrence by making a pre-emptive first strike less dangerous to an aggressor. This logic led the superpowers to sign the Anti-Ballistic Missile Treaty (ABMT) in 1972' (Krause 1999: 126). Put simply, a working NMD system might encourage America to adopt dangerously reckless policies in international relations safe in the knowledge that the homeland was insured against the threat of retaliation from ballistic missiles. Of course, all military technologies have limits, and NMD would not have been effective in the face of asymmetric attacks such as 9/11 but, in a worrying trend down this path, the US has recently withdrawn from the ABM treaty,[10] which suggests it desires to actively pursue the NMD option.

It has been estimated that the size of the US stockpile of nuclear weapons will fall from around 3,800 warheads in 2007 to between 1,700 and 2,200 by 2012 (*Strategic Survey 2003/04* 2004: 20). According to the *Strategic Survey 2003/04* (2004: 20–1), the 'planned "legacy triad" will eventually consist of 14 *Trident* ballistic-missile submarines, 500 *Minuteman* III intercontinental ballistic missiles (ICBMs), 76 B-52H bombers armed with cruise missiles and gravity bombs, and 21 B-2s armed with gravity bombs'. Put in context with a medium-sized nuclear power such as Britain that currently has 'fewer than 200'[11] operational nuclear warheads, it is still an awesome amount of disposable military force, and these large numbers of warheads with their associated delivery systems are more than enough to destroy any foreseeable future threat. The most controversial element of the NPR is the reactivation of research into low-yield nuclear weapons or 'mini-nukes' (that fall within the tactical nuclear weapons category) in order to investigate the possibility of developing more effective 'bunker busting' weapons. The 'robust nuclear earth penetrator' (*Strategic Survey 2003/04* 2004: 21–2) weapon has to overcome a variety of different challenges in order to be effective, not least of which is the ability to bury itself deep enough into its target to reduce the amount of nuclear contamination. The practical problems of using such weapons are illustrated in the following analysis:

> Even when they are made of the hardest steel, earth-penetrating warheads can only survive an impact of about one kilometre per second, giving a three-metre long warhead the ability to penetrate about 12 metres of steel-reinforced concrete. A penetration this shallow probably would not contain the explosive blast produced by the smallest nuclear warheads currently available, creating the prospect that nearby areas would be heavily contaminated by radioactive fallout.
>
> (*Strategic Survey 2003/04* 2004: 23)

This raises the question of whether mini-nukes designed for such a purpose are technologically feasible and, equally important, whether their use will merely lower the current threshold between conventional and nuclear weapons. If so, then US policy, should it initiate 'first use' of mini-nukes in a conflict, far from preventing the spread of these weapons, will in all likelihood encourage their employment in international affairs. Indeed, the development of such weapons could generate an arms race with other states imitating the US. Smaller and more usable nuclear weapons are also more attractive to non-state entities, such as terrorist organizations, that do not possess traditional delivery systems (military aircraft or ballistic missiles), but could smuggle a small device to an intended target. In the final analysis, the costs of developing and using mini-nukes are far outweighed by the disadvantages of setting such a precedent to the US and international society as a whole.

Pre-emptive and preventative approaches

The rejection of traditional shibboleths that have dominated international security for nearly half a century created a permissive environment to put forward and justify a new approach to meet the twin threats of 'radicalism and technology' (Record 2003: 4). Many of its key ideas are apparent in the NSS, yet it is most clearly identified with the part that emphasizes pre-emption, anticipatory action and the dangers posed by imminent threats (White House 2002: 15). In this respect, the document is coldly blunt: 'To forestall or prevent such hostile acts by our adversaries, the United States will, if necessary, act pre-emptively' (ibid.). Robert Jervis (2003: 365) neatly sums up the doctrine's basic thrust:

> The doctrine has four elements: a strong belief in the importance of a state's domestic regime in determining its foreign policy and the related judgment that this is an opportune time to transform international politics; the perception of great threats that can be defeated only by new and vigorous policies, most notably preventive war; a willingness to act unilaterally when necessary; and, as both a cause and a summary of these beliefs, an overriding sense that peace and stability require the United States to assert its primacy in world politics.

The Bush Doctrine has sparked a wide-ranging debate in academic journals (see Lafeber 2002; Litwak 2002–3; Freedman 2003; Heisbourg 2003; Jervis 2003; Rhodes 2003; Slocombe 2003) concerning the meaning of this specific aspect of future US strategy. Indeed, it is interesting how the debate has focused around the idea of preventive war even though the NSS specifically refers to pre-emption. Why the confusion? Antony Blinken (2003–4: 35) helpfully clarifies this critical point:

> The NSS is written in terms of 'pre-emption' but in fact makes a case for 'preventive' action. It's a distinction with an important difference: imminence. One acts 'pre-emptively' against an adversary whose fist is cocked. One acts 'preventively' against an adversary whose fist is not even raised, but who has been muscling up and might decide to strike you sometime in the future.

There is nothing new about the use of anticipatory self-defence in international relations, but it has been quite unusual, and the often-cited examples are the *Caroline* incident of 1837 (ibid.), when British soldiers used lethal force to neutralize an American vessel (the *Caroline* was in US waters at the time) that was supplying weapons to Canadian insurgents and, more recently, Israel's strike against Egyptian forces in 1967 (ibid.). The dangers, however, of the US explicitly adopting such actions are numerous. It may, for instance, cause a general destabilization of the international system – manifested in a proliferation of conflicts – or encourage the emergence of a new norm of intervention in international relations that 'could give licence to other states to do the same' (Litwak 2002–3: 59). As Francois Heisbourg (2003: 80) argues, 'International affirmation of the Bush doctrine could directly challenge the existing rules pertaining to the use of force in the world.' In the absence of a world government and the frailty of the UN that was so clearly exposed in the build-up to the invasion of Iraq in 2003, it is difficult not to envisage the spread of pre-emption – unless nation-states accept the 'exceptional' status of the US.

The concept of preventive war, however, is far more controversial than the idea of pre-emption. As Lawrence Freedman (2003: 107) stresses, the notion 'is cold blooded: it intends to deal with a problem before it becomes a crisis, while pre-emption is a more desperate strategy employed in the heat of crisis'. It is also much rarer in international relations with the best cited case referring not to a war, but rather to a specific action: the Israeli air strike on Iraq's Osiraq nuclear reactor in 1981 (Litwak 2002–3: 60; see also an interesting discussion on the legal aspects of this action in Taylor 2004: 62–3). Furthermore, the legal basis for such actions is highly questionable and often does not fall into the category of anticipatory self-defence that pre-emption can. It is forgotten that, in the aftermath of the Israeli strike, 'the international community roundly condemned them' (Taylor 2004: 62) for the attack. An air strike is one matter, but an all-out war on a state on the grounds of preventive action is quite another, with the implications being on a much higher order of scale. It is also questionable how the destruction of a functioning nation-state with all the associated collateral damage and loss of life among its civilian population can be justified in terms of making America safer. Surely, the consequences of the process will outweigh the benefits of the action and, in fact, the killing/murder/accidental death of innocents will merely generate more enemies of America.

The buzzword of the Bush administration after 9/11 has been regime change. However, regime change is not just a product of Republican dogma. It is a very old idea in international relations that has been evident throughout history: from the age of empires to the Cold War when the Soviet Union advanced into and occupied the states of Eastern Europe after World War II and, eventually, Afghanistan in 1979. The question remains as to how the US can persuade the international community that its leader's idea of regime change is not just neocolonialism clamouring to be liberal democracy, especially in those countries they are occupying. As Edward Rhodes (2003:

140) observes, 'While America's power imposes a special responsibility, Bush makes clear that the moral duty to defend and extend liberalism knows no borders. Societies and states are not free to eschew liberalism.' Again, as with pre-emption, a key danger is that the Bush administration is opening up a Pandora's box of preventive war – eyes wide shut – and, in fact, is ushering in a new age of uncertainty and interstate conflict as other powerful states may copy its example.

The Bush Doctrine in practice

The impact of the Bush Doctrine on international society over the years since 2001 has been immense. The war on terror has offered a very different portrait of the US in terms of internationalism and commitment to foreign adventures as opposed to the nation that agonized over casualties in Somalia in 1993.[12] In just two years, US military forces destroyed the Taleban regime in Afghanistan in 2001, scattered the al-Qaeda network and, in the face of widespread international opposition, invaded Iraq in 2003. Alongside these measures, it has strengthened its own homeland security with extraordinary laws such as the PATRIOT Act and set up, in the face of international condemnation, a holding/interrogation/torture camp in Cuba for suspected al-Qaeda operatives. If nothing else, 9/11 has demonstrated that the US, the only remaining superpower, can and will act unilaterally in international relations if it so desires, regardless of norms, conventions or treaties. Powerful words that have regulated international diplomacy since the end of World War II such as containment, sovereignty and status quo have been discarded in favour of a new vocabulary of power politics that ranges from the 'axis of evil' to regime change. Nevertheless, despite the awe-inspiring pace of change in global society initiated by America in response to 9/11, the war on terror is going badly. The wars in both Afghanistan and Iraq have proved to be indecisive, despite the initial successes. Osama bin Laden has not been captured, and unrest in Afghanistan continues to tie down significant numbers of US forces.[13] Iraq has metamorphosed into a massive military quagmire and, despite the memorable (CNN friendly) three-week charge on Baghdad, the growing insurgency is rapidly turning into a nightmarish commitment that has resulted in the death of more than 2,000 troops with over 9,000 wounded[14] (not to mention the civilian deaths that range from 16,000 to 100,000). It also absorbed approximately 150,000 American troops[15] by January 2005 to ensure security for the national elections.

The remarkable aspect of the Bush Doctrine is how it has managed to turn a generally sympathetic global population in September 2001 (that spanned religions, creeds and beliefs) into a polarized and deeply divided world by 2004. Part of the reason for this radical change in opinion has stemmed from the inconsistent and uneven application of the Bush Doctrine, from Afghanistan to Iraq. The clear linkage between Afghanistan and bin Laden meant that US military operations were considered quite justified. The level of global support for operations against the alliance between the Taleban and al-Qaeda could be measured by the number of states in important regional alliances such as NATO whose leaders were willing to take up 'out of area' operations in places such as Kabul.[16] It was an unprecedented step in the alliance's history and promised perhaps a new vision of international security in which the world's premier security organization intervened in conflicts around the world and not just in Europe. However, the Iraq invasion was perceived very differently. After all, Iraq had nothing to do with 9/11, despite numerous disingenuous suggestions emanating from the Bush administration.[17] Nor did it possess WMD as claimed by Bush and his most prominent ally, Tony Blair. Nevertheless, Iraq was an obsession among many members of the Bush administration, not least the highly prominent neo-conservatives,[18] and conveniently possessed vast quantity of oil reserves – a vital strategic resource for the 'gas-guzzling' US economy. It is impossible to ignore these two factors in the calculations to embark on one of the most unpopular wars of choice in recent memory.

Furthermore, the Iraq war has profoundly affected international society in a way that is normally more associated with larger systemic events such as the Cold War's, or even World War II's, end. It has generated levels of polarization in international relations on an unprecedented scale between regions and religions. In a regional sense, 'old' Europe as Donald Rumsfeld famously remarked[19] was firmly against the war, whereas 'new' Europe (the former communist states) was happy in the main to support the US-led coalition. The vast majority of the Middle East and Africa – excluding Israel, the Gulf states and Saudi Arabia – were against the war, as was much of Asia, apart from the usual suspects of South Korea and Japan (traditionally strong American allies). The polarization among religious communities bears equal significance as well in the light of the unexpected direction of the war on terror. It is an indisputable, but often overlooked, fact that both wars have been fought against largely Islamic populations. The non-regime costs of the Iraq war fluctuate immensely, according to different surveys, on account of the occupying forces' refusal to keep a publicly accessible record of civilian deaths; however, the battle for Fallujah, despite the careful media choreography[20] by US forces, showed a massive amount of destruction within the city using battlefield weapons such as heavy artillery and air strikes. It does raise the question of whether such disproportionate force would be used or, for that matter, be acceptable against non-Muslim communities. In addition, the existence of global media means that the daily horrors of the fighting in Iraq are continuously beamed back to the large Islamic communities in Europe and North America. Consequently, there is a significant danger that this polarization of communities could lead to a widening of the conflict and give the vociferous yet remarkably small number of Islamic fundamentalists a wider constituency within the diaspora Muslim communities residing in the west. If so, then al-Qaeda need not travel long distances to mount their next attacks because the polarization effect will have provided them with a new generation of recruits already in place in the target countries.

Conclusion

Iraq has sucked up virtually 'all of the Army's 10 divisions'[21] (deployed in theatre, preparing to go or having just returned) and the fighting has seriously intensified. The battle for Fallujah cost the US Marines a 10 per cent casualty rate with 71 dead and 600 wounded[22] fighting against 'low-tech' insurgents armed with just AK-47s, RPG-7s and improvised explosive devices (IEDs). Brian Gifford offers a more worrying perspective about the fighting in Iraq that ostensibly (in the context of previous wars) seems quite sustainable:

> The United States had 12 million active-duty personnel at the end of World War II and 3.5 million at the height of the Vietnam War, compared with just 1.4 million today. Adjusted for the size of the armed forces, the average daily number of killed and wounded was 4.8 times as many in World War II than in Iraq, but it was only 0.25 times greater in Vietnam – or one-fourth more.[23]

The costs of the continued fighting in Iraq are clearly much higher when put in this context, and the demands of the counterinsurgency campaign in Iraq could tie down the US military for years, as well as effectively precluding substantial military operations against another 'rogue' state or even the remaining two members of the 'axis of evil', Iran and North Korea. Of more significance, should the US pacification strategy in Iraq fail (a likely outcome given the ineptitude of the grand and operational strategy orchestrated by the Pentagon), then the entire neo-conservative project in the Middle East, of Iraq being the key to a 'democratic transformation' (Ikenberry 2004: 11) of the region, is in jeopardy. Rather than generating 'a benign form of domino dynamics' (Jervis 2003: 368) with Iraq as the initiator, its destabilization may produce exactly the opposite effect with serious consequences for US-friendly regimes in the region.

The inadvertent widening of the war on terror from a narrow focus on al-Qaeda to a much wider aperture that encompasses 'rogue' states has magnified the level of risk facing the US by several orders. States are infinitely more powerful than transnational terrorist organizations and have the ability to develop WMD as well as effective delivery systems. The key lesson of the Iraq war is that cooperation with international organizations will not prevent the US from taking unilateral military operations to provoke regime change. Consequently, isolated states may be less willing to cooperate with international bodies and, in the face of an early build-up of US forces, may be tempted to use pre-emptive military force because delay, in the light of the events of spring 2003, will be tantamount to regime suicide. Indeed, US unilateralist behaviour may also encourage pariah states to engage in co-operation to meet the common threat, which could encompass the transfer of knowledge and materials concerning WMD. Such a scenario would make a poor, and historically flawed, choice of words ('axis of evil') turn into an actual reality. The development and possible use of mini-nukes is perhaps one of the most disturbing future trends, as it will in all likelihood encourage the proliferation of such devices and lower the nuclear threshold. In sum, it could precipitate the very situation that the US has stated that it is trying to prevent: the acquisition of deployable nuclear weapons by terrorist groups from rogue states either as a last act of desperation from a threatened regime or as part of a calculated strategy to take a much wider struggle to the US mainland.

The fight against global terrorism demands a concerted effort, yet unilateral actions will detract from this struggle as well as allow ideological rifts to become established between America and the rest of the world. Such actions will ultimately be to the detriment of the US, as isolation will inevitably mean that the label 'rogue' may be more appropriate to it than to others. In addition, the focus on Iraq (which is likely to grow rather than diminish in the short term) has allowed al-Qaeda to recover its strength in preparation for another major attack on the US. Adding to this troubling idea, the alienation of indigenous Muslim communities by the polarizing effect of the Bush Doctrine may facilitate the next assault. It is important not to forget that making bombs of a devastating magnitude, as demonstrated by the domestic American terrorist, Timothy McVeigh, in Oklahoma in 1995, when he destroyed a federal building (killing 167 people in the blast) with a bomb made out of agricultural fertilizer and motor fuel hidden in a truck, is not a terribly far-fetched idea. Finally, if Iraq becomes the 'rule' rather than the 'exception' in global affairs, then military intervention is likely to become the hallmark of international security for the foreseeable future as 'great power' states utilize the medium of force to gain access to strategically valuable territories, regardless of the protestations of international organizations. Such a prospect bodes ill for the stability of international relations and could herald the return to an environment more akin to the dark days of the interwar years when strong nations ignored the collective will of international bodies such as the League of Nations by embarking on expansionist foreign policies that eventually led to global conflagration. In sum, international security is undergoing profound alterations as a consequence of the Bush Doctrine that have the potential radically to alter global perceptions about the legitimacy of the existing order and the preponderance of the US.

Notes

1 The prominent neo-conservatives are Donald Rumsfeld, Paul Wolfowitz, Douglas Feith, John Bolton and Richard Perle. See Kampfner (2004: 83).
2 This rather dark, selective and sanitized version of world history and its possible future is encapsulated by the neo-conservative writer Robert Kagan (2003).
3 The latest estimate of al-Qaeda's strength suggests that it may have '1,000+' active personnel. See *The Military Balance 2004–5* (2004: 367).
4 Kagan (2003) reveals that the annual US defence budget is 'heading toward' the $400 billion mark.

5 The US has 1,433,600 personnel in its armed forces. Of these, just over half a million are in the US Army with a shade under 200,000 in the US Marine Corps. See *The Military Balance 2004–5*, pp. 23–7.

6 Freedman highlights the tendency of strategists to reach for this 'dark side to the strategic imagination that picks up intimations of disorder at times of stability' (see Freedman 2002: 340).

7 The failure to find a link between al-Qaeda and Iraq is a classic case.

8 The anthrax attacks in 2001 killed just five people. See Julian Borger, 'Anthrax leads leave FBI baffled: Frenzied bloodhounds, a biowarfare background, a terror novel plot – then nothing', *Guardian*, 5 August 2002.

9 Condoleezza Rice used the phrase, 'We don't want the smoking gun to be a mushroom cloud' in a CNN interview on 8 September 2003.

10 The US withdrew from the ABM treaty on 13 June 2002.

11 *The Military Balance 2004–5*, p. 73.

12 The incident, immortalized by the film, *Black Hawk Down*, cost the US Army 18 dead soldiers. See Farrell (2002: 293).

13 The US has around 18,000 personnel in Afghanistan. See *The Military Balance 2004–5*, p. 14.

14 See 'US troops wounded in Iraq War tops 9000', *Washington Post*, 23 November 2004.

15 See Nick Childs, 'Troop increase may spur Pentagon critics', *BBC News*, 2 December 2004.

16 'On 11 August 2003, NATO assumed responsibility for the International Security Assistance Force (ISAF) in Kabul'. See *The Military Balance 2004–5*, p. 35.

17 The most vociferous proponent of the link between Iraq and al-Qaeda has been Vice-President Dick Cheney. See Dan Eggen, 'No evidence connecting Iraq to Al Qaeda, 9/11 panel says', *Washington Post*, 16 June 2004.

18 This obsession revealed itself after 9/11 when Paul Wolfowitz and Donald Rumsfeld, in the face of all the evidence pointing to al-Qaeda, pushed Iraq back on the agenda (see Clarke 2004: 30–1).

19 Rumsfeld was referring to Germany and France as 'old Europe' at a Pentagon press briefing on 22 January 2003.

20 Embedding or placing journalists within military units has become very popular since the invasion of Iraq occurred in 2003. It is clearly part of a conscious media strategy that allows the US Department of Defense to have a much greater degree of control over the flow of information to journalists.

21 Michael Kilian, 'Fears grow of military spread thin', *Chicago Tribune*, 3 December 2004.

22 Patrick Cockburn, 'US death toll in Iraq at record level', *Independent*, 2 December 2004.

23 Brian Gifford, 'The costs of staying the course: conditions in Iraq and in past wars cast casualty tolls in a different light', *Washington Post*, 29 November 2004.

12 The global economy

Daphne Josselin

On 17 September 2002, 20 months into his presidency, George W. Bush released his administration's National Security Strategy (NSS). There, for the first time, the various elements of what became know as the 'Bush Doctrine' were formally articulated, for many confirming a historic shift in American foreign policy. Interestingly, the NSS not only reaffirmed preventive action as the approach of choice to deal with rogue states and terrorists harbouring weapons of mass destruction, it also made foreign economic policy a major tool of America's grand strategy. As part of its fight against terrorism, the US would 'ignite a new era of global economic growth through free markets and free trade' and 'expand the circle of development' (White House 2002). This chapter explores the consequences of Bush's military and economic priorities for the global economy.

The war on terror: costs and consequences

As befits an economic 'hyper-power', US decisions over public spending and monetary policy have often been taken with scant attention to their consequences on the global economy. The early 2000s have been no exception. Between 2000 and 2004, the US budget moved from a surplus estimated at $5.5 trillion to a $412 billion deficit, deterioration equivalent to nearly 6 per cent of gross domestic product (GDP). At the time of writing, White House forecasts point to a record $427 billion budget deficit for 2005. Presidential pledges to cut the deficit in half by 2009, to 1.5 per cent of US GDP, have been widely derided by economists.[1] This massive shift can hardly be blamed solely on the war on terror: according to the Office of Management and Budget, rising expenditures on military and domestic programmes only accounted for about a quarter of the deterioration, versus about half for the economic slowdown and another quarter for Bush's tax cuts.[2]

Yet military costs undoubtedly played a role, as did reconstruction in 'cleaned-up' territories, with no end in sight. Fiscal year 2005 saw a record $105 billion being devoted to military operations in Iraq and Afghanistan, followed in early 2005 by yet another supplemental budget request for fiscal year 2006, this time of $82 billion, pushing the total for both conflicts to nearly $300 billion. Other budgetary figures have reflected similar trends: in the 2005 budget, spending on armed forces and homeland defence increased by 7 and 10 per cent respectively; for fiscal year 2006, Bush requested another 4.8 per cent increase for the Defense Department (bringing the total increase since 2001 to 41 per cent), nearly 7 per cent more for the Department of Homeland Security and nearly 16 per cent more for State Department spending on foreign operations. Some have warned that the combined Iraq and homeland security costs could well match those of the Vietnam War, a cumulative 12 per cent of gross national product (GNP) (Nordhaus 2002).

The consequences of Bush's spendthrift policies for the world economy have so far been largely beneficial, making the US the 'engine' of world growth in a context of persisting economic sluggishness in Europe and Japan. However, by early 2005, the combination of rising budget deficit and spiralling external imbalances is raising serious fears. Increasingly, parallels are being drawn between the present situation and that of the early 1970s: then, as now, the US ran large budget deficits, had a soft money policy and faced open-ended security costs in a context of rising oil prices.[3] The result was the demise of the Bretton Woods system of fixed exchange rates, higher interest rates and a drop in global output.

Largely reflecting lower investor confidence, as of February 2005, the dollar has fallen by 35 per cent against the euro from its early 2002 rate. Yet America's current account deficit continues to widen, 2004 estimates placing it between $600 and $670 billion, well over 5 per cent of GDP. While economists disagree on the sustainability of such a deficit, few dispute the risks should financial markets finally turn around (for an overview of the main issues, see Bergsten and Williamson 2004). A crash in the value of the dollar would push US inflation and interest rates upwards, force other countries to offset declining trade surpluses and raise the spectres of financial crises and world recession. Already there are warnings that the scale of the financing required is outgrowing the willingness of the central banks that have so far agreed to provide it.[4] The change in leadership due to take place at the Federal Reserve Board within the next year is also looked upon with some worry.[5] Hence renewed calls for a trimmer budget deficit (together with higher interest rates to curb consumer spending), so far only heeded in principle by a newly re-elected president.

Even the optimists, those for whom the US is on track to manage another 'soft landing', note rising protectionist pressures, hardly favourable to Bush's ambition to 'ignite a new era of global economic growth through free markets and free trade'. Partly, these are due to the very size of the trade deficit (likely to be around $620 billion for 2004); partly, to the manner of its financing. While private inward investment has slumped, Asian central banks have intervened heavily to hold down their currencies against the dollar and keep their exports cheap, increasing their reserves by about $700 billion from the end of 2001 to 2003 and possibly by another $700 billion in 2004 alone.[6] China, in particular, has been cast as world villain and has come under growing pressure to revalue its currency.

There are also worries that world recession might come from another quarter: energy prices. After months of concerns about the Iraq situation (from the summer of 2002 to the spring of 2003, world oil prices were said to embody a premium of about $4–5 per barrel) (Mussa 2003), many had predicted a fall in crude oil prices following the Iraq intervention, in line with the price response that had followed the first Gulf War.[7] Yet, by September 2004, crude oil prices were 56 per cent higher than at the war's end. Observers have compared the current price hike with previous oil shocks, notably that of the early 1970s, and warned that the consequences of persistent high oil prices for the world economy could be severe, possibly slowing the US and G7 economies by between 0.3 and 1 per cent.[8]

While the reflection of a number of global trends (such as the emergence of China and India as major buyers), the recent 'oil shock' is partly the result of enduring concerns over geo-political risks in the Middle East, one estimate pointing to a 'fear premium' of between $4 and $8 per barrel.[9] Significantly, market participants greeted the fact that Iraq's elections on 31 January 2005 passed without further pipeline sabotage with relief.[10]

But the US government has also been accused of contributing to speculative frenzy, and thus to high oil prices, through its insistence on buying oil to fill the country's Strategic Petroleum Reserve (SPR). Following 9/11, Bush directed the Department of Energy to fill the SPR to its full 700 million barrel capacity to 'maximize long-term protection against oil supply disruptions'. In the following two years, the US increased the SPR by 83 million barrels and did so regardless of a Senate non-binding resolution calling on the administration to stop purchases. Not only has this policy lent further credibility to market worries over the possibility of terrorist attacks on oil infrastructures,[11] it has also directly compounded pressures on world oil prices, possibly by as much as $8 per barrel.[12] One author wryly notes that the decision to fill the reserve, and more generally to maintain – or even expand – American oil consumption, is also boosting cash flow to the terrorist cause.[13]

Overall, there is no doubting the impact of Bush's foreign and macroeconomic policies on the global economy. Notwithstanding the beneficial effect of US consumption on world growth in the first half of the 2000s, the huge costs of the war on terror have fuelled rising budget deficits, thus contributing to the deterioration in US current account deficits. Larger deficits mean growing protectionism and dollar vulnerability. A collapse of the dollar or a soaring budget deficit (not to mention a further oil shock) might all generate higher inflation and interest rates, at great cost to the world economy. But questions have also been raised regarding the impact of US foreign economic policies.

The impact of competitive liberalization

To a large extent, Bush's determination to use economic means to strengthen the 'coalition of the willing' has exerted a positive influence on trade liberalization and growth. In the summer of 2001, the prospects of launching a new trade round were dim, with huge divisions on what the agenda of the proposed negotiations should cover. By November, Doha had become a symbol of unity in the war against terrorism. Importantly, the US was a prime mover behind the launch of the millennium round of World Trade Organization (WTO) negotiations, placing politically sensitive US trade policies on textiles and apparel, agriculture, anti-dumping and countervailing duties on the table for the first time.

Some have also drawn a link between China's cooperation in handling North Korea and fighting Islamic terrorism and Bush's reluctance to give in to growing protectionist pressures. Whether motivated by foreign policy concerns or by a genuine commitment to free trade, the White House has imposed few safeguard tariffs on Chinese imports and only taken up one complaint with the WTO (on semi-conductors), preferring to iron out differences with Beijing informally.[14]

However, the administration's record on the trade front is not unblemished. Bush's first major decision in the field was to impose safeguard tariffs on steel imports in March 2002, a move long resisted by his predecessor. Two months later, the US farm bill promised a significant increase in America's agricultural subsidies. Officials claimed that such moves were the political price to pay for securing fast-track negotiating authority from a reluctant Congress, an authority that had eluded Bill Clinton and was an essential prerequisite for progress in international trade negotiations (see also Bergsten 2002). If so, the approach was successful: in December 2001, the fast-track legislation, renamed trade promotion authority or TPA, was pushed though the House of Representatives by a narrow margin (the three key votes by margins of three or fewer); it passed the Senate eight months later.

Since then, the Bush team has been anything but idle in its pursuit of what then US trade negotiator Robert Zoellick referred to as 'competitive liberalization': the simultaneous negotiation of bilateral, regional and global trade agreements. As of December 2004, 12 bilateral free trade agreements have been signed, and 12 more are in the pipeline. And while the Free Trade Area of the Americas seems to have stalled, a free-trade deal with Central America is currently sitting in Congress. As for the Doha Round, enduring protectionist pressures have failed to derail the process, thanks largely to Zoellick's determination. Effecting what some regarded as a U-turn after the badly received 2002 farm bill, Washington made a substantial offer in June 2002 to reduce agricultural subsidies and trade protection. Moreover, while US refusal to compensate cotton-exporting countries for the adverse impact of its cotton subsidies may have played a part in the collapse of the Cancún multilateral trade talks in 2003, the US continued to press ahead in 2004.[15]

For its proponents, competitive liberalization can provide 'leverage for openness in all negotiations, established models of success that can be used on many fronts' and develop 'a fresh political dynamic that puts free trade on the offensive'.[16] For its critics, however, it is doubtful whether this approach truly advances the cause of free trade. Some of the bilateral agreements, for instance that with Australia, exclude important and highly protected sectors, such as sugar. Moreover, the Bush administration's choice of partners has been seen as arbitrary, if not downright driven by foreign policy considerations: many drew a link between the US–Australia agreement and the latter's involvement in Iraq. By the same token, the opening up of negotiations with Thailand in 2004 had been widely expected following the close collaboration between US officials and the Royal Thai police around the capture of terrorist kingpin Hambali in 2003.[17] That trade policy is partly being subordinated to security objectives is even clearer in the case of Middle East partners: the negotiations initiated with Bahrain in January 2004 were hailed as a clear symbolic tool in the war on terror, while the agreements with Oman and the United Arab Emirates announced in November 2004 were deemed to be 'important steps' towards boosting growth and democracy in the Middle East. In contrast, the economic benefits expected from this flurry of regional and bilateral initiatives appear to be quite limited, explaining lack of support both in Congress and in the American business community. The Central America Free Trade Agreement (CAFTA), in particular, has triggered significant opposition from US trade unions, environmentalists and sugar producers, leading observers to forecast a cliffhanger vote in Congress. Some even warn that regional free trade arrangements are ultimately incompatible with US national interests, prompting the creation of other preferential trading areas, notably in East Asia, from which the US might soon find itself shut out (Gordon 2003).

On the whole, few can doubt that the US post-9/11 has proved a key force behind the launch and continuation of the Doha Round of multilateral trade negotiations. But neither global economic welfare nor the GATT/WTO system seems likely to be significantly enhanced by the many bilateral and regional trading arrangements currently being negotiated by the Bush administration.

Monetary carrots and sticks

In 9/11's aftermath, monetary channels have also been used to promote America's foreign policy goals, isolating enemies, rewarding friends and addressing the security threats raised by global poverty. Terrorist financing was an early target with Title III of the US PATRIOT Act and pressures were exerted overseas. As early as October 2001, the Financial Action Task Force (FATF), an international body established to fight money laundering, published eight recommendations to combat terrorist financing and prepared to take measures against countries that flouted them. Bowing to US pressure, the Saudi government agreed to introduce controls. By 2004, the US government prided itself on having blocked over $136.8 million in terrorist assets.[18]

In what was hailed as 'one of the greatest surprises of George W. Bush's presidency so far', the US administration also announced a dramatic rise in US developmental assistance. In Monterrey on 14 March 2002, after over a decade of falling aid commitments, Bush revealed a plan to increase US bilateral development aid by 50 per cent, starting in 2004 and reaching an added $5 billion a year by 2006. The full increase in funding would set up a new Millennium Challenge Account (MCA) to promote growth in reform-oriented governments, namely those 'ruling justly, investing in their people, and establishing economic freedom'. In April, the administration pledged to increase US funding for the World Bank by 18 per cent over three years provided the institution met certain performance criteria. In September, the NSS gave rare prominence to development and aid alongside defence and diplomacy. Then came the 2003 State of the Union address, in which Bush called for $10 billion in new funding ($15 billion in total) over the next five years to combat HIV/AIDS in Africa and the Caribbean.[19]

This flurry of new initiatives can be seen in large part as one element in the administration's post-9/11 approach. For one, aid can play a key role in the war on terror by supporting front-line countries and weak states: the 2004 budget thus called for $4.7 billion in aid for key states, including $657 million for Afghanistan, $460 million for Jordan, $395 million for Pakistan and $255 million for Turkey. More generally, the new policy reflects 'a growing awareness that Washington must start using both "hard" and "soft" power if it is going to make the world a safer and more secure place', as illustrated quite strikingly by the juxtaposition of the HIV/AIDS initiative and the Iraq strategy in the 2003 State of the Union address (Radelet 2003a: 2).

From the start, the MCA initiative was explicitly linked to broader foreign policy considerations, with Bush making it clear that 'we fight against poverty because hope is an answer to terror'. Not surprisingly, questions have been raised regarding its potential contribution to US policy on development and poverty reduction (Brainard *et al.* 2003). The grants are administered by the Millennium Challenge Corporation (MCC), a new government entity overseen by a board composed of cabinet officials and chaired by the Secretary of State: how will its action be articulated with that of the 7,000-strong United States Agency for International Development (USAID)? Will its staff of 100 be up to the task of administering $5 billion of grants per year? Most worryingly for those who have long pressed for a depoliticization of US aid-giving, how will the recipients be selected? In the first two years, only countries with per capita incomes of less than $1,435 were included. This, together with the 16 eligibility criteria explicitly defined, seems to guarantee fairer and more effective US aid-giving. From the third year, however, lower middle-income countries will join the pool, such as Jordan, Egypt, Turkey, Russia and Colombia, leaving scope for a geo-political bias (see the survey by Radelet 2003b: 171–87). Conversely, there is a strong risk that the poorest countries will not meet the MCA's eligibility criteria, leaving most of sub-Saharan Africa in the doldrums, alongside those failed states most likely to harbour terrorism.

As of February 2005, it is of course too early to assess the likely impact of Bush's ambitious aid programmes on development. Funding in particular remains an unknown: out of the $2.5 billion requested by the president to fund the MCA in fiscal year 2005, only $1.5 billion was authorized by Congress. Even if the $3 billion requested by Bush for fiscal year 2006 meets with a more generous response, it is unlikely that the programme will be fully operational by the announced date of 2006. Scale-up on the HIV/AIDS programme has been similarly slow. Yet this important shift in US policy towards the developing world could still exert a significant influence on the world economy, especially if backed up by greater trade liberalization.

Conclusion

At the time of writing, many from economists to officials at the IMF and the UN share the view that 'the defining feature of the global economy right now is the $660 billion US current account deficit'.[20] The Bush administration itself seems to have finally acknowledged the scale and urgency of the problem, even if the remedies envisaged remain contested, to say the least. Blaming the deficit on others (Europeans for their slow growth, Asian partners for their repressed exchange rates) might trigger more protectionist pressures at home and defiance abroad. The budget cuts announced by the president have failed to convince. Eventually, addressing the issue might require cuts in military spending and foreign aid, possibly undermining the very objectives that the Bush administration is trying to pursue. Yet failing to act creates genuine risks of a world recession.

The picture is similarly mixed when it comes to trade and aid policies. Back in 2002, the launch of the Doha trade round, together with the granting of 'fast-track' trade negotiating authority to the Bush administration were seen by one observer as 'among the most significant and positive ways in which the September terrorist attack has affected the outlook for the global economy' (Granville 2003). Three years on, the US remains a leader in the field, but the proliferation of regional free trade agreements is not devoid of risks, nor are mounting demands to clamp down on Chinese imports and the outsourcing of US jobs. The year 2005 is set to see a tough battle for the renewal of 'fast-track' negotiating authority, without which the US will have to relinquish trade leadership and, with an ambitious domestic agenda to push through Congress, it is unclear how much political energy Bush will be willing to expend on the trade front. More battles will probably also have to be fought in support of the MCA and HIV/AIDS programmes. Against the background of called-for budgetary stringency, the US might yet revert to its traditional laggard position as regards aid-giving and fail to tackle one of the critical issues facing the world economy: rising inequality.

All these point to profound contradictions in the Bush Doctrine as it pertains to global economic trends: between short-term achievements and long-term prospects, and between claimed objectives and actual policies. Addressing these contradictions will be one of the key challenges facing the administration in its second term.

Notes

1 For instance, using Congressional Budget Office figures, Nouriel Roubini calculates a 2009 budget deficit of about $600 billion, or 4 per cent of GDP, excluding social security reform. Nouriel Roubini's Global Economics Blog, 7 February 2005; accessed at http://www.roubiniglobal.com/archives/2005/02/budget_lies_it.html.
2 Office of Management and Budget, Mid-year Budget Review, 15 July 2003.
3 Maurice Obstfeld and Kenneth Rogoff, 'The unsustainable US current account position revisited', NBER Working Paper Series, WP 10869, October 2004; Fred Bergsten, 'The risks ahead for the world economy', *Economist*, 11 September 2004, pp. 81–3.
4 In 2003, the world's central banks financed 90 per cent of the US's $530 billion current account deficit; estimates place their share at 70 per cent for 2004, or $465 billion. Nouriel Roubini and Brad Setser, 'Will the Bretton Woods 2 regime unravel soon? The risk of a hard landing in 2005–2006', February 2005; accessible at http://www.stern.nyu.edu/globalmacro/.
5 Alan Greenspan's term in office was due to end on 31 January 2006.
6 Nouriel Roubini and Brad Setser, 'Will the Bretton Woods 2 regime unravel soon? The risk of a hard landing in 2005–2006', February 2005; accessible at http://www.stern.nyu.edu/globalmacro/.
7 'The economic fog of war', *Wall Street Journal*, 12 February 2003.
8 Nouriel Roubini and Brad Setser, 'The effects of the recent oil price shock on the US and global economy', 2004; accessible at http://www.stern.nyu.edu/globalmacro/. See also Philip K. Verleger, *Energy: The Gathering Storm*, Institute for International Economics, September 2004.
9 Nouriel Roubini and Brad Setser, 'The effects of the recent oil price shock on the US and global economy', 2004; accessible at http://www.stern.nyu.edu/globalmacro/.
10 'Crude falls with no disruption in Iraq or change in OPEC output', Bloomberg, 31 January 2005. Recent incidents had included an attack on a duct transporting crude oil from Iraq's northern fields in December 2004 and sabotage to Persian Gulf oil terminals in southern Iraq in early January 2005.
11 'A burning question', *Economist*, 27 March 2004, pp. 93–4.
12 Philip K. Verleger, *US Energy Policy: In Conflict with the War on Terrorism*, Institute for International Economics, August 2004, p. 7.
13 Ibid.
14 At the end of 2004, the administration finally appeared to relent and considered imposing safeguard quotas on Chinese textiles in case of threat of market disruption. However, a federal judge found in favour of a large coalition of textile importers who had filed a suit against the government, possibly to the relief of the Bush team.
15 Whether US commitment to the Doha Round would endure past the departure of Robert Zoellick, newly appointed Deputy Secretary of State, and in the face of mounting protectionist pressures, remained to be seen.
16 Robert B. Zoellick, United States Trade Representative, *The President's Trade Policy Agenda*, 1 March 2004.
17 C. Preble, *Free Trade a Potent Weapon Against Terror*, Cato Institute, 20 October 2003; accessed at http://www.cato.org/cgi-bin/scripts/printtech.cgi/research/articles/preble-031020.html.

18 Office of Management and Budget, *Summary of Accomplishments and Future Challenges*, 2004.

19 The US–Middle East Partnership Initiative (MEPI), established by Secretary of State Powell in December 2002 to promote education, economic opportunity and the rule of law in the region, provided yet another relevant – though, with $74.4 million in 2004, more modest – illustration of this new emphasis on 'soft' aid power.

20 Nouriel Roubini and Brad Setser, 'Will the Bretton Woods 2 regime unravel soon? The risk of a hard landing in 2005–2006', February 2005; accessible at http://www.stern.nyu.edu/globalmacro/. See also Anne O. Krueger, 'How stable is the global economy?', 11 February 2005, at http://www.imf.org/external/np/speeches/2005/021105.htm; and 'UN urges global action on US debt', *New York Times*, 27 January 2005.

13 The United Nations

Stephen Ryan

The publication of the National Security Strategy (NSS) of the United States of America on 17 September 2002 was one of the most significant and controversial foreign policy events of recent years. The document is wide ranging and many parts are predictable. Much of it is concerned with how to respond to 'shadowy networks of individuals' and 'rogue states'. There is a defence of free markets and free trade that, it is claimed, will 'ignite a new era of global economic growth'. There is a strong link made between development and democracy. However, one paragraph stood out. This stated that 'to forestall or prevent such hostile acts by our adversaries, the United States will, if necessary, act pre-emptively'. It was this idea that summed up 'the Bush Doctrine', a label in use since a presidential speech at West Point in June 2002. As Madeleine Albright (2003a: 2) has noted, it appeared that 'reliance on alliance had been replaced by redemption through prevention'.

Some have argued that nothing much has changed with the Bush Doctrine. Melvyn Leffler (2004), for example, states that the Bush foreign policy should not be described as revolutionary, unprecedented or a radical departure from Clinton's policies because there is much in the Bush approach that resonates with traditional themes. There is some truth here, but the continuity thesis underestimates the jolt caused by the explicit adoption of a policy of preventive war, which is a fundamental challenge to the United Nations (UN). Under the UN Charter, states are only allowed to use force or the threat of force in self-defence or where the Security Council decides that there is a threat to international peace and security. Interestingly, chapter VIII of the NSS, which deals with agendas for cooperation with the other main centres of global power, makes no reference to the UN at all. Nor is the UN mentioned in chapters dealing with strengthening alliances, working to defuse regional conflicts or expanding circles of development. In fact, the UN does not appear to have any role at all in the new US strategy.

Nonetheless, the application of this doctrine to Iraq and the prospect of future action against North Korea and Iran created an impression that a major conflict had arisen between the global 'hyper-power' and the UN. Many observers certainly predicted more troubled times ahead. Jonathan Steele, for example, remarked that the US president 'is hijacking the anti-terrorist agenda and crashing it into the most sacred skyscraper in New York: the headquarters of the UN. If his doctrine is not rapidly rejected by other states ... Article 51 of the UN charter will have suffered a mortal blow.'[1] Richard Falk echoed this, claiming that the doctrine 'repudiates the core idea of the United Nations Charter (reinforced by decisions of the World Court in The Hague), which prohibits any use of international force that is not undertaken in self-defence after the occurrence of an armed attack across an international boundary or pursuant to a decision by the Security Council'.[2] Just before Bush addressed the General Assembly in September 2003, Kofi Annan warned that the logic of preventive strike 'represents a fundamental challenge to the principles, on which, however imperfectly, world peace and stability have rested for the last 58 years'.[3] Michael Glennon (2003) has argued that, at this time, the entire UN edifice came crashing down because of the changing nature of international politics.

This chapter will explore in more depth the threat that the Bush Doctrine presented to US–UN relations. It will argue that, when placed in historical context, apocalyptic visions were exaggerated. Whereas the Bush Doctrine, along with other aspects of the foreign policy of the administration, is a threat to some basic UN principles such as non-aggression and respect for sovereignty, the actual record suggests that the relationship is more complex than it might seem at first glance.

US–UN relations in historical perspective

The UN has always provoked mixed feelings in the US. The world body is, of course, an American creation. The principal drafter of the Charter was the Roosevelt administration (see Hoopes and Brinkley 1997). The support that this administration gave to the UN can be seen as an expression of what Walter Russell Mead (2001) has identified as the Wilsonian tradition in thinking about US foreign policy. Wilsonians are idealistic internationalists who believe that the US should 'strengthen the role of international judicial and political institutions, to usher in an era of law-based international relations' (Mead 2001: 284).

However, Mead (2004: 84) claims that the Wilsonians lack the domestic political strength to implement their ideas and have to compete with three other world views that are less sympathetic to international organizations. These are 'economic nationalists' (Hamiltonians), 'isolationists' (Jeffersonians) and 'populist nationalists' (Jacksonians). These traditions have encouraged suspicion and even outright hostility to the UN, and this is especially true of the Jacksonians, who have the 'least regard for international law and international practice' (Mead 2004: 246). Examples of such attitudes are easy to find. Senator McCarthy's attacks on the UN in the late 1940s and early 1950s forced UN Secretary-General Trygve Lie to allow the FBI to vet US appointments to the organization, thus compromising its reputation for impartiality. Hostility increased because of the loss of US dominance caused by an influx of newly independent former colonies in the 1960s and the admission of communist China at the expense of Taiwan in 1971. In the 1970s, the antagonistic mood was evident in the actions and statements of the UN Ambassador Daniel Patrick Moynihan, who carried out a sustained assault on the UN for its inability to promote and protect civil and political rights and because of its anti-Israel resolutions. Opposition peaked, however, in the 1980s when the Reagan administration took the US out of UNESCO, refused to cooperate with an International Court of Justice verdict that the US had acted illegally in Nicaragua, refused to ratify the Law of the Sea Treaty and caused severe financial difficulties for the UN when it withheld funds from the organization. Most of these attacks came from conservatives but, in the 1990s, many liberal internationalists were also critical of the UN because of its failures to protect human rights in Rwanda and Bosnia.

The most significant US foreign policy stance towards the UN since 2000 has emerged from the neo-conservative tradition (see, for example, Durham 2004; Halper and Clarke 2004). This argues that multilateral institutions are harming the US national interest and that US governments should exploit the strong US position in world politics to ensure continued dominance. Freedom of action for the US involves relegating the UN to a trivial role because it could place roadblocks to impede decisive US actions. This mode of thinking can be traced back to the draft Defense Policy Guideline (DPG) of 1992, drafted by Paul Wolfowitz and Lewis Libby.[4] This was shelved at the time but, in 1997, the ideas it contained resurfaced at the recently created Project for a New American Century. Members of this body included Dick Cheney, Donald Rumsfeld, Paul Wolfowitz, Lewis Libby and Richard Perle. It combined some hardheaded realist analysis with a strong belief in US exceptionalism. The claim is that the US is both a hegemonic power and a moral beacon.[5]

A letter written by members of the Project to Clinton in January 1998 called for a new US security policy that should include the removal of Saddam Hussein (Singer 2004: 189). In May 1998, a similar letter to the House Speaker and the Senate Majority Leader criticized the UN as a 'chimera . . . from whom Saddam would conceal his programmes for developing weapons of mass destruction. The result would be the emboldening of other regimes in pursuit of such weapons and the putting of American troops and American allies in danger' (Durham 2004).

With so many of these individuals placed in important foreign policy and defence positions in 2001, it was no surprise that it was the neo-conservative roadmap that the administration followed when foreign policy became a vital issue after 9/11. For 'far more than anyone else, they had their responses in place and targets fixed . . .. Saddam's coordinates were already entered into the computer' (Halper and Clarke 2004: 33). However, it promised a serious collision with the UN for, as Ivo Daalder and James Lindsey noted, the neo-conservative hegemonist world view of the Bush administration believes 'that multilateral institutions and agreements are neither essential nor necessarily conducive to American interests' (Daalder and Lindsay 2003: 108).

The unilateralism of the Bush administration

To argue that the Bush Doctrine marks the end of US multilateral policy and the beginning of a new unilateralist approach to foreign affairs would be an oversimplification. Whatever the stance of particular administrations, it has never been US government policy to give the UN too much of an influence on foreign policy decision-making. Indeed, no president has really accepted the primacy of the Charter principles of collective security and the peaceful settlement of disputes when they conflict with perceived US vital interests. The UN was effectively excluded from, or played only a marginal role in, the Cuban Missile Crisis, the Vietnam War and the invasions of the Dominican Republic, Guatemala, Grenada and Panama. It is true that there was a brief period at the start of the 1990s when, carried away by 'new world order' rhetoric, Washington seemed to regard the UN in a more positive manner. But this did not last for long, and the liaison did not survive the disasters in Mogadishu. After this, it was the Clinton administration that refused to participate in international action against the genocide in Rwanda; introduced Presidential Decision Directive 25 that curtailed US support for UN peace-keeping; ensured that Boutros-Ghali did not get a second term as Secretary-General although the majority of UN members were in favour of this; and launched a war against the Serbs over Kosovo even though this was not authorized by the UN Security Council. In Iraq, as Falk and Krieger have pointed out, it 'undermined and corrupted the UN inspection process by using UN inspectors to conduct espionage'.[6]

Nonetheless, the first 18 months of the Bush administration were marked by a number of foreign policy decisions that showed that a more argumentative and consistent unilateralism had been introduced into US foreign policy. During this time, the US refused to sign the Kyoto Accords; announced its withdrawal from the US–Soviet Anti-Ballistic Missile Treaty of 1972 in order to develop its 'son of Star Wars' missile defence technology; 'unsigned' the Rome Statute that established the International Criminal Court (ICC); opposed a Comprehensive Test Ban Treaty; refused to ratify the UN Convention on the Rights of the Child, although it has ratified its two optional protocols (only the US and Somalia have failed to ratify this landmark UN treaty); and opposed a number of other international conventions, including the Convention on the Elimination of All Forms of Discrimination Against Women, a Biological Weapons Convention and the Ottawa Convention on Land Mines (also opposed by Clinton).

Until 9/11, however, there was no explicit or coherent underpinning to these actions, outside of the work previously carried out by the neo-conservatives already mentioned. This strategic perspective began to emerge in June 2002 when, in an address at West Point, Bush stated 'the war on terror will not be won on the defensive. We must take the battle to the enemy, disrupt his plans, and confront the worst threats before they emerge.'[7] The speech made not a single reference to the UN.

As Mead (2004: 84) points out, the neo-conservatives cannot be shoe-horned into one of his four traditions, nor are they trying to create a fifth one. Rather they are 'trying to take over all of the four older parties and remake them'. So the neo-conservative (Mead prefers the term 'American revivalist') approach contains elements of all the others, including the Wilsonian liberal internationalist position. However, in the revivalist version, the traditional Wilsonian active interventionism has been kept, but support for 'rule-based global institutions' such as the UN has been abandoned (Mead 2004: 88). Thus, the Bush policy on Iraq, Mead claims, contains three separate lines of argument that are the result of an amalgamation of Jacksonian and Wilsonian thinking (Mead 2004: 116). The Jacksonians saw a clear danger arising from the spread of nuclear weapons to Iraq, while the Wilsonians recognized opportunities to remove a repulsive regime and spread democracy throughout the Middle East. The third strand was to find an alternative to the policy of containment of Iraq, which was destabilizing Saudi Arabia and causing great suffering in Iraq.

The Bush administration, the UN and Iraq

One of the consequences of 9/11 was a close working relationship between the US and the UN on the issue of international terrorism. On 28 September 2001, under Chapter VII of the Charter, Security Council resolution 1373 addressed the issue of the support and funding of terrorism, deciding that all states shall 'prevent and suppress the financing of terrorist acts' and 'refrain from providing any form of support ... to entities or persons involved in terrorist acts'. It also calls on states to increase cooperation in the fight against international terrorism. Under the authority of this resolution, Annan created a Counter-Terrorism Committee of the Security Council to monitor implementation of the resolution.[8] In return, the US was willing to release more funds to the UN.

The determination of the Bush administration to bring down the Saddam Hussein regime in Baghdad, however, showed that such multilateralism did not spill over into other important areas. Iraq seemed to be the obsession of this administration and, as we have seen, the idea of military action against Iraq had formed in the minds of many key individuals even before they took up their posts in the Bush government. Several of them, most notably the vice-president, opposed any UN involvement, believing that Saddam would try to engage the organization in endless debate and delay. Bob Woodward's authoritative account of the lead-up to war is revealing. Cheney was 'not the steady, unemotional rock that he [Powell] had witnessed a dozen years earlier during the run-up to the Gulf War. The vice-president was beyond hell-bent for action against Saddam. It was as if nothing else existed' (Woodward 2004:

175). Indeed, the vice-president held these views so strongly that he appears to have continued his opposition to the UN even after Bush, during a speech to the General Assembly in September 2002, signalled a willingness to seek UN approval for a strong line against Baghdad.

This, however, did not mean that the White House was going to make many concessions on its Iraq policy: the president's attitude seems to have been that the UN needed to catch up with decisions already made in Washington (Eisendrath and Goodman 2004). Nonetheless, the policy seemed to bear fruit with Security Council resolution 1441 of November 2002. This established an enhanced system of inspections by the United Nations Monitoring, Verification and Inspection Commission (UNMOVIC) and the International Atomic Energy Agency. Iraq was warned in the resolution of the 'serious consequences' that would follow from non-compliance, but there was no direct authorization of military force in this event. In fact, the Security Council determined that it would remain 'seized of the matter', and France, Russia and China as well as several of the non-permanent members made statements that the resolution did not mean that there were now 'hidden triggers' or that military force could be used without an explicit authorization by the Council (see, for example, Singer 2004: 156–7).

This, though, was the highpoint of US–UN cooperation on this issue, because some permanent members of the Security Council had significant doubts about an aggressive policy towards Iraq. Whereas the Blair government strongly supported the White House, the French and the Russians were opposed. Here, it might not have helped that, since the publication of the NSS, the Iraq policy could be viewed as a manifestation of not just a new unilateralism, but a new hegemonic drive. Thus, Mead notes that American statements in the run-up to war meant that a 'perfectly justifiable military action against the rogue regime in Iraq was effectively and widely portrayed as an assault by the United States against the foundations of international order' (Mead 2004: 160). The Bush Doctrine of preventive war was meant to frighten enemies of the US, but it also alarmed many of its traditional allies (Halper and Clarke 2004: 142).

Powell's support for UN involvement was severely undermined in January 2003 when the French Foreign Minister de Villepin stated that nothing justified war. The more the Security Council looked deadlocked on this issue, the less leverage the UN would have over Iraq. After the comments, Powell, according to Woodward (2004: 285), was 'so furious he could barely be contained' and, on 21 January, the Secretary of State concluded that the inspections would not work (Glennon 2003). In fact, there was always a flaw in the Powell/Blair policy of working through the UN on the basis of Security Council resolution 1441. The prediction appears to have been that either UN pressure on Iraq would have forced Saddam to abandon cooperation with the weapons inspectors or these weapons inspectors would discover evidence of 'material breach'. Either way, the regime would have been compromised and stronger action would gain wider acceptance. However, as Christoph Bluth

(2004: 880) has noted, 'the US and Britain were caught in a trap of their own making: There was no "smoking gun", no unambiguous material breach; and at the same time Hans Blix, the chief weapons inspector, had convinced many that the inspection process was worthwhile.'

Against a background of some Iraqi cooperation with the inspectors and doubts about the veracity of some claims made about non-compliance, the US and the UK were not able to persuade enough members of the Security Council to give them a second resolution authorizing military force, as was envisaged at the time of Resolution 1441. In a sense, Cheney was right, the US was snagged by the UN. Nonetheless, firmly set on a war course, Washington and London now brushed aside the UN and began the war anyway. However, the failure to get explicit UN endorsement was significant as it undermined the legitimacy of the action and boosted the cause of those who opposed the war.

One more point has to be made about the impact of Iraq on the UN. This is that, in order to justify its use of military force, the administration implemented a policy of attacking the integrity of the organization. This took several forms. Security Council members were accused of lacking the will or the courage to stand up to a tyrant who had flouted the organization's resolutions. Attempts were made to undermine the credibility of the chief weapons inspectors Blix and El Bharadei (Blix 2004: chs 10 and 11). UN personnel were also accused of corruption – most notably those associated with the Iraq 'Oil for Food' programme.

This allowed the US to claim that it was saving the UN from the consequences of its own inaction. So, Bush informed the General Assembly on 23 September 2003 that the Security Council was 'right to warn of serious consequences if Iraq refused to comply. And because there were consequences, because the coalition of nations acted to defend the peace, *and the credibility of the United Nations*, Iraq is free . . .'.[9] Here, one should record the observation of Hans Blix (2004: 9) that 'it is an interesting notion that when a small minority has been rebuffed by a strong majority it is the majority that has failed the test'.

Overall, then, the aftermath of the Iraq debate left the UN weakened with a deeply divided Security Council and a lingering US hostility not just to France, but also to 'old Europe' in general. Britain's reputation as an internationalist and pro-UN state was severely compromised; a precedent was set for preventive war in violation of the Charter; and leaders such as Sharon and Putin were handed ready-made justifications for their policies towards Palestine and Chechnia respectively. Arab states could not help but note the hypocrisy of the US in calling for strict implementation of UN resolutions on Iraq while turning a blind eye to Israeli violations of other UN resolutions. Just 18 months after the US worked effectively with the UN to create an international coalition to bring down the Taleban regime and establish a strong international response to the threat posed by al-Qaeda, Zbigniew

Brzezinski (2004: 214) noted that the 'global solidarity with America has increasingly been transmuted into American solitude'.

Bush and the UN: areas of cooperation

Anyone looking for confirmation of a terminal crisis between the UN and Washington will be disappointed by the evidence that the US continues to give support to the organization in a wide number of areas and through a wide range of activities. Shashi Tharoor (2003: 75) points out that, 'even while disagreeing on Iraq, the members of the Security Council unanimously agreed on a host of other vital issues, from Congo to Côte d'Ivoire, from Cyprus to Afghanistan. Indeed, the Security Council remains on the whole a remarkably harmonious body.' Albright (2003b: 17) seems to agree, claiming that 'beyond the Council itself, the United Nations' ongoing relevance is evident in the work of the more than two dozen organizations comprising the UN system'.

It is true that there have been tensions in other areas. Two in particular stand out. The first is the ongoing US opposition to the International Criminal Court. This is not a UN body but, in 2002, the US threatened the UN's peace-keeping role because of a fear that American personnel serving on such missions could be prosecuted for war crimes. In June that year, it even vetoed a resolution to extend the UN peace-keeping operation in Bosnia. Eventually, a compromise was worked out in Security Council Resolution 1422 of 12 July 2002. This exempted officials or personnel from a contributing state not a party to the Statute from investigations or prosecutions for acts or omissions committed on UN-authorized operations unless this was authorized by the Security Council, where the US, of course, holds a veto. This exemption was to last for a year, but it was extended for another 12 months in June 2003 by Security Council Resolution 1487, against the wishes of the Secretary-General. France, Germany and Syria abstained in this vote, but Paris did not use its veto. However, in June 2004, against the background of the Abu Ghraib prison scandal, the US abandoned its attempts to get the exemption extended for another year when it became clear that it would not obtain nine votes in favour in the Council. In retaliation, the US withdrew two small US contingents from the peace-keeping missions in Eritrea/Ethiopia and Kosovo – a total of just nine people.

Another area of tension is the Bush administration's policy on birth control and abortion. One of the first acts of the Bush presidency was to reinstate President Reagan's 'Mexico City Policy' or the 'Global Gag Rule', which states that US funding will only be provided to organizations that refuse to support abortion as a family planning method. Since 2002, the US has withheld between $25 million and $34 million a year earmarked for the United Nations Population Fund and has frozen some funds for the World Health Organization (WHO) (Singer 2004: 40). The US government claims that this is because they indirectly support forced abortion or sterilization in China, although little evidence has been put forward to substantiate this claim, and it is denied by the organizations themselves. Critics of US policy claim that it has had an adverse effect on the health of women in many countries because it has led to closures of health clinics and outreach programmes offering prenatal care and family planning advice, resulting in a significant rise in unwanted pregnancies and an increase in HIV/AIDS infection rates. The administration has also opposed the Convention on the Elimination of All Forms of Discrimination Against Women, because it affirms the reproductive rights of women.

Yet, in many other areas, as Tharoor indicates, there is ongoing cooperation. In the international struggle against international terrorism, the US State Department has pointed out the results achieved by working with the UN. They include the launch of an initiative to identify and secure radioactive sources; the creation of an audit programme to facilitate compliance with international aviation standards; and enhanced security of ports.[10] Indeed, one of the key US priorities for the UN in the coming years will be to strengthen the Security Council's capacity to deal with threats to international peace and security that arise from international terrorism and the spread of weapons of mass destruction (WMD).[11]

Evidence of US support comes from funding to various UN bodies and programmes. In April 2003, the US announced an additional $10 million for the UN High Commissioner for Refugees (UNHCR) to support return programmes in Bosnia, help Burmese refugees in Thailand and assist projects to help women and children refugees. This was in addition to $125 million already donated to UNHCR in that financial year and $44 million for refugee programmes in Iraq, Afghanistan and parts of Africa. The same year, the US contributed 17 per cent of the United Nations Children's Fund (UNICEF) budget, 25 per cent of the budget of the International Atomic Energy Agency and 22 per cent of the core budget of the World Health Organization.[12] Although it is opposed to the ICC, Washington contributed $57 million in 2003 to support the two ad hoc war crimes tribunals for the former Yugoslavia and Rwanda and $6 million for preparatory work to renovate the UN headquarters on the East River.

In 2004, the US paid 22 per cent of the UN's regular budget. It also paid 25.6 per cent of the peace-keeping budget and was willing to authorize new missions in Ivory Coast, Liberia, Haiti and Burundi. It has also been responsible for initiatives such as the appointment of a Gender Advisor, Amy Smith, to the UN peace-keeping mission in the Republic of Congo and has offered to the UN mission in Liberia the assistance of its Weapons Removal and Abatement Office. In the same year, the US contributed 57 per cent of the budget of the World Food Programme, 33 per cent of the budget of UNHCR, 17 per cent of the budget of UNICEF and 14 per cent of the core budget of the United Nations Development Programme. This year, Washington also announced $600,000 for the UN High Commissioner for Human Rights for monitors in Darfur.

Also worthy of note has been the growing participation of US police officers in UN civilian police (CIVPOL) activities. In 2004, although only 27 US
military personnel were serving with UN peace-keeping missions, US civilian
police were participating in several CIVPOL deployments. This development was facilitated by PDD-71 of February 2000 on Strengthening Criminal
Justice Systems in Support of Peace, which is the responsibility of the State
Department's Bureau for International Narcotics and Law Enforcement Affairs. This body has prescreened and trained officers to make them available
for rapid deployment and has enhanced existing training programmes. In
the same month as the Bush Doctrine was published, there were US civilian police in Kosovo (555 plus 18 police trainers), Bosnia and Herzegovina
(200) and Macedonia (16). It is envisaged that 75 US CIVPOL officers will
help to train and advise the new Liberian police force. Despite the downsiz-
ing of the UN mission in East Timor, with the change from the United Nations Transitional Administration in East Timor (UNTAET) to the United
Nations Mission of Support in East Timor (UNMISET), the US continued
to play a role, as they did with a police training programme in Serbia. The
recruitment, selection and deployment of these officers is subcontracted to
DynCorp, which also retains offices in mission areas to support them.

Under pressure from Senate Majority leader Bill Frist, the US has also
made a significant contribution to the international battle against AIDS ($12
billion over five years), although, in line with its general policy, one-third of
this must be used to promote abstinence (Singer 2004: 125). Maybe the most
interesting development is the surprising decision by Bush to rejoin UNESCO
'as a symbol of our commitment to human dignity', despite the fact that its
headquarters is in Paris, the epitome of 'old Europe'. This was announced at
his address to the General Assembly on 12 September 2002, with the decision
taking effect a year later. The new Director-General of UNESCO, Koichiro
Matsuura, has made vigorous efforts to reform the organization, including
cutbacks in staffing and reversals of promotions agreed by his predecessor,
much to the anger of many of his own staff. But this seems to have impressed
the US administration, which has decided that many UNESCO programmes
advance a 'wide range of US interests', including the promotion of universal
education and literacy and freedom of the press.[13] In September 2003, Laura
Bush, the President's wife, led the delegation that participated in the rejoining ceremony. President Reagan took the US out of this organization in
December 1984 because of its 'budgetary expansion', mismanagement and
'hostility' to the free market and a free society. The decision to rejoin was
opposed by many on the right, including the Heritage Foundation, which
issued a report calling for a more cautious approach and an annual audit by
the US General Accounting Office.[14] In a shrewd move, the UNESCO Secretary-General has appointed Laura Bush as UNESCO Honorary Ambassador
for the United Nations Decade of Literacy. Not only did the US rejoin, it
has also become the largest financial contributor to the organization, but US

membership is also likely to lead to energetic disagreements on issues such as bioethics, overstaffing, intellectual property rights and 'politicization'.

The US, the UN and the future

To date, Iraq is the only case of preventive war by the Bush administration. Afghanistan can be viewed as a response based on the inherent right to self-defence and had the support of the UN. So a general assessment of the Bush Doctrine's impact is difficult on the evidence of just one example. It has even been suggested by Martin Indyk that we should not see Iraq as a consequence of the Bush Doctrine, rather that the Bush Doctrine was a response to the Iraq issue that is not likely to be applied in other cases.[15]

However, it is clear that the potential for US–UN conflict remains. At present, there is no sign that the US is going to abandon the preventive doctrine. On the other hand, it does not appear that the UN is willing to endorse such a principle. On 23 September 2003, at the start of the General Assembly session, for example, Annan rejected this idea and reaffirmed the principle of collective security as set out in the Charter. Bush, who spoke to the Assembly shortly after, gave no indication in his address that he was willing to reject preventive war in response to Annan's comments. So future clashes on this issue are a real possibility, but they are unlikely to be fatal. As we have noted, the US continues to cooperate with the UN on a wide range of issues. The UN also needs the US, and it is interesting that the feeling that the US has acted illegally has not led to any acts of censure against Washington from within the organization. There has, for example, been no move to involve the International Court of Justice for an advisory opinion on the legality of US actions towards Iraq.

There are observers who believe that a key factor in explaining Bush's foreign policy is his strong Christian beliefs. If there is any truth in such arguments, then we have one reason why Bush might sideline the organization in any test of US policy – if God is on his side, why does he need the UN? In reality, of course, this is too simplistic. We cannot blame the decline in US–UN relations on just one individual. There are a number of features of contemporary international politics that have impacted on this relationship. They include structural factors (the emergence of the US as the dominant military power), cultural factors (the rise of neo-conservatism in the US) and scientific factors (technological advances that make the spread of WMD a frightening prospect).

At the structural level, John Ikenberry (2002) has pointed out that there may be a profound geo-political change under way that will alter US relations with other states. This seems to be what Kagan means by the claim that 'today's transatlantic problem, in short, is not a George Bush problem. It is a power problem.'[16] These structural changes have also affected US–EU relations. The Europeans, freed from the Soviet threat, have become more willing to criticize the US. American policy-makers, on the other hand, may no longer regard the alliance with Europe as its most important foreign policy interest (Mead 2004: 123).

At the cultural level, Erik Voeten, in an analysis of UN voting patterns, has noted a growing 'preference gap' between the US and the rest of the world that has widened at a constant rate between 1991 and 2001. The conclusion is that 'US hegemony has elicited almost universal resistance' and this is before the impact of the Bush administration could be assessed (Voeten 2004: 747). Yet, despite these shifts, opinion polls have consistently shown that the US public is pro-UN. As Brzezinski (2004: 199) noted, 'as late as February 2003 . . . the majority of the American people believed that war should not be taken outside the UN framework'.

The pragmatist that one assumes exists in any US president would have to concede that the UN can help to promote US interests. It can offer legitimacy, experience, expertise and face-saving strategies. In addition, how the US treats the UN can have an important impact on how it is perceived by international opinion. Joseph Nye (2003b, 2004) has pointed out that the UN can serve US interests in a number of areas, but attacks on the UN may backfire in ways that reduce American soft power. Ironically, the US seemed to be relying on soft power to smooth the post-invasion transition in Iraq. As a result, it might have overestimated the welcome that US troops would receive once Saddam was toppled. Before the war, John Lewis Gaddis (2002) argued that the strategy relied on getting cheered, not shot, at. If so, it went disastrously wrong.

The evidence is that US soft power is in decline, for an assertive unilateralism adds to global distrust of and hostility to the US, which makes it harder to translate power into influence (Berger 2004). Albright (2003b: 17) points to a Pew Global Attitudes Project survey of 16,000 individuals in 20 countries. It found a sharp decline (15 percentage points or more) in positive attitudes to the US in states such as Brazil, France, Germany, Jordan, Nigeria, Russia and Turkey. The irony of this has been noted by Brian Urquhart (formerly a senior UN official), who points out that the US 'has antagonised international opinion at a time when worldwide solidarity against fundamentalist terrorism is desperately needed . . . to have drastically eroded, in less than four years, the position of respected international leadership built up by the United States over the past hundred years or more is an extraordinary achievement'.[17]

In the run-up to the Iraq invasion, Bush threatened that the UN would become irrelevant if it did not enforce its own resolutions. Yet, in September 2004, in what has become an annual address to the General Assembly, the president argued that 'the UN and its member nations must respond to Prime Minister Allawi's request, and do more to help build an Iraq that is secure, democratic, federal, and free'.[18] In the same speech, Bush seemed to want to work with the UN in a number of areas, including reducing Third World debt, obtaining a global ban on human cloning, confronting human trafficking, fighting AIDS and providing assistance to the people of Darfur.

He also proposed a new 'Democracy Fund' within the UN that would 'lay the foundations of democracy by instituting the rule of law and independent courts, a free press, political parties and trade unions'. The Fund would also support the work of election monitors. In the same month as the Bush address, the State Department set out five priority themes for the 59th General Assembly for 2004–5.[19] These are promoting democracy; economic freedom; furthering the roadmap to Middle East peace; ending trafficking in persons, particularly child sex tourism; and the banning of human cloning

So the Bush White House appears to have accepted that there are advantages in working with the UN, especially in areas that have been christened by Annan as 'problems without passports' because they defy unilateral solutions. These include nuclear proliferation, global terrorism, HIV/AIDS and drugs. Given this, what we are likely to see is a continuation of selective engagement with the UN. This will entail cooperation when interests overlap, but marginalization of the organization if it appears to adversely affect US interests. This is likely to happen whatever the future of the Bush Doctrine. As for this doctrine at the time of writing, it is hard to predict its future. Because a taboo has been broken and a preventive war has been launched by an American president, next time it might be easier to do so again. On the other hand, the experiences of war have triggered a sort of Kantian process called unsocial sociability. Kant (1991) famously pointed out how, when reason failed to stop wars, the experience of the miseries caused by armed conflict would in fact result in greater support for international cooperation to stop them in the future. It cannot be denied that problems arising from its first real test of the Bush Doctrine in Iraq, caused by what Stanley Hoffmann (2002) has called 'rhetorical overkill and ill-defined designs', have given many pause for thought, and it may be much harder to mobilize for similar actions on subsequent occasions. Indeed, as Indyk points out, US policy towards North Korea, Iran and Libya, all states presumed to have had well-advanced WMD programmes, suggests that the doctrine is no longer a guiding principle but just a foreign policy option.[20] The Iraq invasion has not dealt a mortal blow to international terrorism – in fact, quite the opposite. Weapons of mass destruction became 'weapons of mass disappearance' (Blix 2004: 255). Iraq has not become a peaceful and democratic state and, if it has transformed the Middle East, it is in the direction of even greater hostility to the US. As Mead has noted, you 'have a feeling that even Bush isn't saying, "Hey this was great. Let's do it again".'[21]

There will be a number of tests that might allow us to engage in a more accurate estimate of the state of US–UN relations. These include the elections due in Iraq in early 2005, the Middle East peace process and the willingness of a Republican-controlled House and Senate to release funds for the UN. On the last of these issues, there are signs that there could be troubled waters ahead. In September 2004, for example, the Senate Appropriations Committee cut $173.38 million from the Bush administration's request for the assessed payments to international organizations and $76 million from the peace-keeping request. Interestingly, the Committee criticized the lifespan of some deployments and expressed a view that private companies might be able to undertake peace-keeping missions in a more efficient manner.[22] Annan could also become the target of Congress because of controversies about the UN-sponsored 'Oil for Food' programme, which is now under investigation by both the UN and Congress. There are no suggestions that the Secretary-General behaved improperly, but there have been accusations that his son, Kojo Annan, was receiving payments from one of the companies involved in this programme. Congress has called on the UN investigation panel, led by former US Federal Reserve Chairman Paul Volcker, to release all papers connected with this case, but so far this request has been refused.[23]

It will also be worth examining the US reaction to the report of the 16-member High-Level Panel on Threats, Challenges and Change, created by Annan in September 2003 to recommend clear and practical measures for ensuring effective collective action. The report, entitled *A More Secure World: Our Shared Responsibility*, was released in December 2004.[24] The US representative on this panel was Brent Scowcroft, a national security adviser to both Ford and Bush Senior and a critic of the Iraq policy of the Bush White House. The report was a direct response to the failures of collective security during the run-up to the US invasion of Iraq and, at present, the Secretary-General is working on how to implement its recommendations. These will be discussed at a special summit of world leaders at the UN in September 2005.

The report identifies many of the areas that the US regards as priorities for international action, including WMD proliferation, terrorism, HIV/AIDS, human trafficking and the promotion of human rights. On the other hand, it also represents a strong re-endorsement of collective action, claiming that 'all states have an interest in forging a new comprehensive collective security system that will commit all of them to act cooperatively in the face of a broad array of threats' (para. 28). It also comes out strongly against unilateral preventive action, arguing that it presents a 'risk to global order . . . Allowing one to so act is to allow all' (para. 191). The report calls for reform of the Security Council but does not threaten the US veto because 'we see no practical way of changing the existing members' veto powers' (para. 256). This is because any permanent member can veto any proposal that would take the veto away. However, the same paragraph claims that the veto has 'an anachronistic character' and asks the permanent members to restrict its use. Whatever reforms are adopted, it is recommended that there be no expansion of the veto to other states.

Conclusion

What we are now presented with are two clear, but very distinct, visions about how to respond to the changing nature of global politics: the official US response, set out in the Bush Doctrine, and the official UN response, set out in the High-Level Panel on Threats, Challenges and Change. The first is unilateralist and endorses preventive war. The second is multilateralist and rejects preventive war in favour of a reformed version of collective security.

The current evidence is that the Bush administration will not transform itself in its second term. It will take the presidential election victory as a mandate to continue as it has in the past four years, which will mean more conflicts within the UN not just over preventive war, but also population policies, the environment and a range of other issues. But it need not be this way. The landmark West Point speech by Bush contains an interesting comment by the president. He declared that 'our nation's cause has always been larger than our nation's defence. We fight, as we always fight, for a just peace . . .'. Here, we catch a glimpse of the Wilsonian component in the neo-conservative position. If the balance between this and the Jacksonian element was to tilt in favour of the former, then it might encourage a belief that the promotion of US interests does not have to mean wounding the UN. Indeed, the High-Level Report contains useful ideas about how to create a more peaceful and just international system.

Some commentators refuse to take the idealistic dimension of the neo-conservative agenda seriously. Unlike Mead, for example, Halper and Clarke (2004: 19) argue that this is 'little more than window dressing'. However, they also point out that Bush did not enter office 'predisposed toward the neo-conservative agenda' (ibid.: 112) and has, on several occasions, expressed continuing support for multilateral institutions (ibid.: 330). So maybe there is some room for change. As the UN moves towards its 60th anniversary, it is probably about to embark on major reforms. It would be encouraging to see the US participate in this process with the same constructive and generous manner that it displayed at the organization's creation.

Notes

1 Jonathan Steele, 'The Bush Doctrine makes a nonsense of the UN Charter', *Guardian*, 7 June 2002.
2 Richard Falk, 'The new Bush Doctrine', *Nation*, 27 June 2002.
3 In Evelyn Leopold, 'Annan challenges US doctrine of preventive action', *Common Dreams Newscenter*, 23 September 2003.
4 Paul Wolfowitz is now Deputy Defence Secretary and Lewis Libby is Vice-President Cheney's Chief of Staff. Wolfowitz was offered the post as Ambassador to the UN by Powell before the Bush administration took office.
5 The Project for a New American Century's attitude to the UN is illustrated by looking at the sort of articles it supports on its web pages. See, for example, the reprint of Stephen Schwartz's article in the *Weekly Standard* 'UN go home', at www.newamericancentury.org/iraq-20030407a.htm. The basic thrust of the article is that the UN has done such a lousy job in Kosovo that no-one in their right minds should entrust the organization with a key role in Iraq. *Weekly Standard* is edited by William Kristol. After the Iraq 'victory', it carried a headline 'On to Iran'.
6 Richard Falk and David Krieger, 'Subverting the UN' at www.transnational.org/pressinf/2002/PF165_SubvertingUN.html.

7   A full text of the address is available at www.whitehouse.gov/news/releases/2002/06/print/20020601-3.html.

8   For a description of recent work by this body, see UN Press Release SC/8221. There is a full analysis of the UN's response to terrorism before and after 9/11 in Boulden and Weiss (2004).

9   www.un.org/webcast.ga/58/statements/usaeng030923.htm. Italics added.

10 usinfo.state.gov/is/Archive/2004/Mar/24-699579.html.

11 www.state.gov/p/io/c9703.htm.

12 usinfo.state.gov/is/Archive/2004/Mar/24-531091.html.

13 US State Department, *The United States Rejoins UNESCO: A Fact Sheet*, Washington, State Department, 22 September 2003.

14 See Brett D. Schaefer, *Not the Time for the United States to Rejoin UNESCO*, Background Paper no. 1405, Washington: Heritage Foundation, 2001, available at www.heritage.org/Research/InternationalOrganizations/BG1405.cfm.

15 See Martin S. Indyk, 'How Bush's doctrine of pre-emption was ambushed by reality' at www.brookings.edu/views/op-ed/indyk/20040326.htm. Indyk was an Assistant Secretary of State in the Clinton administration.

16 'Power and weakness', *Policy Review*, June 2002, at www.newamericancentury.org/kagan-20020520.htm.

17 Brian Urquhart, Contribution to 'The election and America's future', *New York Review of Books*, 4 November 2004, p. 16.

18 www.whitehouse.gov/news/releases/2004/09/20040921-3.html.

19 www.un.int/usa/ga59obj.htm.

20 Martin S. Indyk, 'How Bush's doctrine of pre-emption was ambushed by reality' at www.brookings.edu/views/op-ed/indyk/20040326.htm.

21 Walter Russell Mead, 'Iraq occupation erodes Bush doctrine', *Washington Post*, 28 June 2004.

22 www.globalpolicy.org/finance/docs/2004/0917senate.htm.

23 See, for example, 'Annan "disappointed" son didn't tell all', www.cnn.com, 29 November 2004; see also 'Destroying the UN: US should worry about the witch-hunt against Kofi Annan', *Financial Times*, 4 December 2004.

24 See www.un.org/secureworld/.

14 International law and human rights in a pre-emptive era

Malcolm D. Evans

No academic citations are necessary to make the point that one of the most frequently repeated mantras since 11 September 2001 is that human rights have been one of the most prominent casualties of the war against terror and of the more visible realities of Operation Enduring Freedom in Afghanistan and Operation Iraqi Freedom. It is an easy case to make. The sights and sounds of war themselves resonate with human suffering. The plight of those detained by the US at Guantánamo Bay (for a recent general account, see Rose 2004) – graphically (if not strictly speaking accurately) described as a legal black hole (Styen 2004) – and the revelations of the treatment of Iraqi detainees in the Abu Ghraib prison in Baghdad speak for themselves.[1] Daily news bulletins and newspapers bring stories of suffering into our homes.[2] One of the consequences has been to undermine the credibility of the US and the UK as exemplars and advocates of respect for human rights, and this has been reinforced by the introduction of draconian legislation ostensibly aimed at furthering the protection of the people from further acts of terror but which also challenge many of the well-entrenched orthodoxies of the civil rights movement and well-established safeguards against the misuse of authority. Another consequence has been to let loose a debate about the legitimacy of torture and ill-treatment of detainees in quarters where, even five years ago, it would have been thought unthinkable. Does all of this mean that the era of human rights, ushered in by the horror of World War II, is in retreat?

Human rights in the international arena

Over the last 50 years, a great deal has been said about international law and human rights, and a great deal has been achieved. Indeed, possibly not since the state-centred system of international law and international relations came into being at the end of the wars of religion in seventeenth-century Europe has an emerging concept so radically transformed our way of thinking about global order. It is, however, also true that, during this period, far too much was invested in the possibility of international law providing an effective means of addressing the human rights concerns held by individuals, civil society and governments at a time when it was – or should have been – clear that the structures, systems and presuppositions of the international legal community were inimical to such an endeavour.[3] The rhetoric of an international legal commitment to protect human rights tended to become an end in itself, and the effective realization of the legal obligations that were put in place was little more than an aspiration. Human rights diplomacy ran the risk of focusing more upon the facilitation and realization of more general political objectives than of improving the lot of those subject to human rights abuses on a day-to-day basis. Thus, human rights sank into the warp and weft of international discourse, colouring but not transforming it.[4] Change – although real – has been incremental and, while international law now provides the template against which the practice of states falls to be assessed, it still has not proved capable of generating the mechanisms through which states can properly be held to account.[5]

International legal obligations are, for the most part, derived from treaties entered into by states themselves or emerge from the process of customary law formation, this being based on the practice of states coupled with a belief in the legal quality of that practice. If we were to conduct a stock-taking of the situation in the early 1990s, the position might have been recorded as follows: numerous human rights treaties have been created and entered into force at the global and regional level which have their own specific implementation regimes. These include critical scrutiny of self-assessments through reporting procedures, inspectoral commitments and, of course, quasi-judicial and judicial procedures including the UN Human Rights Committee and the European and Inter-American Courts of Human Rights. Compliance with these procedures is, however, limited. Beyond this, the UN Charter – itself an international treaty – provides the platform for the work of the UN Commission on Human Rights and the many procedures that operate under its auspices and are subject to political scrutiny and oversight. Customary international law now embraces the protection of many of the more basic human rights, although the mechanisms of international accountability associated with them were comparatively feeble. In short, much remained to be done, but the changed geo-political climate following the collapse of the Soviet Union proved to be a pivotal moment, opening up the prospect of change.

In 1993, the UN World Conference on Human Rights adopted the Vienna Declaration and Plan of Action,[6] yet this sent out mixed messages. Whatever intrinsic significance this has is greatly outweighed by the significance of the debate that it fostered, this being the question of the universality of human rights and of cultural relativism (see Bauer and Bell 1999). The underlying issue was even simpler and starker: does the realization of international human rights commitments depend upon the existence of democracy? Although the question was not directly posed in that fashion at Vienna, it might well have been because the states lining up to challenge the universalist human rights paradigm were largely non-democratic countries seeking to retain their international and internal political legitimacy (see, for example, Bayef-sky 1996). The stance they took was certainly bold – arguably, desperate – but one cannot fault their logic, as the logic of human rights does indeed lead back to democracy and the logic of universal human rights to the universal-izing of democracy.

Resort to the language of 'human rights' can fulfil various functions, one of which is akin to the role of 'Bills of Rights' within domestic constitutions, which provide the bases upon which the relationship between power and pop-ulace is policed, setting out principles that guide the examination of activities that take place in the borderlands between the acceptable and unacceptable conduct of both state and citizen. In this guise, they form a key component of a given form of 'constitutional compact' – that of democratic, constitutional governance. They are designed for and work within a given type of 'legal space'. International human rights can also fulfil an entirely different func-tion that flows from the perception that humans are being 'wronged' (Booth 1999). Whether this is 'true' is immaterial: indeed, it is (in human terms) unknowable. International law has converted these claims into a language of rights that are to be espoused and reflected in their national legal order.[7] If, then, states simply ignore their 'international human rights' commitments within their domestic legal orders, it seems inevitable that there will be pres-sure to draw on the other mechanisms of the international legal system to assist in bringing about their domestic realization.

This is exactly what happened during the 1990s when all these nascent trends and frustrations coalesced into the claim that the international com-munity was justified in authorizing collective intervention in order to avert humanitarian disaster and, in the wake of this, that, in the absence of a clear collective decision to intervene for humanitarian reasons, states were enti-tled to take such action unilaterally, with 'humanitarian' being understood as the alter ego of the 'gross violations of human rights' (for an overview of these debates, see Holzgrefe and Keohane 2003). These claims reached their high watermarks in the debates surrounding the no-fly zones imposed over Iraq in order to protect the Shia and Kurdish populations from violence and the NATO intervention in Kosovo in 1999 (Wheeler 2000: 139–71 (Iraq) and 242–84 (Kosovo)). Influential writers advocated the use of force not only to prevent the continuation of human rights abuses but also in order to bring about the conditions in which human rights could be protected. Thus, writ-ers as influential as John Rawls (1999) could argue in favour of extending the protections of the liberal international community only to those illiberal societies that could nevertheless be deemed 'decent', while Michael Riesman (2000) and Fernando Téson (2003) are among the more well-known names in an increasing group who called for spreading democracy as a necessary precursor to the full realization of human rights and freedoms. Others, in-cluding Alan Buchanan (2004), have called for the wholesale reorientation of the international legal system around a moral theory that has the realization of human rights as its primary objective. Crusades for human rights were all but with us,[8] and the best that legal 'purists' might do was to resort to the view that, although illegal, such interventions were nevertheless legitimate[9] – though without paying too much thought as to the consequences of decoupling legitimacy from legality.

The Bush Doctrine of pre-emptive self-defence can easily be seen as the most radical outworking of this approach yet advanced because it calls for the protection of democratic society by the propagation of democratic society. Whereas others have argued that the peoples within a state have a right to democratic governance, the claim that it implicitly makes is that all states have the right to call for, and work towards, the establishment of democratic governance in all states, as this is the necessary precondition for the realization of human rights, which forms the bedrock of international peace, international security and international justice. Yet, rather than being seen as a means through which human rights thinking finally shakes off the shackles of a self-serving state-centred international legal system, the idea of using the tools of international law and of the international community to delegitimize states that routinely perpetrate wholesale violations of human rights and of bringing the force – literally – of the international community to bear upon them has receded from view.

All moral purposes pursued through force end up mired with the misery that their pursuit produces, and this is no exception. It seems to me, however, that there is something different – or, at least, additional – here. Although capable of being projected in the fashion outlined above, the Bush Doctrine has not in fact been used in this way at all: rather, it has been premised on the more cautious, and introspective, grounds of national security. It has become a means to justify the 'taking out the threat' rather than as a means of encouraging the export of standards of governance. It is only when all other justifications have failed that the US and UK have fallen back on the humanitarian justifications for Operation Iraqi Freedom, which therefore seem completely devoid of credibility. There seemed to be a failure of imagination or of will at a moment that could have changed the way in which we view the international order and when the direction of international law could have been radically transformed. But it did not happen and the moment was lost.

What are the consequences for human rights? The focus of attention has now veered back towards its more traditional locus, the manner in which each state treats those under its jurisdiction subject to a degree of general international scrutiny and oversight. Where there is real evidence of ongoing abuse, then the international community may attempt to assert itself – as with Sudan at the time of writing[10] – but the sense of expectation that the world community was on the brink of seriously engaging with the worst of its human rights violators by exorcizing them from the society of civilized nations and striving to replace dictatorship or tyranny with participative democracy as a tool in the universal realization of basic human rights has been lost. You can put genies back into bottles, it seems. At this level, at least, then, it is true to say that the quest for the realization of human rights through international intervention has been a victim of the war against terror.

Human rights in the domestic arena

The feature of the post-9/11 world that has attracted the most attention is the manner in which the world's leading democracies have seemingly trenched upon their human rights commitments in order to pursue the war against terror. In the US, this is best exemplified legislatively by the PATRIOT Act[11] and, of course, by the attempt by the administration to classify those detained in Afghanistan as 'unlawful combatants' at the US base at Guantánamo Bay in Cuba in order to try to ensure that their detention was beyond the reach of the constitutional protections offered to detainees held within the US. In the UK, the response has in some ways been even more dramatic as it has entailed issuing a notice derogating from its obligations under Article 5(1) of the European Convention on Human Rights in order that it might detain foreign nationals suspected of posing a threat to national security indefinitely and without moving to trial.

In both the US and the UK, debates have also been ignited on the legitimacy of using previously impermissible degrees of force during interrogation in order to acquire information. In the US, this has found voice through Alan Dershowitz's argument[12] in favour of a controlled 'licensing' approach that does not so much prevent as delay legal scrutiny of the evidence upon which the permission to interrogate in such a fashion was based. In this way, it is argued, such interrogation remains within the orbit of the rule of law. Alternative approaches have included manipulating the received view of what forms of physical and psychological pressure are to be considered illegitimate – in effect, raising the threshold of what is to 'count' as ill-treatment – and to be creative in formulating possible defences to domestic criminal prosecution.[13] In the UK, there has been a focus on the legitimacy of using information allegedly acquired through torture or other forms of ill-treatment at the hands of non-UK nationals in order to justify the detention of aliens without trial. Further curtailments of civil liberties continue to be mooted in the interests of the war against terror, the most recent being the suggestion of the removal of trial by jury for those suspected of terrorist offences. Such is the totemic power of the all-pervasive and yet unseen threat that it is difficult to gauge the point at which general tolerance of such erosions might lie.

There are, however, a number of obvious but important points that need to be taken into account when drawing up the domestic balance sheet. The first is that all these developments have been subject to intense public scrutiny and debate, the legitimacy of which has remained unquestioned. Although the debates surrounding the rights and wrongs of these responses to the threat to national security posed by international terrorism have often been acrimonious, no attempt has been made to curtail those debates 'in the interests of national security', this being the point past which no democratic state can go without forfeiting its position as a democratic society. However, this is not saying much more than that the major democracies of the world have not wholly abandoned their democratic and human rights credentials. But there is more to record.

Whatever the horrors and iniquities of Guantánamo Bay, it remains the case that the US Supreme Court has not allowed the administration to evade judicial oversight and has insisted that the grounds of detention be open to challenge.[14] In simple terms, the argument presented by the executive was that the relevant provision of the US Code, SS. 2241(a), which provided that 'Writs of habeas corpus may be granted by the Supreme Court, any justice thereof, the district courts and any circuit judge within their respective jurisdictions', could not apply to the detainees at Guantánamo Bay for the obvious reason that it was not within the jurisdiction of any of these courts or judges as it was not sovereign US territory. In *Rasul v. Bush*, the Supreme Court took the view that it was sufficient that aliens were being detained by the executive in a territory over which it exercised 'plenary and exclusive' jurisdiction. It is unclear whether this is the same thing as 'effective control' for the purposes of international legal responsibility but, whatever the case, there is some truth in the observation made by the three dissenting Justices that the Supreme Court was potentially extending its jurisdictional reach to the 'four corners of the earth' in that it was (arguably) permitting aliens captured in a foreign theatre of combat to bring a petition for habeas corpus before the US courts and thus permitting judicial scrutiny of aspects of the conduct of conflict in a previously unheralded fashion.[15] It does not matter whether this is considered to be a plus or a minus: what is incontrovertible is that the Supreme Court chose to rise to the challenge and has carved out a potentially wide-ranging and significant jurisdictional capability through which to explore the legitimacy of executive action in the pursuit of the war on terror – and, in passing, war in general. Nor has Abu Ghraib been lost from sight, and the first of those involved in the ill-treatment of detainees that took place there have recently been sentenced by military juries to ten years' imprisonment.[16]

In the UK, the House of Lords has also risen to the challenge presented by the 2001 Anti-Terrorism, Crime and Security Act. The Court of Appeal had dismissed a claim that the Act was incompatible with the terms of Article 5 in conjunction with Article 14 of the European Convention on Human Rights on the ground that, although it discriminated between UK nationals and non-UK nationals suspected of involvement in terrorism, there were legitimate grounds for such different treatment.[17] However, in December 2004, eight of the nine Law Lords hearing the appeal agreed that, not only was the 2001 Act incompatible with those provisions, but the measures were also a disproportionate response to the situation facing the UK in the wake of 9/11.[18] As Lord Hope put it, 'It is the first responsibility of government in a democratic society to protect and safeguard the lives of its citizens . . . and it is the duty of the court to do all it can to respect and uphold that principle.

But the court has another duty too. It is to protect and safeguard the rights of the individual'.[19] A declaration of incompatibility does not render an act invalid and, early in 2005, the Government responded by introducing the Prevention of Terrorism Act 2005, adopted on 11 March 2005 after a parliamentary struggle of epic proportions. The last of those detained under the 2001 Act were released on that day, but a number of them were immediately made subject to the draconian restrictions provided for by its successor, and it seems likely that the issue will still be taken up under the European Convention on Human Rights. Whatever the final outcome, the obvious point is that these matters are being challenged before the courts in a fashion that demonstrates the potency of human rights considerations within the domestic legal system. Proponents of human rights may disapprove of where that balance is struck, but is it human rights thinking that continues to provide the relevant conceptual paradigm? What is more, this is a major departure from what might have been expected based on the previous practice of the courts in both the US and the UK. Writing at the end of 2003, Eyal Benevenisti (2004) pointed to the tendencies and traditions of deference to the executive in previous court decisions in both the US and the UK regarding challenges to its practices in times of war, and such tendencies were certainly in evidence at that time. A year later, however, a very different picture has emerged, which suggests a major change in judicial attitude and approach.

Beyond these high-profile courtroom set pieces lies a point of much greater long-term significance. The idea that the leading democracies are somehow 'immune' (in a non-legal sense) from the demands of human rights compliance has been shattered. This is not a new revelation to the UK, which had this truth brought home to it vividly in relation to the proceedings brought against it before the European Commission and Court of Human Rights regarding internment in Northern Ireland. But the lesson seems to have been lost a little during the 1990s with the rise of a 'for export only' culture by government in relation to human rights. For the US, it is perhaps its first major confrontation with the need to balance human rights considerations against the demands of national security, and it appears to have been shaken by the strength of global reaction to its attempts to manoeuvre its way around the international legal framework. Some of the more aggressive elements of US practice in the international sphere have been toned down.[20] At the same time, the US came in for renewed attention from the regional and international human rights communities and mechanisms, notably the Inter-American Commission on Human Rights, whose jurisdiction in relation to US activities in the Americas is unquestioned.[21] There was no legal black hole – what was lacking were enforcement agencies whose work carried clout.

The UK has, however, certainly felt the direct force of engagement with international human rights bodies in relation to its war on terror. For example, the European Committee for the Prevention of Torture has now visited those detained under the 2001 Anti-Terrorism, Crime and Security Act twice, in February 2002[22] and March 2004, and the UN Committee against Torture expedited its consideration of the UK's regular report in the light of the publicity concerning Abu Ghraib and other allegations and, in November 2004, issued a broad-ranging series of recommendations that challenge elements of the 2001 Anti-Terrorism, Crime and Security Act and the use of evidence suspected of having been acquired through torture abroad.[23] The UN Committee for the Elimination of Racial Discrimination (CERD) has also expressed its deep concern about the Anti-Terrorism, Crime and Security Act, focusing on its discriminatory treatment of non-nationals.[24]

These incidents may seem like pin pricks – and indeed they are. But add to this the activism within the UN and elsewhere[25] in response to Guantánamo Bay and Abu Ghraib and, although it is too soon to predict with certainty, one of the more paradoxical outcomes of the application of the Bush Doctrine may yet prove to be the reinvigoration and renewed potency of the human rights dimension in the scrutiny of executive and administrative action at both domestic and international levels. Human rights have been infringed – grievously – in the wake of 9/11 and their legitimacy challenged, but the idea of human rights has not succumbed to the pressures placed upon it. On the contrary, the resilience and potency of human rights thinking has won through, which suggests that it has not become a victim of the war on terror.

Conclusion: a strengthening tide?

The human rights of many individuals have been gravely violated by the prosecution of the war against terror and systems and structure established that have the potential seriously to erode the freedoms long enjoyed and taken for granted by many within the western democracies. The seriousness of this is not to be dismissed. However, despite the obvious and visible erosions of human rights, and despite the rather dismissive rhetoric that has sought to marginalize human rights in the interests of national security, there is evidence that suggests that the power that the idea of human rights now holds within the international community is not weakening, but is in fact strengthening.

Slowly but surely, some of the more resilient barriers to the effective implementation and enforcement of human rights obligations are wearing thin or wearing away. The traditional claim that human rights are a matter of internal affairs and not a matter of international concern is now no longer heard or tolerated. Criminal responsibility now attaches to an ever-growing list of violations of fundamental human rights and personal immunity of perpetrators denied before international tribunals and increasingly challenged before domestic tribunals in respect of an ever-broadening list of defendants in both criminal and civil proceedings. Universal jurisdiction is now being asserted in practice as well as in theory. Domestic human rights commissions continue to multiply and improve in quality and effectiveness. Beyond the headlines, there is solid evidence of continued achievement and recognition of human rights values and approaches. The reality of implementing the Bush Doctrine has taken the wind out of the sails of those who advocate the forcible export of democracy in the interests of human rights and dispelled domestic complacency concerning human rights. The tragedy is that there remains so great a need to be vigilant.

Notes

1 See, for example, Amnesty International Report, 'USA: Pattern of brutality – war crimes at Abu Ghraib', issued 7 May 2004, and the UN Commission on Human Rights, 'Report on the present situation in Iraq', UN Doc E/CN.4/2005/4 (9 June 2004). See also the accounts and documentation in Danner (2004).

2 See, for example, the survey by Bronwen Madox, 'Human rights clash with terror war', *The Times*, 11 November 2004, pp. 39–40, extracting from and commenting on the United Kingdom Foreign and Commonwealth Office Human Rights Annual Report 2004 (Cm 6564), published that day.

3 This can be gleaned from a critical reading of numerous works devoted to exploring the emergence of the human rights 'regime' within international law in general and the UN in particular. See, for example, Alston (1992) and Alston and Crawford (2000).

4 See, for example, Mullerson (1997), which concluded in a rather downbeat fashion that, during the Cold War, the west's human rights diplomacy 'played a certain positive role in the improvements which we now see in many countries'.

5 There has been considerable progress regarding holding individuals to account for the more egregious human rights abuses that may qualify as either international crimes or offences attracting universal jurisdiction. See, for example, Ratner and Abrams (2001); Reydams (2003); Romano *et al.* (2004). There has, however, been comparatively little progress regarding the holding of states to account, and the most notable development in recent years has been the abandonment of the idea of holding states criminally responsible for their actions at all under international law. For an overview, see Crawford (2002: 16–20).

6 For the text and an overview of the process, see 1993 *Human Rights Law Journal* 14: 346.

7 For an exploration of the interplay between international human rights obligations and domestic change, see Risse *et al.* (1999).

8 If the use of that terminology might be deemed offensive within parts of the Muslim world, then such offence could only have been compounded by the European Court of Human Rights when it pronounced what most thought unpronounceable: that the realization of human rights required the existence of democratic structures, that states were entitled to take steps to protect themselves from forces that challenged their democratic structures and the introduction of Sharia law was one such challenge, because 'sharia is incompatible with the fundamental principles of democracy, as set forth in the Convention'. See *Refah Partisi v. Turkey*, [GC], Judgment 13 February 2003, para. 123, Reports of Judgments and Decisions, 2003-II, (2003) 37 European Human Rights Reports 1. For a critical examination of this case in the context of an exploration of the war against terrorism, see McGoldrick (2004: 163–8).

9 See, for example, the conclusions of the Independent International Commission in *The Kosovo Report: Conflict, International Response and Lessons Learnt* (Oxford: Oxford University Press, 2000).

10 See UN Commission on Human Rights Report on the Situation in the Darfur

Region of Sudan, 3 May 2004 and UN SC Resolution 1564, 18 September 2004 which, acting under chapter VII of the UN Charter, established the Commission of Inquiry on Darfur, the Report of which was released on 25 January 2005. On 31 March 2005, the UN Security Council, in Resolution 1593 (2005) and acting under chapter VII of the UN Charter, referred the situation in Darfur to the Prosecutor of the International Criminal Court in the Hague.

11 The Uniting and Strengthening America by Providing Appropriate Tools to Intercept and Obstruct Terrorism Act of 2001 (USA PATRIOT Act), PL 107-05.

12 See, generally, Dershowitz (2002) and 'Opinion: torture warrants', *Spectator*, 1 May 2004.

13 Both approaches are found in the classified but widely trailed US Working Group Report on Detainee Interrogations in the Global War on Terrorism of March 2003. There was, however, something of a retreat from the extreme views expressed in this report in the subsequent Levin Memorandum issued by the US Department of Justice on 20 December 2004.

14 See *Hamdi et al. v. Rumsfeld, Secretary of Defense*, No. 03-6696 Decision of June 28 2004 (as regards US citizens) and *Rasul et al. v. Bush, President of the United States*, No. 03-344, Decision of June 28 2004 (as regards non-US nationals).

15 Ibid. Dissenting Opinion of Judge Scalia (joined by Chief Justice Rehnquist and Judge Thomas). A similar result was given by the UK Court of Appeal in R (on the application of *Al Skeini and Others v. The Secretary of State for Defence*, 14 December 2004, [2004] EWHC 2991 (Admin)), in which it was decided that the court was able to exercise jurisdiction on the basis of the 1998 Human Rights Act in the case of a claim made in respect of a detainee who died in the custody of British Forces in Iraq, operating with the consent of the Iraqi authorities. (The court rejected the broader claim that it could exercise jurisdiction over five other representative cases concerning claimants killed as a result of military operations in the field. See paras 281–8.)

16 Special Charles Graner was sentenced to ten years' imprisonment and dishonourably discharged from the US Army for his role in abusing detainees by a military jury in Fort Worth, Texas, in January 2005. See Reuters News Report, 16 January 2005.

17 *A and Others v. Secretary of State for the Home Department*, [2002] EWCA Civ 1502, [2004] QB 335, 25 October 2002, allowing an appeal against the original decision of the Special Immigration Appeals Commission, [2002] HRLR 1274, 30 July 2002.

18 *A and Others v. Secretary of State for the Home Department*, [2004] UKHL 56, 16 December 2004. In another related judgement, the Court of Appeal had also rejected a claim that the Secretary of State was not entitled to reply on evidence potentially acquired through torture or ill-treatment committed by non-UK nationals abroad when determining whether to detain non-nationals under the terms of the Act (see *A and Others v. Secretary of State for the Home Department*, 11 August 2004, [2004] EWCA Civ 1123). The latest House of Lords judgement did not have to address this question, and the matter was left open pending a direct challenge to the legitimacy of the detention orders issued under Section 23 of the 2001 Act. See *A and Others v. Secretary of State for the Home Department*, [2004] UKHL 56, paras 71 (Lord Bingham) and 220 (Baroness Hale).

19 Ibid., para. 99.

20 For example, the US was singularly unsuccessful in its attempt to halt the adoption of an Optional Protocol to the UN Convention against Torture in 2002 which, once in force, will ultimately permit visits to all places of detention by an international visiting body. See Evans and Haenni-Dale (2004) and Dennis (2003). It also backed down from its attempt to continue to secure a resolution from the UN Security Council exempting US servicemen taking part in UN-authorized military activities abroad from the reach of the International Criminal Court.

21 See Inter-American Commission on Human Rights, Detainees in Guantánamo Bay, Cuba: Request for Precautionary Measures, Decision of 12 March 2002 (see *Human Rights Law Journal*, 2002, 23: 15).

22 The report arising from this visit is published as CPT/Inf (2003) 18 and the response of the UK to this Report as CPT/Inf (2003) 19 (both published in February 2003). Also, in a previously unheralded preface to its 14th General Report, (CPT/Inf (2004) 28, published 21 September 2004), the CPT went as far as to observe that: 'There is also a growing body of evidence that the methods of detention and interrogation employed in various locations, in the context of the fight against terrorism and of military operations it has spawned, have on occasion violated that prohibition. The treatment meted out to some persons detained by Coalition forces in Iraq, revealed in a graphic manner by material placed in the public domain earlier this year, is but one illustration.'

23 See UN Committee against Torture, CAT/C/CR/33/3, issued 25 November 2004.

24 See UN Committee for the Elimination of Racial Discrimination, CERD/C/63/C0/11, issued 10 December 2003. The committee reiterated this general point in its most recent General Recommendation, No. 30 adopted in March 2004.

25 For a concise summary, including the establishment and work of the UN Counter Terrorism Committee under UN Security Council Resolution 1373 (28 September 2001), see von Schorlemer (2003).

15 United States unilateralism in a multilateral legal order

Phoebe Okowa

The legal order that the United States subscribed to in 1945 was decidedly multilateral in structure and outlook. As is well known, in the scheme contained in the Charter of the United Nations, all states unilaterally agreed to renounce the use of force in interstate relations. The renunciation in Article 2 (4) provides that: 'All members shall refrain in their international relations from the threat or use of force against the territorial integrity or political independence of any state, or in any other manner inconsistent with the purposes of the United Nations.' In return, a collective security framework was put in place which gave the five permanent members authority to monopolize the use of force on behalf of the international community. In order to ensure that decisions were not taken on the basis of narrow self-interest, it was made a condition that all decisions involving the use of force would require the unanimous consent of all the five permanent members. The concurrence of all the permanent members was put in place to prevent the taking of rush decisions and to allow time for reflection and accommodation as to the best course of action. The possible use of a veto by any one of the five permanent members was an indispensable element of this new legal regime. There was implicitly a commitment on the part of the selected five that all their actions would be taken in the collective interest. In taking their seats on the Security Council, the permanent members were in effect accepting that they would assume extended and onerous responsibilities on behalf of the international community. The resulting legal regime, as is widely acknowledged, was far from perfect. It was frequently violated by states who at times found its constraints stifling but, as the Secretary-General of the UN has recently stated, it also provided a framework for peaceful coexistence that has lasted for 58 years.[1]

The post-1945 legal order also entrenched in the international system a principle of formal equality. Juridically, all states had the same rights and, in practical terms, this meant membership of international organizations on the same terms and an equal entitlement to vote and take part in the deliberations of international institutions (except for the Security Council) (Jennings and Watts 1992: 340). For instance, Monaco and the US would have the same vote in the deliberations of the General Assembly. Juridical equality was also accompanied by a formal commitment to the principle of non-interference in the internal affairs of all states. Article 2 (7) of the Charter firmly reiterated the principle of non-interference in matters regarded as being essentially within the sphere of domestic jurisdiction. However, formal equality was also tempered by an element of realism – contributions to the UN budget, for instance, were weighted to take into account the economic ability of the member states. A second element of the juridical equality entrenched in the legal regime since 1945 was the acceptance of the entirely consensual nature of the international legal order – only those norms that had received the assent of the community of states could be regarded as binding on them (Jennings and Watts 1992: 341; Roth 2003: 236).[2] A state could thus opt out of legal rules at the formation stage if it felt that subscribing to them was not in its national interest. The refusal by the United States to join the many multilateral treaty regimes, such as the Law of the Sea Convention,[3] Comprehensive Test Ban Treaty,[4] Convention on Biodiversity,[5] 1997 Ottawa Landmines Convention,[6] Kyoto Protocol on Climate Change,[7] the Rome Statute on the International Criminal Court,[8] although viewed by many as obstructive unilateralism, is perfectly consistent with the consensual nature of the international legal order (Scharf 2000). The situation is different, however, once there is a formal commitment to treaty obligations – non-compliance is strictly speaking not permissible except on the treaty's or customary law's own terms.

As is well known, for most of the Cold War period, the collective security regime enshrined in the Charter never worked as was intended. With a few notable exceptions, the US has largely remained committed to the form of the multilateral arrangements in the UN Charter and its organizing principles. In practice, though, the interpretation placed by it on the Charter regime has been self-serving and designed to advance personal interests. But there are very few examples of explicit rejection of the multilateral framework by the US. The best and most frequently cited is the statement made by the American Secretary of State Dean Acheson at the time of the Cuban Missile crisis. He argued that 'the power, position and prestige of the United States had been challenged by another state; and law simply does not deal with such questions of ultimate power . . . No law can destroy the state creating the law. The survival of states is not a matter of law.'[9] According to Acheson, the crisis was not a legal issue. In other contexts, the US ironically argued that, insofar as the Charter had failed to function as intended, the obligations contained in it were no longer binding on its members. Implicit in this was the view that individual member states possessed something akin to a default power, which could be exercised should the organization fail to function. Indeed, it is in this area of use of force that the US has felt most at liberty to disregard the restraining norms.

This justification put forward by Acheson has not been relied on subsequently but, taken to its logical conclusion, it would irredeemably undermine the contextual framework on which the legal restraints on the use of force are grounded. The position nevertheless remains isolated and, in subsequent contexts, although interpreting the law to advance its own self-interest, the US has remained largely committed to the view that the Charter framework remains applicable and that disputes concerning the use of force may be subjected to external third-party scrutiny if the rule of law is to be maintained. In 1984, Nicaragua's Sandinista regime led by Daniel Ortega brought an action before the international court accusing the US of giving armed support to the Nicaraguan opposition forces that were fighting to overthrow Ortega's socialist regime. Specifically, the government of Nicaragua argued that the support given violated the established norms prohibiting the use of force and non-intervention in the internal affairs of another state. Although contesting the jurisdiction of the international court in that case, the US nevertheless accepted the applicability of legal standards and the possibility of scrutiny by the political organs including the Organization of American States (OAS) and the Security Council.[10] The argument that the US was the sole judge of whether military action in any instance was aggressive or defensive was not advanced at all in the many arguments put forward before the international court.

Many of the contestable uses of force during the Cold War period were paradoxically always justified by reference to the Charter principles. Thus, the interventions in Grenada, the Dominican Republic and Panama were justified by reference to democracy as a basic and inalienable Charter right and, as a corollary, a corresponding obligation on member states to restore the democratic ideal even if this included overthrowing undemocratic regimes not based on the consent of the governed (Chesterman 2001: 91). A related argument proceeded on the premise that undemocratic regimes not based on the consent of the governed could not claim to speak on behalf of the state; sovereignty in such situations rested with the people, and the forcible overthrow of these regimes did not violate the principles on non-use of force (Roth 2000: ch. 7). In other instances where there had been violations of human rights, the US argued that a use of force to ensure respect for particular human rights was consistent with the Charter. State sovereignty, it was suggested, should not be allowed to stand in the way of human rights. This argument rested on a hierarchical construct of international law, with human rights at the pinnacle. The alleged priority given to human rights was also frequently put forward as a justification for humanitarian intervention – the over-riding purpose of the UN, the argument went, was to protect human rights even if this involved using force against and without the consent of the territorial sovereign. The justification was put forward in relation to the humanitarian relief operations in southern Iraq and, more dramatically, when the US acted as part of NATO's controversial humanitarian intervention in Kosovo.[11]

The interpretation placed by the US on the content and parameters of self-defence has also generally been regarded as self-serving and going be-

yond what international law as it stands permits. Nevertheless, the arguments have been firmly based on the collective framework in the Charter.
This includes the view that the right to use force is available not only against
attacks by states but also in response to threats that are merely anticipated
as well as those that are imminent. Thus, the US has consistently argued
that, given the nature of threats from terrorists and other non-state actors,
it would be unrealistic to expect it to wait until an attack had materialized
before taking defensive action – the nature of threats in this context is different from those posed by states, and preventive or pre-emptive action may be
the only realistic way of dealing with these threats.[12] Some of these justifications were put forward in relation to the ill-fated and largely doomed war to
overthrow Saddam Hussein. Although always a minority position, it was by no
means isolated. The claim that a right to use force extended to anticipated
threats and that proportionality of measures must be assessed by reference
not just to what is necessary to repel an actual attack but also to what might
be desirable to deter future threats has also been shared by Israel and to
some extent – at least in relation to the war on Iraq – the United Kingdom.
These interpretations, although widely seen as controversial, have nevertheless acted as a springboard for debate on how to make the UN relevant to the
needs of states in the twenty-first century.[13]

In other contexts, the justification for the use of force has been squarely
grounded on UN Security Council resolutions. Thus, the NATO operation
in which the US took part in Kosovo partly rested on a controversial interpretation of the applicable Security Council resolutions as having either
authorized the action taken or implicitly ratified the action afterwards by
the endorsement of the terms of the peace settlement secured as a result
of the intervention (Chesterman 2001). In each case, it is significant that
these unilateral efforts were broadly seen as consistent with legal and moral
precepts that underpin the collective Charter framework.

Much has been made of the American refusal to take part in the multilateral arrangements in place to combat global climate change and to enforce
accountability for serious violations of international criminal law norms.
Although non-participation in the climate change regime has a longer
history, it will not be considered here for want of space (Obethur and Ott
1999; Birnie and Boyle 2002: 523). The rejection of the Rome Statute of the
International Criminal Court (ICC) and the concerted effort embarked on
by the United States to undermine its key institutions is potentially more
worrying. True non-participation in the ICC treaty was one stance the US
was perfectly entitled to take; treaty regimes remain robustly consensual,
and non-participation is within the sovereign rights of all states. The US had
participated and influenced the final outcome of the treaty text. Many of its
key provisions, such as deferral to national legal systems, limits on prosecuto-
rial discretion and due process guarantees, had been insisted upon and won
by the US (Sewell and Kaysen 2000). In the event, the rejection of the final
instrument can be only be attributed to the fact that the states parties were

not prepared to accord the US any special or privileged status in the resulting instrument.

This rather benign account reveals that, far from rejecting the multilateral legal order outright, the US has largely sought to advance its interests
within it. Yet it is also clear that, in many instances, the interpretation placed
by the US on the content of the law is not so benign but, in fact, amounts to
either an outright rejection of the existing normative regimes and institutions or their modification in ways inimical to their underlying policies. In
the *Nicaragua Case*, the International Court of Justice rejected the US arguments that it manifestly lacked jurisdiction and proceeded to decide the case
on its merits.[14] Having lost the jurisdictional phase, the US refused to take
any further part in the proceedings and ignored the final judgement. The
message here was clear – it was only prepared to take part in multilateral
institutions as long as its own views carried the day. It would bow to the collective will only to the extent that it coincided with its own self-interest.

The protracted debate on the war in Iraq has now been largely laid to rest;
the broad consensus being that, from the point of view of the Charter and
of the UN, it was clearly illegal.[15] However, more than any other previous
incident, it does reveal contempt for the multilaterally agreed constraints
in situations where they stand in the way of US self-interests. The argument
put forward by the US and the UK that a use of force even without UN
authorization was legitimate in order to prevent the unreasonable use of the
veto by the other permanent members was clearly unsustainable. Arguably, it
is precisely with these kind of difficult cases in mind that the veto was put in
place to prevent hasty and ill-thought decisions; far from indicating failure,
the disagreements between members of the Security Council on the legality
of the war demonstrated that the veto working as intended.

Conclusion: implications for the international legal order

The perceived unilateralism pursued by the US has not always been inimical
to the international legal order. In some cases, the robust rejection of the
privileges and special exemptions that the US has sought for itself has
reinforced faith in the multilateral legal order and the institutions charged
with enforcing it. Indeed, the US refusal to participate in the *Nicaragua Case*
and its final rejection of the court's judgement in that case restored the court's
battered reputation that occurred in the wake of its controversial judgement's
in the *South West Africa Case*[16] and the *Nuclear Tests Cases*.[17] In the aftermath
of those judgements, the majority of states in the international community
were disenchanted with the International Court of Justice as a neutral forum
for upholding the rule of law. The long fallow period that accompanied those
decisions only came to an end after the judgement in the *Nicaragua Case*.
The judgement confirmed the continuing vitality of international law as a
yardstick against which unilateral state action is to be measured.

The many controversial instances of self-serving interpretations of the content and quality of the normative restraints on the use of force put forward by the US both during the Cold War and afterwards have contributed to the development of the legal regimes in unexpected ways. Rejection of the US-led NATO intervention in Kosovo resolutely confirmed that no principle of humanitarian intervention enjoyed general acceptance as a matter of positive law.[18] These excessive claims of entitlement to use force, although indefensible on their own terms, have nevertheless provided the opportunity to test the efficacy of the legal regimes. Both Kosovo and Iraq, although decisively seen as lacking in legitimacy, nevertheless led to unprecedented soul searching, including in the UN itself, as to how the 1945 legal framework can be adapted to meet the requirements of substantive justice and deal with the changing character of conflicts and threats to state interests.[19]

Two lessons may be drawn from the US-led intervention in Iraq. The complete impotence of the international community to take any action against the US has potentially done untold damage to the vitality of the norms constraining the use of force as a set of neutral rules that applies equally to all. The contempt may trigger others to take unilaterally serving actions and in ways that may be inimical to the very interests that the US sought to safeguard in the first place. On the other hand, the spectacularly unfortunate breakdown in law and order that accompanied the war, no doubt unforeseen at the time of the invasion, will, it is suggested, serve as a cautionary tale for any future state that decides to go it alone. It is interesting that, in the aftermath of the war, both the US and the UK have cautiously moved in the direction of multilateralism and sought to engage the UN in the final settlement of the Iraq story.

As far as non-participation in the ICC goes, the Rome Statute has already entered into force, American absence notwithstanding, and the first investigations are under way.[20] It is of course impossible to ignore the very real difficulties presented by the absence of the US, especially given its potential to derail the Court by using its veto power in the Security Council, in those circumstances where a specific role has been preserved for the Council. Nevertheless, the coming into operation of the ICC is a reaffirmation of the potency of multilateralism even in the face of superpower defiance.

Notes

1 Secretary-General's address to the General Assembly, New York, 23 September 2003, at http://www.global org/reform/initiatives/panels/high/0903 address.htm.
2 1970 Declaration on Principles of International Law Concerning Friendly Relations and Co-operation Among States in accordance with the Charter of the United Nations, GA Resolution 2625, 24 October 1970.
3 UN Convention on the Law of the Sea (Montego Bay), Misc. 11 (1983), cmnd 8941.
4 1996 Comprehensive Nuclear Test Ban Treaty, http:pws.ctbto.org/.
5 Convention on Biological Diversity, 31 ILM (1992) 818.

6 Convention on the Prohibition of the Use, Stockpiling, Production and Transfer of Anti-personnel Mines and their Destruction, 1997, 36 ILM 1507.

7 Protocol to the Framework Convention on Climate Change (Kyoto), 37 ILM (1998) 22.

8 37 ILM (1998) 999.

9 D. Acheson, remarks 57 AJIL proc. 13, 14 (1963).

10 *Military and Paramilitary Activities in and against Nicaragua* (*Nicaragua v. United States*) 1984 ICJ Reports 392, 432–6, paras 91–8.

11 See I. Brownlie, C. Chinkin, C. Greenwood and V. Lowe, *Kosovo House of Commons Foreign Affairs Committee*, 4th Report June 2000, 49 ICLQ 876.

12 US National Security Strategy 2002 at http:www.whitehouse.gov/nss.html.

13 Report of the Secretary-General's High-Level Panel on Threats, Challenges and Change, 2 December 2004, GA A/59/565.

14 1986 ICJ Reports, p. 1.

15 See statement by United Nations Secretary-General Kofi Annan to the BBC, http://news.bbc.co.uk/1hi/world/middle-east/3661134/stm.

16 ICJ Reports 1966, p. 6.

17 *Nuclear Tests Cases* (*Australia v. France*) (1974) ICJ Reports p. 253 and *New Zealand v. France* ICJ Reports, p. 257.

18 Report of the Secretary-General's High-level Panel on Threats, Challenges, and Change; see also Group of 77 South Summit Declaration (April 2000), http://www.G77.org/Docs/Declaration-G77Summit.htm.

19 UN Secretary-General's Annual Report to the General Assembly, UN Press Release Doc. SG/SM/7136, GA/9596 (20 September 1999).

20 Three states parties have referred situations to the office of the prosecutor: the Central African Republic, the Democratic Republic of Congo and the Republic of Uganda, see http://www.icc.cpi.int/home.

Bibliography

The 9/11 Commission Report. 2004. Final Report of the National Commission on Terrorist Attacks Upon the United States. London: W.W. Norton and Co.

Ahmed, Nafeez Mosaddeq. 2003. *Behind the War on Terror: Western Secret Strategy and the Struggle for Iraq*. Forest Row, Essex: Clairview Books.

Albright, Madeline. 2003a. 'Bridges, Bombs, or Bluster', *Foreign Affairs* 82: 2.

Albright, Madeline. 2003b. 'United Nations', *Foreign Policy* 138: 17.

Alperovitz, Gar. 1995. *The Decision to use the Atomic Bomb and the Architecture of an American Myth*. London: HarperCollins.

Alston, Phillip, ed. 1992. *The United Nations and Human Rights*. Oxford: Oxford University Press.

Alston, Phillip and James Crawford, eds. 2000. *The Future of UN Human Rights Treaty Monitoring*. Cambridge: Cambridge University Press.

Alterman, Jon B. and J. Stephen Morrison. 2003. 'Is it Time to Engage Libya', CSIS Middle East Note Africa Notes. Washington, DC: CSIS Africa Programme, Center for Strategic and International Studies.

Andreani, Gilles. 2004–5. 'The "war on terror": good cause, wrong concept', *Survival* 46 (4): 31–50.

Andreasen, Steve. 2004. 'Reagan was right: let's ban ballistic missiles', *Survival* 46 (1): 118.

Arend, Anthony Clark. 2003. 'International law and the preemptive use of military force', *Washington Quarterly* 26 (2): 89–103.

Ash, Timothy Garton. 2004. *Free World: Why a Crisis of the West reveals the Opportunity of our Time*. London: Allen Lane.

Asmus, Ronald, Philip P. Everts and Pierangelo Isernia. 2004. *Transatlantic Trends 2003, Power, War and Public Opinion: Thoughts on the Nature and Structure of the Trans-Atlantic Divide*. Ann Arbor, MI: Inter-university Consortium for Political and Social Research.

Barker, Geoffrey. 2003. *Sexing it up*. Sydney: UNSW Press.

Barzilai, Gad, Aharon Klieman and Gil Shidlo, eds. 1993. *The Gulf Crisis and its Global Aftermath*. London: Routledge.

Bauer, Joanne R. and Daniel A. Bell. 1999. *The East Asian Challenge for Human Rights*. Cambridge: Cambridge University Press.

Bayefsky, Anne F. 1996. 'Cultural sovereignty, relativism and international human rights: new excuses for old strategies', *Ratio Juris* 9: 42–59.

Baylis, John, James Wirtz, Eliot Cohen and Colin S. Gray, eds. 2002. *Strategy in the Contemporary World.* Oxford: Oxford University Press.

Baylis, John and John Garnett, eds. 1991. *Makers of Nuclear Strategy.* London: Pinter Publishers.

Beazley, Kim. 1998. 'Diplomacy and strategy' in William Tow, ed. *Australian–American Relations.* South Yarra: Macmillan.

Beeson, Mark. 2003. 'Australia's relationship with the United States', *Australian Journal of Political Science* 38 (3): 387–405.

Benevenisti, Eyal. 2004. 'National courts and the "war on terrorism"', in Andrea Bianchi, ed. *Enforcing International Law Norms Against Terrorism.* Oxford: Hart Publishing, pp. 307–29.

Berger, Samuel R. 2000. 'A foreign policy for the global age', *Foreign Affairs* 79 (6): 36.

Berger, Samuel R. 2004. 'Foreign policy for a democratic president', *Foreign Affairs* 83 (3): 47–63.

Bergsten, C. Fred. 2002. 'A renaissance for United States trade policy?', *Foreign Affairs* 81 (6): 86–98.

Bergsten, C. Fred and John Williamson, eds. 2004. *Dollar Adjustment: How Far? Against What?* Washington, DC: Institute for International Economics.

Birnie, P. and A. Boyle. 2002. *International Law and the Environment.* Oxford: Oxford University Press.

Blinken, Antony J. 2003–4. 'From pre-emption to engagement', *Survival* 45 (4): 35.

Blix, Hans. 2004. *Disarming Iraq.* London: Bloomsbury.

Bluth, Christoph. 2004. 'The British road to war: Blair, Bush and the decision to invade Iraq', *International Affairs* 80: 880.

Bobbitt, Philip. 2003. *The Shield of Achilles: War, Peace and the Course of History.* London: Penguin.

Booker, Salih, William Minter and Ann-Louise Colgan. 2003. 'America and Africa', *Current History* May: 195–9.

Booth, Ken. 1991. 'Bernard Brodie', in John Baylis and John Garnett, eds. *Makers of Nuclear Strategy.* London: Pinter Publishers, p. 50.

Booth, Ken. 1999. 'Three tyrannies' in Tim Dunne and Nicholas Wheeler, eds. *Human Rights in Global Politics.* Cambridge: Cambridge University Press, pp. 31–70.

Boulden, Jane and Thomas G. Weiss, eds. 2004. *Terrorism and the United Nations.* Bloomington: Indiana University Press.

Brainard, Lael, Carol Graham, Nigel Purvis, Steven Radelet and Gayle Smith. 2003. *The Other War: Global Poverty and the Millennium Challenge Account.* Washington, DC: The Brookings Institution Press.

Broinowski, Alison. 2003. *Howard's War.* Melbourne: Scribe.

Brzezinski, Zbigniew. 2004. *The Choice: Global Domination or Global Leadership.* New York: Basic Books.

Buchanan, Allen. 2004. *Justice, Legitimacy and Self-Determination: Moral Foundations for International Law.* Oxford: Oxford University Press.

Buckley, Mary. 2001. 'Russian perceptions', in Mary Buckley and Sally N. Cummings, eds. *Kosovo: Perceptions of War and its Aftermath.* London: Continuum, pp. 156–75.

——. 2002. 'Russian foreign policy and its critics', *European Security* 11 (4): 29–45.

——. 2003. 'Former superpower: the Russian Federation', in Mary Buckley and Rick Fawn, eds. *Global Responses to Terrorism: 9/11, Afghanistan and Beyond.* London: Routledge, pp. 221–38.

Burke, Anthony. 2001. *In Fear of Security.* Annandale: Pluto Press.

Burke, S.M. and Lawrence Ziring. 1990. *Pakistan's Foreign Policy*. Karachi: Oxford University Press.

Campbell, David. 1998. *Writing Security: United States Foreign Policy and the Politics of Identity*. Manchester: Manchester University Press.

Capling, Ann M. 2003. 'Democratic deficit, the global trade system and 11 September', *Australian Journal of Politics and History* 49 (3): 372–9.

Chesterman, S. 2001. *Just War or Just Peace, Humanitarian Intervention and International Law*. Oxford: Oxford University Press.

Clarke, Richard A. 2004. *Against All Enemies: Inside America's War on Terror*. London: The Free Press.

Cooper, Robert. 2003. *The Breaking of Nations. Order and Chaos in the Twenty-First Century*. New York: Atlantic Monthly Press.

Crawford, James. 2002. *The International Law Commission's Articles on State Responsibility*. Cambridge, Cambridge University Press.

Cummings, Sally N. 2003. 'Negotiating the US presence: the Central Asian states', in Mary Buckley and Rick Fawn, eds. *Global Responses to Terrorism: 9/11, Afghanistan and Beyond*. London: Routledge, pp. 239–51.

Daalder, Ivo H. and James M. Lindsay. 2003. 'Bush's foreign policy revolution', in Fred Greenstein, ed. *The George W. Bush Presidency*. Baltimore: Johns Hopkins University Press, pp. 100–37.

——. 2003. *America Unbound: The Bush Revolution in Foreign Policy*. Washington, DC: Brooking Institution.

Dange, Theodros. 2002. 'Africa and the war on terrorism: the case of Somalia', *Mediterranean Quarterly* Fall: 62–73.

Danner, Mark. 2004. *Torture and the Truth*. London: Granta Books.

Dennis, Michael. 2003. 'Human rights in 2002: the annual sessions of the UN Commission on Human Righs and the Economic and Social Council', *American Journal of International Law* 97: 364–74.

Dershowitz, Alan M. 2002. *Why Terrorism Works*. New Haven, CT: Yale University Press.

Donaldson, Robert H., ed. 1981. *The Soviet Union in the Third World: Successes and Failures*. Boulder, CO: Westview.

Doran, Michael Scott. 2004. 'The Saudi paradox', *Foreign Affairs* 83 (1): 35–51.

Drifte, Reinhard. 2003. *Japan's Security Relations with China Since 1989*. London: Routledge.

Duke, Simon. 2000. *The Elusive Quest for European Security. From EDC to CFSP*. London: Macmillan.

Durham, Martin. 2004. 'The American right and the Iraq war', *Political Quarterly* July–Sept: 257–65.

Eisendrath, Craig R. and Melvin A. Goodman. 2004. *Bush League Diplomacy: How the Neo-conservatives are Putting the World at Risk*. Amherst: Prometheus Books.

Evans, Malcolm and Claudine Haenni-Dale. 2004. 'Preventing torture? The development of the Optional Protocol to the UN Convention against Torture', *Human Rights Law Review* 4: 19–55.

Farrell, Theo. 2002. 'Humanitarian intervention and peace operations', in John Baylis, James Wirtz, Eliot Cohen and Colin S. Gray, eds. *Strategy in the Contemporary World*. Oxford: Oxford University Press, p. 293.

Ferguson, Niall. 2004. *Colossus: The Rise and Fall of the American Empire*. London: Allen Lane.

———. 2005. 'Sinking globalization', *Foreign Affairs* 84 (2): 64–77.

Fiorina, Morris. 2005. *Culture War? The Myth of a Polarized America.* New York: Pearson Longman.

Flitton, Daniel. 2002. 'Perspectives on Australian foreign policy, 2002', *Australian Journal of International Affairs* 57 (1): 37–54.

Freedman, Lawrence. 1988. 'I exist; therefore I deter', *International Security* 13 (1): 177–95.

———. 2002. 'Conclusion: the future of strategic studies', in John Baylis, James Wirtz, Eliot Cohen and Colin S. Gray, eds. *Strategy in the Contemporary World.* Oxford: Oxford University Press, p. 340.

———. 2003. 'Prevention, not preemption', *Washington Quarterly* 26 (2): 105–14.

———. 2004. *Deterrence.* Cambridge: Polity.

Friedman, George. 2004. *America's Secret War: Inside the Hidden Worldwide Struggle between the United States and its Enemies.* London: Little, Brown.

Frum, David and Richard Perle. 2003. *An End to Evil: How to Win the War on Terror.* New York: Random House.

Gaddis, John Lewis. 2002. 'A grand strategy of transformation', *Foreign Policy* Nov./Dec.: 50–7.

———. 2004. *Surprise, Security and the American Experience.* Cambridge, MA: Harvard University Press.

Gao, Zichuan. 2004. 'An analysis of China's peripheral security environment', *Dangdai yatai* 1: 9–10.

Garnaut, Ross. 2002. 'An Australian–United States Free Trade Agreement', *Australian Journal of International Affairs* 56 (1): 123–41.

Garran, Robert. 2004. *True Believer.* Crows Nest, NSW: Allen & Unwin.

Ginsberg, Roy. 2001. *The European Union in International Politics. Baptism by Fire.* Lanham, MD: Rowman & Littlefield.

Glennon, Michael J. 2003. 'Why the Security Council failed', *Foreign Affairs* 82 (3): 16–36.

Goot, Murray. 2003. 'Public opinion and the democratic deficit', *Australian Humanities Review* May. http://www.lib.latrobe.edu.au/AHR/archive/Issue-May-2003/goot.html.

Goredem, Charles. 2003. 'Initiatives against terrorism in southern Africa: implications for human rights', *African Security Review* 12: 91–100. http://www.iss.co.za/Pubs/ASR/12No1/EGored.html.

Gordon, Bernard K. 2003. 'A high risk trade policy', *Foreign Affairs* 82 (4): 105–18.

Gordon, P.H. and J. Shapiro. 2004. *Allies at War: America, Europe, and the Crisis over Iraq.* New York: McGraw-Hill.

Granville, Brigitte. 2003. 'The global economy: What changed?', in Mary Buckley and Rick Fawn, eds. *Global Responses to Terrorism: 9/11, Afghanistan and Beyond.* London: Routledge, pp. 276–83.

Griffith, Samuel B., trans. 1971. *Sun Tzu: The Art of War.* Oxford: Oxford University Press.

Gunaratna, Rohan. 2002. *Inside al-Qaeda.* London: Hurst.

Guo, Xianggang. 2003. 'The shifting of US global strategic priority', *Guoji wenti yanjiu* 2: 17–22.

Haass, Richard N. 2000. 'The squandered presidency – demanding more from the commander-in-chief', *Foreign Affairs* 79 (3): 139.

Halliday, Fred. 2001. *The World at 2000: Perils and Promises.* New York: Palgrave.

Halper, Stefan and Jonathan Clarke. 2004. *America Alone: The Neo-Conservatives and the Global Order.* Cambridge: Cambridge University Press.

Hampton, Mary N. 1966. *The Wilsonian Impulse: US Foreign Policy, the Alliance, and German Unification.* Westport, CT: Praeger.

Hansen, Birthe. 2000. *Unipolarity and the Middle East.* Richmond, Surrey: Curzon Press.

Harries, Owen. 2004. *Benign or Imperial?* Sydney: ABC Books.

Heisbourg, Francois. 2003. 'A work in progress: the Bush Doctrine and its consequences', *Washington Quarterly* 26 (2): 75–88.

Henderson, Gerard. 2004. 'Australia's security: a consistent approach', *New Zealand International Review* 29 (1): 11–14.

Hentz, James J. 2004. 'The contending currents in United States involvement in Sub-Saharan Africa,' in Ian Taylor and Paul Williams, eds. *Africa in International Politics: External Involvement on the Continent.* London: Routledge, pp. 23–40.

Herbst, Jeffrey. 2000. 'Western and African peacekeepers: motives and opportunities', in John W. Harbeson and Donald Rothchild, eds. *Africa in World Politics: The African State System in Flux.* Boulder, CO: Westview Press, pp. 308–23.

Herd, Graeme P. 2002. 'The Russo-Chechen information warfare and 9/11: Al-Qaeda through the South Caucasus looking glass?' *European Security* 11 (4): 110–30.

Herring, Eric. 1995. *Danger and Opportunity: Explaining International Crisis Outcomes.* Manchester: Manchester University Press.

Hitchens, Christopher. 2003. *Regime Change.* London: Penguin Books.

Hoffmann, Stanley. 2000. 'Toward a common foreign and security policy', *Journal of Common Market Studies* 38: 189–98.

Hoffmann, Stanley. 2002. 'Clash of globalizations', *Foreign Affairs* 81: 113.

Hollander, Paul, ed. 2004. *Understanding Anti-Americanism: Its Origin and Impact at Home and Abroad.* New York: Ivan Dee.

Holzgrefe, J.L. and Robert O. Keohane. 2003. *Humanitarian Intervention.* Cambridge: Cambridge University Press.

Hook, Glenn D. *et al.* 2001. *Japan's International Relations.* London: Routledge.

Hoopes, Townshend and Douglas Brinkley. 1997. *FDR and the Creation of the UN.* New Haven: Yale University Press.

Huntington, Samuel. 1996. *The Clash of Civilizations and the Remaking of World Order.* New York: Free Press.

Ikenberry, G. John. 2002. 'America's imperial ambition', *Foreign Affairs* 81 (5): 44–60.

——. 2004. 'The end of the neo-conservative moment', *Survival* 46 (1): 7–22.

Irshad, Muhammad. 2004. 'US won't accept Pakistan, India as N-states', *Defence Journal* 8 (1): 36.

Jawad, Haifa A., ed. 1997. *The Middle East in the New World Order.* London: Macmillan.

Jennings, R. and A. Watts. 1992. *Oppenheim's International Law*, vol. 1. London: Longman.

Jervis, Robert. 2003. 'Understanding the Bush Doctrine', *Political Science Quarterly* 118 (3): 365–88.

——. 2005. *American Foreign Policy in a New Era.* London: Routledge.

Kagan, Robert. 2003. *Paradise and Power: America and Europe in the New World Order.* London: Atlantic Books.

Kampfner, John. 2004. *Blair's Wars.* London: The Free Press.

Kant, Immanuel. 1991. 'Perpetual peace: a philosophical sketch', in Hans Reiss, ed. *Kant: Political Writings.* Cambridge: Cambridge University Press.

Kaplan, Lawrence F. and William Kristol. 2003. *The War Over Iraq: Saddam's Tyranny and America's Mission*. San Francisco: Encounter Books.

Kaplan, Robert. 2002. *Power and Weakness. America and the World. Debating the New Shape of International Politics*. New York: W.W. Norton and Co.

Kerr, Paul. 2005. 'North Korea talks achieve breakthrough', *Arms Control Today*, October. http://www.armscontrol.org/act/2005_10/OCT-NKBreakthrough.asp.

Kerr, Roger. 2004. 'What America means for New Zealand', *New Zealand International Review* 29 (1): 7–10.

Khalidi, Rashid. 2004. *Resurrecting Empire: Western Footprints and America's Perilous Path in the Middle East*. London: I.B. Tauris.

Krause, Keith. 1999. 'Rationality and deterrence in theory and practice', in Craig A. Snyder, ed. *Contemporary Security and Strategy*. London: Macmillan, p. 121.

Krauthammer, Charles. 2004. 'In defence of democratic realism', *The National Interest* 77 (Fall): 15–25.

Kull, Steven, Clay Ramsay and Evan Lewis. 2003–04. 'Misperceptions, the media, and the Iraq War', *Political Science Quarterly* 118 (4): 569–98.

Kux, Dennis. 1993. *India and the United States: Estranged Democracies 1941–1991*. Washington, DC: NDU.

——. 2001. *The United States and Pakistan, 1947–2000*. Baltimore: Johns Hopkins University Press.

LaFeber, Walter. 2002. 'The Bush Doctrine', *Diplomatic History* 26 (4): 543–58.

Laurent, Eric. 2004. *Bush's Secret World: Religion, Big Business and Hidden Networks*. Cambridge: Polity Press.

Leffler, Melvyn P. 2004. 'Bush's foreign policy', *Foreign Policy* Sept./Oct.: 22–8.

Leonard, David K. and Scott Straus. 2003. *Africa's Stalled Development: International Causes and Cures*. London: Lynne Rienner Publishers.

Li, Jingzhi. 2003. 'The changes in the world pattern and great power relations: an analysis of the Iraq War and its impact', *Guoji luntan* 3: 1–8.

Li, Rex. 1999a. 'Unipolar aspirations in a multipolar reality: China's perceptions of US ambitions and capabilities in the post-Cold War world', *Pacifica Review* 11 (2): 115–49.

——. 1999b. 'Partners or rivals? Chinese perceptions of Japan's security strategy in the Asia–Pacific region', *Journal of Strategic Studies* 22 (4): 7–9.

——. 2003a. 'A rising power with global aspirations: China', in Mary Buckley and Rick Fawn, eds. *Global Responses to Terrorism: 9/11, Afghanistan and Beyond*. London: Routledge, pp. 210–20.

——. 2003b. 'The North Korean nuclear crisis and China's strategic calculus', in *Chinese Military Update*. London: Royal United Services Institute for Defence and Security Studies, pp. 8–10.

Lieven, Anatol. 1998. *Chechnya: Tombstone of Russian Power*. New Haven, CT: Yale University Press.

Litwak, Robert S. 2002–3. 'The new calculus of pre-emption', *Survival* 44 (4): 58.

Liu, Jianfei. 2003. 'The impact of the Iraq War on the international situation and China's international strategic choice', *Dangdai shijie yu shehuizhuyi* 4: 28.

Lyon, Rod and William Tow. 2003. *The Future of the Australian–US Security Relationship*. Carlisle, PA: Strategic Studies Institute.

McAllister, Ian *et al*. 2004. *Attitude Matters*. Canberra: Australian Strategic Policy Institute.

Macfarlane, S. Neil. 2005. 'Willing to act', *The World Today* 61 (8/9): 28–9.

McGoldrick, Dominic. 2004. *From 9/11 to the Iraq War 2003: International Law in an Age of Complexity.* Oxford: Hart Publishing.

Manne, Robert. 2001. *The Barren Years.* Melbourne: Text Publishing.

———, ed. 2004. *The Howard Years.* Melbourne: Black Inc. Agenda.

Marquand, Robert. 'As China rises, US taps Japan as key Asia ally', *Christian Science Monitor*, 21 March 2005.

Marr, David and Marian Wilkinson. 2004. *Dark Victory.* Crows Nest, NSW: Allen & Unwin.

Mazari, Shireen M. 2004. 'Rethinking the national security of Pakistan,' in *Changing Global and Geo-strategic Environment: Implications for Pakistan, Margalla Papers 2004.* Islamabad: National Defence College, p. 20.

Mead, Walter Russell. 2001. *Special Providence: American Foreign Policy and How it Changed the World.* New York: Routledge.

———. 2004. *Power, Terror, Peace, and War: America's Grand Strategy in a World at Risk.* New York: Alfred A. Knopf.

Menkhaus, Ken. 2002. *Somalia: Next Up in the War on Terrorism?* CSIS Africa Notes. Washington, DC: CSIS Africa Programme, Center for Strategic and International Studies.

The Military Balance 2004–5. Oxford: Oxford University Press, 2004.

Mills, Greg. 2004. 'Africa's new strategic significance', *Washington Quarterly* 27 (4): 157–69.

Morrison, J. Stephen. 2002. 'Somalia's and Sudan's race to the fore in Africa', *The Washington Quarterly* Spring: 191–205.

Mullerson, Rein. 1997. *Human Rights Diplomacy.* London: Routledge.

Murphy, Emma C. 1997. 'The Arab–Israeli conflict in the new world order', in Haifa A. Jawad, ed. *The Middle East in the New World Order.* London: Macmillan, p. 110.

Musharraf, Gen. Pervez. 2002. 'Inaugural address', in *Peace and Security in South Asia,* Proceedings of the International Conference 19–20 September 2002. Islamabad: Institute of Strategic Studies, pp. 7–8.

Mussa, Michael. 2003. *Global Economic Prospects: Through the Fog of Uncertainty.* International Policy Briefs, no. PB03-2. Washington, DC: Institute for International Economics.

Mutimer, David. 1999. 'Beyond strategy: critical thinking and the new security studies', in Craig A. Snyder, ed. *Contemporary Security and Strategy.* London: Macmillan, p. 90.

Nogee, Joseph L. and Robert H. Donaldson. 1985. *Soviet Foreign Policy since World War II,* 2nd edn. New York: Pergamon.

Nordhaus, William D. 2002. 'The Economic Consequences of a War with Iraq', in Carl Kaysen *et al.*, eds. *War With Iraq: Costs, Consequences and Alternatives.* New York: American Academy of Arts and Sciences.

Nye, Jr, Joseph S. 2003a. *The Paradox of American Power: Why the World's Only Superpower Can't Go It Alone.* New York: Oxford University Press.

———. 2003b 'US power and strategy after Iraq', *Foreign Affairs* 82 (4): 60–73.

———. 2004. 'The decline of American soft power,' *Foreign Affairs* 83 (3): 16–20.

———. 2005. *Soft Power: The Means to Success in World Politics.* New York: Public Affairs.

Obethur, S. and H. Ott. 1999. *The Kyoto Protocol.* Berlin: Springer-Verlag.

O'Connor, Brendon. 2004. 'Perspectives on Australian foreign policy, 2003', *Australian Journal of International Affairs* 58 (2): 207–20.

O'Connor, Brendon and Martin Griffith, eds. 2005. *The Rise of Anti-Americanism*. London: Routledge.

Parmar, Inderjeet. 2005. 'Catalysing events, think tanks and American foreign policy shifts: a comparative analysis of the impacts of Pearl Harbor 1941 and 11 September 2001', *Government and Opposition* 40 (1): 1–25.

Polman, Linda. 2003. *We Did Nothing: Why the Truth Doesn't Always Come Out When the UN Goes In*. London: Penguin Books.

Pond, Elizabeth. 2004. *Friendly Fire: The Near-Death of the Transatlantic Alliance*. Pittsburgh: European Union Studies Association; and Washington, DC: Brookings Institution Press.

Power, Samantha. 2002. *'A Problem From Hell': American and the Age of Genocide*. London: Flamingo.

Rabasa, Angel M. *et al*. 2005. *The Muslim World after 9/11*. Santa Monica, CA: RAND Corporation.

Radelet, Steven. 2003a. 'Bush and foreign aid', *Foreign Affairs* 82 (5): 2.

Radelet, Steven. 2003b. 'Will the Millennium Challenge Account be different?', *The Washington Quarterly* 26 (2): 171–87.

Rais, Rasul Buksh. 2002. 'Pakistan and the United States: Shaping a new Partnership', *Peace and Security in South Asia*, Proceedings of the International Conference held at the Institute of Strategic Studies, Islamabad, 19–20 September 2002, pp. 46–56.

Ratner, Steven and Jason Abrams. 2001. *Accountability for Human Rights Atrocities in International Law*, 2nd edn. Oxford: Oxford University Press.

Rawls, John. 1999. *The Law of Peoples*. Cambridge, MA: Harvard University Press.

Record, Jeffrey. 2003. 'The Bush Doctrine and war with Iraq', *Parameters* XXXIII (1): 4.

Reisman, Michael. 2000. 'Sovereignty and human rights in contemporary international law', in Greg Fox and Brad Roth, eds. *Democratic Governance and International Law*. Cambridge: Cambridge University Press, pp. 239–58.

Reiss, Hans, ed. 1991. *Kant: Political Writings*. Cambridge: Cambridge University Press.

Reno, William. 1998. *Warlord Politics and African States*. London: Lynne Rienner Publishers.

Renshon, Stanley A. 2004. *In His Father's Shadow: The Political Transformations of George W. Bush*. New York: Palgrave Macmillan.

Revel, Jean-Francois. 2002. *Anti-Americanism*. San Francisco: Encounter Books.

Reydams, Luc. 2003. *Universal Jurisdiction*. Oxford: Oxford University Press.

Rhodes, Edward. 2003. 'The imperial logic of Bush's liberal agenda', *Survival* 45 (1): 131–54.

Rice, Condoleezza. 2000. 'Promoting the national interest', *Foreign Affairs* 79 (1): 56.

Risse, Thomas, Stephen C. Ropp and Kathryn Sikkink. 1999. *The Power of Human Rights*. Cambridge: Cambridge University Press.

Romano, Cesare, Andre Nollkaemer and Jann Kleffner. 2004. *Internationalized Criminal Courts*. Oxford: Oxford University Press.

Rose, David. 2004. *Guantanamo: America's War on Human Rights*. London: Faber and Faber.

Ross, Andrew and Kristin Ross, eds. 2004. *Anti-Americanism*. New York: New York University Press.

Roth, B. 2000. *Governmental Illegitimacy in International Law*. Oxford: Oxford University Press.

Roth, B. 2003. 'Bending the law, breaking it, or developing it? The United States and the humanitarian use of force in the post-Cold War era', in M. Byers and G. Nolte, eds. *United States Hegemony and the Foundations of International Law*. Cambridge: Cambridge University Press.

Rundle, Guy. 2001. 'The opportunist', *Quarterly Essay* 3: 1–65.

Scharf, M.P. 2000. 'ICC'S jurisdiction over nationals of non-party states', in S. Sewall and C. Kaysen, eds. *The United States and the International Criminal Court*. Oxford: Oxford University Press, pp. 213–30.

Schlesinger, Jr, Arthur. 2004. *War and the American Presidency*. New York: W.W. Norton.

von Schorlemer, Sabine. 2003. 'Human rights: substantive and institutional implications of the war against terrorism', *European Journal of International Law* 14: 265–82.

Schroeder, P. 1976. *Alliances, 1815–1945: Weapons of Power and Tools of Management; Historical Dimensions of National Security Problems*. Lawrence, KS: University Press of Kansas.

Sewall S. and C. Kaysen. 2000. *The United States and the International Criminal Court*. Oxford: Oxford University Press.

Shahi, Agha. 2002. 'Welcome Address', *Peace and Security in South Asia*, Proceedings of the International Conference, 19–20 September 2002. Islamabad: Institute of Strategic Studies, p. 3.

Sharansky, Natan. 2004. *The Case for Democracy: The Power of Freedom to Overcome Tyranny and Terror*. New York: Public Affairs.

Sicherman, Harvey. 2005. 'US policy in the Middle East: on the brink', Foreign Policy Research Institute, 12 January.

Singer, Peter. 2004. *The President of Good and Evil: Taking George W. Bush Seriously*. London: Granta.

Singh, Robert. 2003. *Contemporary American Politics and Society: Issues and Controversies*. London: Sage.

——. 2003. 'Superpower response: the United States of America', in Mary Buckley and Rick Fawn, eds. *Global Responses to Terrorism: 9/11, Afghanistan and Beyond*. London: Routledge, pp. 52–65.

Slocombe, Walter B. 2003. 'Force, pre-emption and legitimacy', *Survival* 45 (1): 117–30.

Smith, Michael E. 2004. *Europe's Foreign and Security Policy. The Institutionalization of Cooperation*. New York: Cambridge University Press.

Snyder, Craig A., ed. 1999. *Contemporary Security and Strategy*. London: Macmillan.

Stelzer, Irwin, ed. 2004. *Neoconservatism*. London: Atlantic Books.

Strategic Survey 2003/4: An Evaluation and Forecast of World Affairs. Oxford: Oxford University Press, 2004.

Styen, Lord Justice. 2004. 'Guantanamo Bay: the legal black hole', *International and Comparative Law Quarterly* 53: 1–15.

Su, Ge. 2003. 'On the adjustment in the US National Security Strategy', *Guoji wenti yanjiu* 2: 5–10, 22.

Taylor, Terence. 2004. 'The end of imminence?', *Washington Quarterly* 27 (4): 62–3.

Téson, Fernando. 2003. 'The liberal case for humanitarian intervention', in J.L. Holzgrefe and Robert O. Keohane, eds. *Humanitarian Intervention*. Cambridge: Cambridge University Press, pp. 93–129.

Tharoor, Shashi. 2003. 'Why America still needs the United Nations', *Foreign Affairs* 82: 75.

Tow, William. 2004. 'Deputy sheriff or independent ally?', *Pacific Review* 17 (2): 271–90.

Tucker, Robert W. 1993. 'Origins of the New World Order', in Gad Barzilai, Aharon Klieman and Gil Shidlo, eds. *The Gulf Crisis and its Global Aftermath.* London: Routledge.

Verrier, June. 2003. 'Australia's self-image as a regional and international security actor', *Australian Journal of International Affairs* 57 (3): 455–71.

Voeten, Erik. 2004. 'Resisting the lonely superpower: responses of states in the United Nations to US dominance', *Journal of Politics* 66: 729–54.

Volman, Daniel. 2003. 'The Bush administration and African oil: the security implications of US energy policy', *Review of African Political Economy* 98: 573–84.

Wang, Jian. 2003. 'The situation in the Middle East after the Iraq War and the future directions of America's global strategy', *Shijie jingji yanjiu* 8 (8): 47–50.

Webber, Mark. 1997. *CIS Integration Trends: Russia and the Former Soviet South.* London: Royal Institute of International Affairs.

Weller, Pat. 2002. *Don't Tell the Prime Minister.* Carlton North: Scribe Publications.

Weiss, Linda, Elizabeth Thurbon and John Matthews. 2004. *How to Kill a Country.* Crows Nest, NSW: Allen & Unwin.

Wesley, Michael. 2001. 'Perspectives on Australian foreign policy, 2001', *Australian Journal of International Affairs* 56 (1): 47–63.

Wheeler, Nicholas. 2000. *Saving Strangers.* Oxford: Oxford University Press.

White, Brian. 2001. *Understanding European Foreign Policy.* Basingstoke: Palgrave.

White, Hugh. 2002. 'Australian defence policy and the possibility of war', *Australian Journal of International Affairs* 56 (2): 253–64.

White House. 2002. *The National Security Strategy of the United States of America.* Washington, DC: Government Printing Office.

Wilkie, Andrew. 2004. *Axis of Deceit.* Melbourne: Black Inc. Agenda.

Woodward, Bob. 2004. *Plan of Attack.* London: Simon & Schuster.

Wu, Xianbin. 2004. 'The characteristics and motives of the Bush administration's policy towards Taiwan', *Dangdai yatai* 3: 16–23.

Zelikow, Philip. 2003. 'The transformation of national security', *National Interest* 71 (Spring): 17–28.

Zoellick, Robert B. 2000. 'A Republican foreign policy', *Foreign Affairs* 79 (1): 68.

Index